Language and Tourism
in Postcolonial Settings

TOURISM AND CULTURAL CHANGE

Series Editors: Professor Mike Robinson, *Ironbridge International Institute for Cultural Heritage, University of Birmingham, UK* and Professor Alison Phipps, *University of Glasgow, Scotland, UK*

Understanding tourism's relationships with culture(s) and vice versa, is of ever-increasing significance in a globalising world. TCC is a series of books that critically examine the complex and ever-changing relationship between tourism and culture(s). The series focuses on the ways that places, peoples, pasts, and ways of life are increasingly shaped/transformed/created/packaged for touristic purposes. The series examines the ways tourism utilises/makes and re-makes cultural capital in its various guises (visual and performing arts, crafts, festivals, built heritage, cuisine etc.) and the multifarious political, economic, social and ethical issues that are raised as a consequence. Theoretical explorations, research-informed analyses, and detailed historical reviews from a variety of disciplinary perspectives are invited to consider such relationships.

Books in this series are externally peer-reviewed.

Full details of all the books in this series and of all our other publications can be found on http://www.channelviewpublications.com, or by writing to Channel View Publications, St Nicholas House, 31-34 High Street, Bristol BS1 2AW, UK.

TOURISM AND CULTURAL CHANGE: 54

Language and Tourism in Postcolonial Settings

**Edited by
Angelika Mietzner and
Anne Storch**

CHANNEL VIEW PUBLICATIONS
Bristol • Blue Ridge Summit

DOI https://doi.org/10.21832/MIETZN6782
Library of Congress Cataloging in Publication Data
A catalog record for this book is available from the Library of Congress.
Names: Mietzner, Angelika, editor. | Storch, Anne, editor.
Title: Language and Tourism in Postcolonial Settings/Edited by Angelika Mietzner
   and Anne Storch.
Description: Bristol, UK; Blue Ridge Summit, PA: Channel View Publications, 2019.
   | Series: Tourism and Cultural Change: 54 | Includes bibliographical references
   and index.
Identifiers: LCCN 2018055386 (print) | LCCN 2019002785 (ebook) |
   ISBN 9781845416799 (pdf) | ISBN 9781845416805 (epub) | ISBN 9781845416812
   (Kindle) | ISBN 9781845416782 (hbk : alk. paper) | ISBN 9781845416775
   (pbk : alk. paper)
Subjects: LCSH: Tourism—Social aspects—Developing countries. | Language and
   culture—Developing countries. | Sociolinguistics—Developing countries.
Classification: LCC G155.D44 (ebook) | LCC G155.D44 L35 2019 (print) |
   DDC 306.4/819—dc23
LC record available at https://lccn.loc.gov/2018055386

British Library Cataloguing in Publication Data
A catalogue entry for this book is available from the British Library.

ISBN-13: 978-1-84541-678-2 (hbk)
ISBN-13: 978-1-84541-677-5 (pbk)

Channel View Publications
UK: St Nicholas House, 31-34 High Street, Bristol BS1 2AW, UK.
USA: NBN, Blue Ridge Summit, PA, USA.

Website: www.channelviewpublications.com
Twitter: Channel_View
Facebook: https://www.facebook.com/channelviewpublications
Blog: www.channelviewpublications.wordpress.com

Copyright © 2019 Angelika Mietzner, Anne Storch and the authors of individual chapters.

All rights reserved. No part of this work may be reproduced in any form or by any means without permission in writing from the publisher.

The policy of Multilingual Matters/Channel View Publications is to use papers that are natural, renewable and recyclable products, made from wood grown in sustainable forests. In the manufacturing process of our books, and to further support our policy, preference is given to printers that have FSC and PEFC Chain of Custody certification. The FSC and/or PEFC logos will appear on those books where full certification has been granted to the printer concerned.

Typeset by Deanta Global Publishing Services Limited.
Printed and bound in the UK by Short Run Press Ltd.
Printed and bound in the US by Thomson-Shore, Inc.

Contents

Contributors		vii
Preface: cape coast caper *Tawona Sitholé*		x
1	Linguistic Entanglements, Emblematic Codes and Representation in Tourism: Introduction *Angelika Mietzner and Anne Storch*	1
2	Transformations of the 'Tourist Gaze': Landscaping and the Linguist behind the Lens *Christiane M. Bongartz*	18
3	Backpacking Performances: An Empirical Contribution *Luís Cronopio*	38
4	'We Have Our Own Africans': Public Displays of Zār in Iran *Sara Zavaree*	49
5	Cameras as Barriers of Understanding: Reflections on a Philanthropic Journey to Kenya *Angelika Mietzner*	66
6	Heritage Tourism and the Freak Show: A Study on Names, Horror, Race and Gender *Anne Storch*	81
7	Postcolonial Performativity in the Philippine Heritage Tourism Industry *Raymund Vitorio*	106
8	The Hakuna Matata Swahili: Linguistic Souvenirs from the Kenyan Coast *Nico Nassenstein*	130

Afterword: Between Silence and Noise: Towards an Entangled
Sociolinguistics of Tourism 157
Adam Jaworski

Bookend: cape ghost 168
Alison Phipps

Index 170

Contributors

Christiane M. Bongartz is Professor of English Linguistics at the University of Cologne. Her research focuses on the understanding of languaging: how are languages learned and used in multilingual contexts? Situated at the intersection of traditional psycho- and sociolinguistic perspectives, her projects are increasingly concerned with the deconstruction of these paradigms. Forthcoming publications include a volume on narratives in bilingual research in her series *Inquiries in Language Learning* (Peter Lang) and a research report on referential production in *Linguistic Approaches to Bilingualism* with Jacopo Torregrossa and Ianthi Tsimpli. She is advising editor of the journal *The Mouth*.

Luís Cronopio is a master student and researcher of African Culture at the University of Cologne. His academic background combines nursing sciences, tropical health and anthropology. His main research interests focus on political philosophy, art history of the 20th century, socio-anthropology of health and anthropology of drugs.

Adam Jaworski is Chair Professor of Sociolinguistics at the School of English, University of Hong Kong. He was formely at Adam Mickiewicz University Poznań, Birkbeck University of London and Cardiff University. His research interests include language and globalisation, display of languages in space, media discourse, nonverbal communication and text-based art. His most recent book is *The Elite Discourse* (Routledge, 2018, with Crispin Thurlow). He is a member of the editorial board of the following journals: *Discourse, Context & Media*, *Discourse & Society*, *Journal of Language and Politics*, *Journal of Sociolinguistics*, *Language in Society*, *Linguistic Landscape*, *The Mouth*, *Multilingua* and *Visual Communication*, among others. With Brook Bolander, he co-edits the Oxford University Press book series, *Oxford Studies in Sociolinguistics*.

Angelika Mietzner is a research fellow at the Institute for African Studies and Egyptology, University of Cologne. Her research interests cover descriptive and sociolinguistic aspects of Nilotic languages, language styles in fleeting relationships and tourism, and critical heritage studies. Her main research was conducted in Kenya where topics of all research interests can be met.

Nico Nassenstein is Junior Professor (assistant professor) of African Linguistics at the Johannes Gutenberg University Mainz. His main focus is on sociolinguistics, especially related to contexts of migration, globalisation, conflict and tourism. He is interested in matters of language change, variation and diversity and has mainly worked on the languages Kiswahili, Lingala and Kinyarwanda-Kirundi (East and Central Africa). He has recently developed a strong interest in changing language practices in tourism contexts, both along the East African coast and in Majorca, Spain. Currently, he is co-editing a special issue of the *Journal of Language and Culture* with colleagues from Cairns (Australia) and Cologne (Germany), and a volume on swearing and cursing with Anne Storch. Nico Nassenstein is co-editor of the journals *Afrikanistik-Ägyptologie-Online* (AAeO), *Swahili Forum* and *The Mouth*.

Alison Phipps is UNESCO Chair in Refugee Integration through Languages and the Arts at the University of Glasgow, Professor of Languages and Intercultural Studies, and Co-convener of the Glasgow Refugee, Asylum and Migration Network. She received an OBE in 2012, is a Fellow of the Royal Society of Edinburgh and the Academy of Social Sciences. Alison regularly advises public, governmental and third sector bodies on migration, arts and languages policy and was appointed Chair of the New Scots Core Group in 2018. Author of numerous books and articles, she is a published poet and a regular international keynote speaker and broadcaster.

Tawona Sitholé, better known as Ganyamatope (my ancestral family name), my heritage inspires me to make connections with other people through creativity, and the natural outlook to learn. I am widely published as a poet and playwright, and short story author. A storyteller and musician, I am co-founder of Seeds of Thought, a non-funded arts group. I am currently UNESCO artist-in-residence at the University of Glasgow, with research and teaching roles in the school of education and medical school. Other educational roles are with Glasgow School of Art, University of the West of Scotland, University of Stirling and Newcastle University

Anne Storch is Professor of African Linguistics at the University of Cologne. Her work combines contributions to cultural and social contexts of languages, the semiotics of linguistic practices, colonial linguistics, heteroglossia and register variation, epistemic language and metalinguistics, as well as linguistic description. Her publications include

Secret Manipulations (2011), *A Grammar of Luwo* (2014), and several other volumes. A book on linguistics and tourism written by her and Ingo Warnke and a volume on colonial linguistics, co-edited together with Ana Deumert and Nick Shepherd, are forthcoming. She is co-editor of the journal *The Mouth* (https://themouthjournal.com/).

Raymund Vitorio is a joint PhD candidate (Language Studies) at the National University of Singapore and King's College London. His dissertation explores the discursive construction of citizenship in Singapore through the lens of linguistic ethnography and metapragmatics. His research interests also include the sociolinguistics of globalization, linguistic landscapes, tourism, and performativity.

Sara Zavaree is a PhD candidate at the Institute of African Studies and Egyptology in the University of Cologne and is currently working on Zār spirit possession rituals in southern Iran. Her research interests include ritual studies, the Indian Ocean (slave) trade networks and the history of slavery in the Persian Gulf.

Preface
cape coast caper

Tawona Sitholé

if there is one thing
about this place
it's the noise
the many many volumes
of history
the rusty rusty ringing
of decibels
the ruthless lashes
of the waves
the fiery rage
of the sea
the high-pitched voices
of the traders
trying
to shout above each other
trying
to shout above the noise
it's more than you can stand

in the discord
the wind is whistling

you must leave it here
your name
you must leave it here
otherwise
they won't let you past

and so you do
and as you enter

in the discord
the wind is whistling

gold coast cape coast
put on your mask
put on your mask
for the mask'eraid
gold coast cape coast
put on your cape
put on your cape
for the escapade
the mass parade
the mass parade
they all line up for
the mass parade

and as they fade
what appears to be your guide appears
and starts walking
instinctively you follow the momentum
but this only leads to a stall
with percussive triangles
with shirts and blouses
with hearts on sleeves
fancy tightrope
to skip a generation
soothing lotions
and
calming creams
to rub on wounds
and paste on scars
it's more than you can take

the guide is speaking
but is drowning
in the discord
instead
what you can hear
is a spirited voice
not loud
but crisp
against the noise

this is not why i came
this is not what i came
to be
known as
known for

a shadow steals by
can't tell whether
a vendor
defender
or
pretender

the one thing about this place
is the appearance
facing the sea
the darkened house
with whitewashed walls
with rooms rooms
passages and guns
pointing in all directions
at invisible enemies
and beneath
the courtyard
tunnels tunnels
cavities and cells
with no
no windows
you could swear
this house is darkening
you could swear
these walls are whitening
it's more than you can stand

in the discord
the wind keeps whistling

the mask'eraid
the escapade
they all line up for
the mass parade

and as they fade
you wonder whether
the other visitors
can see them too
the shadows
and the more you look
the less you see
the less there seems to be

the guide is walking
instinctively you follow the momentum
but this only leads to another stall
with hides hidden
in exquisite bracelets
in a variety of complexions
shades and tones
some for wrists
some for ankles
some for minds
it's more than you can take

the guide is speaking
but is drowning
in the discord
instead
what you can hear
is a spirited voice
not loud
but clear
above the noise

borrowed time
has side effects
and too many to count
like visits of the tide

another shadow steals by
can't tell whether
a dweller
seller
or
sell-out

the guide is walking
instinctively you follow the momentum
but this only leads to another stall
with refreshments
special brew
a blend
of floods
of held-back tears
of cocktails
of emotions
one sip

sharp taste
two sips
bitter taste
it's more than you can take

in the discord
the wind keeps whistling

the mask'eraid
the escapade
they all line up for
the mass parade

and as they fade
the guide is speaking
but is drowning
in the discord
instead
what you can hear
is a spirited voice
not loud
but clean
across the noise

when will this end
in fact
when will this begin
i don't want to leave
but
take me to another place

one thing about this place
is the atmosphere
only thing that comes close
is the utmost fear
just like a restless survivor
the air is never still
and
between areas of pressure
winds keep blowing
nothing more chilling
than a trade wind
that keeps whistling
after the home is blown
and this one lingers

on the opaque walls
between
long unbroken silences
between
quiet solemn reflections
some of what is
blown in
some of who are
blown away
in the
unending argument
between land and sea

land is solid
water is fluid
sun is smiling
wind is whistling
and
heart is beating

seems like any other
ordinary day
but this is not any other
ordinary place
on any day
at any time
by any law
in any tongue
what happened
happens
here
lies beyond
this final
point of
the tour
the door
of no return

in the discord
you seem to hear
what seems to lie
beyond
seems like
the wind is whistling
not sure if

the voices are
sounds of harm
or
harmony

gold coast cape coast
put on your mask
put on your mask
for the mask'eraid
gold coast cape coast
put on your cape
put on your cape
for the escapade
the mass parade
the mass parade
they all line up for
the mass parade

1 Linguistic Entanglements, Emblematic Codes and Representation in Tourism: Introduction

Angelika Mietzner and Anne Storch

We begin with a banal example. In this image (Figure 1.1), a group of souvenirs are placed on the sand of Diani Beach in Kenya. These objects form part of a larger supply of carvings that are found in a dozen or so souvenir stalls in front of a hotel that caters to international, though mostly German, package tourists.

What is offered to these tourists are carvings of animals that they might have seen and taken pictures of during a safari to a national park that usually takes place prior to the beach holiday. There are also masks, bowls and candleholders that will help to create memories of the 'real Africa' one has been to: exotic, mysterious and traditional. Upon asking the souvenir vendors – men well in their fifties with decades of experience in the business – who designs these objects and who accounts for the entire assortment at sale here, the men replied that almost all the designs came from Europe or were at least decided upon there. Traders in the Netherlands and in Germany, they said, would select certain objects out of an entire catalogue of souvenirs at offer, and have them carved and painted in Kenya. The beach is just a small part of the business; Christmas markets, one-world emporiums and interior decoration shops are more profitable and reliable, the men claimed. Creativity is controlled by those who own these businesses: fair-trade and pro-poor organisations and arts and crafts dealers in Europe.

We (two linguists with a specialisation in African linguistics and professional experiences that almost always relate to postcolonial and neocolonial spaces) asked the men about the story behind the midsized figures that are in the centre of the picture: three black statues with red paint on their hands, bellies and buttocks, and with exaggerated heads turned to the beholder. Wide-eyed stares fixate us, and we look at a mouth that contains white, bared teeth. The entire figure looks like the caricature of the cannibal, the ultimate Other. The vendors explained

Figure 1.1 Figures on a beach (photo A. Storch)

that these sculptures were part of an entire set that represents 'characteristic Africans': Maasai, Somali, Makonde and Ghanaians. The figures in question are Ghanaians, we are told. 'There are no cannibals here,' a vendor concluded.

This is a sentence that sounds familiar after having been to the beach even for just a couple of days, where we worked on a project that deals with the acquisition and use of heteroglossic repertoires there. This beach is not only a business area for souvenir vendors, but also of people who offer anything from a necklace to sex. A visit to the beach and a swim in the warm waters entails haggling it seems, though not so much over the price of a certain object or service, but rather over the beach itself: in order to go there, does one have to buy or may one turn down what is offered? The following dialogue is one among many similar ones that were recorded at Diani Beach in September 2017; a beach vendor, or beach boy, approaches a tourist, a woman from Germany who stays in the same hotel we are staying in, by greeting her in a form of Swahili that is largely reserved for tourism communication (Nassenstein, 2016 & this volume). The woman, who has explained that she finds it difficult to relate to the many dealers at the beach, replies only reluctantly, perhaps trying to fulfil a minimum of politeness, but moves on without returning the offered greeting gesture. The vendor tries to attract more attention by suggesting that they have already met, but he receives just another refusal, a faint waving and a nod of her head. At the end of the encounter, the beach vendor seems to suggest that there is no need to be so reluctant, or even afraid, this is a safe space, no cannibals here:

Vendor	*Jambo!*
	'Hi!'
	\<offers high five\>
Tourist	*Äh jambo!*
	'Mh, hi!'
	\<moves on\>
Vendor	*Aber hallo, ich hab dich schön gesehn!*
	'Wow, hello, I have already/nicely seen you!'
Tourist	*Jaja...*
	'Well, well.'
	\<hostile / refusing gesture\>
Vendor	*Wir sind hier keine Kannibalen, wir beißen nicht. Wir fressen dich nicht.*
	'We are no cannibals over here, we won't bite. We won't eat you.'

This dialogue might seem simple, but it is, at a closer look, complex and rather deep. Together with the objects that are produced in a nearby community but by order of international players and intended to serve as a portrayal of AFRICA, this communicative event illustrates what the language of tourism might be: first of all, and most obviously, perhaps, there is a presence of several languages, namely Swahili and German, as well as English. Swahili seems appropriate only in its form as a tourist code, in a much too brief greeting, which, however, at the same time is commodified language, printed on cups, towels and t-shirts (Figure 1.2). German is spoken at the beach as well, and it seems to be equally commodified: as a working tool it is indispensable to those selling to tourists in Diani, who use it in highly efficient ways, playing with stereotypes, idiomatic language and irony. Yet, language remains curiously constrained by its context.

At the beach, we heard the remark on the cannibals many times, usually as an expression of contempt over reluctant buyers. The beach, as a prototypical tourism site, does not offer much space for encounters that are not shaped by its commodification. Its sections are partitioned by different players – hotel management, tourists, fishermen, beach boys, among others – and interactions and conversations run along scripted lines.

It is interesting that the figure of the cannibal is reproduced by the hybrid players at the beach in these scripted, ever-recurring dialogues that happen at the beach and the tourism spots surrounding it. *Kannibale* in this environment may be part of a mimetic interpretation of ironic comments by Germans, as a way of speaking back: 'we know what you think of us.' But it also has a deeper layer: colonial imagery of the monstrous

4 Language and Tourism in Postcolonial Settings

Figure 1.2 *Jambo* on a cup (photo A. Storch)

Other produced and continues to produce mistranslations of narratives on historical experiences (such as Europeans and Africans suspecting each other of cannibalism during earlier colonial encounters; cf. Behrend, 2013), and the frequent emergence of the cannibal in beach discourse not only hints at such colonial continuities, but also at the dynamics which are inherent in them. After all, the discursive violation of the cannibalism taboo (suggesting the addressee might consider the speaker a cannibal) elicits strong emotions: anger, irritation and contempt, which ultimately attract the attention needed in order for some business to be done in an utterly competitive environment of which many different players claim ownership (Andrews, 2014). Therefore, even though the cannibal is an offensive discursive turn, making all too obvious that this is, ultimately, a spoilt paradise, it can be played with in profitable ways, as a technique that helps to create an affective vendor–buyer relationships. While greetings need to be quick (but sound impolite to our ears trained in *Kiswahili sanifu* – Standard Swahili of the classroom) in order to get immediate hold of a potential client, access rituals need to be emotionally bonding. The discursively disturbing cannibal therefore bears multiple meanings: this is a comment on a shared violent past, a play with being othered, an unpleasant comment on a presumably failed interaction (nothing sold...), but it is also part of a communication that will be carried on, later, during the following days. And here, the cannibal phrase turns into an access ritual – disturbing yet grasping attention and creating conscience.

The tourists we met in the all-inclusive hotel that was one of the foci of our research projects, and their comments that we read in the guest books and online fora dedicated to Diani Beach almost unequivocally expressed their disdain about the communicative interactions they had at the beach. What easily takes on the form of the 'quick' (Phipps, 2007) is as often turbulent language practice that leaves us with contradictory feelings – confused and angry and yet trying to make sense of the encounter.

***

This volume is dedicated to a deeper understanding of the relationships between researchers, tourist sites and their different players, language and performance in postcolonial and neocolonial spaces. Who are we there, and as whom are we constructed by those who are there with us? Turning the gaze to tourist sites of the 'global south' reveals not only that colonial continuities shape limitations in engaging with one another, but also that the politics of current global mobilities are very much the politics of movements that resemble, in their directedness and economies, movements in the era of colonialism. This might seem a statement that contradicts current perspectives on migration as most saliently being a movement of people from the 'global south' to the 'global north', as refugees and as 'global poor'. However, the seemingly more commonplace mobilities from the north into about every part of the globe involve considerably larger numbers of people and result in foreign presences of unrivalled extent, worldwide: tourism is not only among the world's largest industries, but it also forms part of mobilities that outnumber those that are so much in focus now – those of refugees and 'southern' migrants. This blurred perspective is as much rooted in our colonial history as are the directions in which these mobilities take place. As Esther Lezra (2014) writes, a collective way of thinking, dominated by European colonial paradigms still results in projections of white guilt onto black monstrosity, which makes it rather easy, we suspect, to portray the presences of 'the southern poor' in the 'global north' as menacing or, at least, disturbing. Yet, 'the multigeneric, multispatial, and multilingual social archive' (Lezra, 2014: 52) that we can explore and analyse in order to deepen our understanding of the art of demonising others, of continuously consolidating foreign interests in the formerly colonised parts of the world, and of the neocolonial dynamics at stake, also offers access to' 'the literary and artistic documents that – disjointed and yet together – transform the archive into a narrative of relentless anti-colonial struggle' (Lezra, 2014: 52). The neocolonial dynamics of tourism, in terms of its political economies, cultural production and linguistic performativity, are, therefore, also confronted with the overarching contradictory and contradicting possibility of leaving hegemonic paradigms, becoming someone else and turning White guilt into White virtue (Lipsitz, 2014; Roque, 2015; Hunt, 2015, among others).

Hence, even though the tourism industry is produced and based on the perfect consumption of its sites, the continuous implementation of hegemonic (European) thought and practice, and the continuation of colonial categorisations, its inherent need for rupture, confusion and adventure (Ruf, 2007) reveal the simplifications that underlie simple binaries such as 'northern' and 'southern', 'colonial' and 'colonised', and so on. Tourism, as one of the most ubiquitous and powerful sites of mobility and cross-linguistic interaction, is a complex context in which historically rooted entanglements (linguistic, ideological, economical) are played out by the different participants. Consequently, a sociolinguistics of tourism increasingly needs to turn a gaze to the settings in which the discovery of ourselves as well as the production of the Other takes place – contexts of power inequalities, resistance and subversion, social injustice and struggle. This is not so much about language simply seen as a monolithic structure or as multilingual wealth and diversity, but about language as a possibility painted by ideologies and objectifications, as well as language as a living, messy practice that allows for the interpersonal and 'quick' (Phipps, 2007).

In other words, tourism – its mobilities, dynamics and consumptions alike – is a context in which language might be merely an idea, such as this Swahili lessons offered at a southern Kenyan hotel, which were not more than an advertisement, and never were held (Figure 1.3).

The advertisement completed an entire assemblage of announcements, for example on tour buses, booking tariffs, restaurant opening times. But unlike these, it was of little interest, and a bit hidden, as the tourists who would book the offered courses and lessons had not come for a while. Kenyan beaches do not attract international tourists as before, and the hotel, for a couple of years already, catered to Kenyan conferences and family holidays, to guests, in other words, who were not the target group of a Swahili lesson because they were likely to already know this language.

Yet, Swahili, or any other language at stake, actually might be acquired during one's stay at the touristic 'homeless home' (Ruf, 2007): emblematic words quickly learnt and taken home as phrases printed on t-shirts and cups, as well as linguistic representation in touristic performance and mimetic interpretations of what is foreign and different are among the seemingly everyday contexts in which language is enregistered, objectified and transmitted. Local grassroots learning (e.g. Schneider, 2016) as well as the multispatial commodification of language (Heller, Pujolar & Duchêne, 2014) have been in the spotlight recently as crucial contexts of language as practice and representation

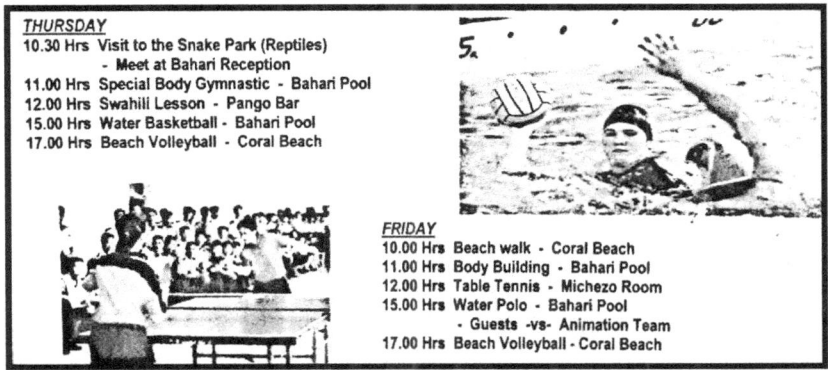

Figure 1.3 Promised language, among other lessons (photo A. Storch)

alike. These and other current contributions to the sociolinguistics of tourism (e.g. Jaworski & Pritchard, 2005; Thurlow & Jaworski, 2010; Heller *et al.*, 2014; Blackwood *et al.*, 2016; Nassenstein, 2016) increasingly help us understand that language in tourism contexts is also about anti-colonial performance and stance, and subversive play. Normative and standardised language and the possibility of a single interpretation of what is said are equally challenged: talk may consist of any resource available, and 'feel good' as long as it is permitted to be open and fluid; multilingual proficiency in standard languages, in contrast, may be seen as work and as a working tool that is tedious to use (Storch & Nassenstein, forthcoming). And while we travel along colonial routes, it seems we encounter colonial images and concepts – those of VILLAGES, TRIBES, the INDIGENOUS, the MONSTROUS OTHER.

Yet, we may find it disturbing to travel and consume along such lines of thought, and the rupture offered by travel also allows for the creation of communality and humanity. In an ambiguous way, the cracks that open and that become visible there are among the problematic legacies of colonialism that not only shape globalised mobilities of tourists but also the ways in which language incipiently defies the grasp of linguistics. If there is nothing that is good in what is bad, as Christiane M. Bongartz remarks in this volume, then our good intentions in trying to acknowledge language as a messy humane practice remain contradictory attempts to liberate what we need to control – at least, the object of our discussion is still LANGUAGE, something that is whole and separate, and that still must be categorised, using terms that remind us of our good intentions, such as 'World Englishes' and 'Beach Swahili', which in the end would still be imperfect and substandard, and broken. Colonial language ideologies and terminology resist our good intentions, it seems, and yet, on a beach, become part of subversive play that hurls the ruins of these colonial monuments at our feet.

This is also relevant to how tourism not only includes the here and now, but it is in many ways connected to culture and language – and as such very much linked to the ANCIENT or LOST culture and the language spoken in these cultures in former times. Travelling abroad does not only mean travelling in space but also travelling in time where history plays an important role. But 'time' in tourism is a relatively blurred concept: it can refer to centuries and millennia, as in the Pharaonic Village in Cairo, where tourists immerse themselves in history, accompanied by people disguised as ancient Egyptians (http://www.pharaonicvillage.com/):

Figure 1.4 Travel back in time

'Time' in tourism may also refer to a time which has not yet passed, but is conceptualised as TRADITIONAL and UNDERDEVELOPED – time that seems to signify the 'not yet', the stage that 'still is', for example, in the AFRICAN VILLAGE, as the tourism blogger Jim Heck (2011) observes:

> The market for village visits is so strong that even today, when traditional villages just don't exist, they are being reconstructed, and thousands of visitors return from Africa every day believing they have seen "an African village" in exactly the same way conservatives leave church each Sunday believing Satan is a Muslim. [...] By the 1980s and certainly 1990s Africa was developing as fast as information technology. Primitive people weren't primitive, anymore. But primitive and "savage" and "diseased" and "deprived" were the "physical, psychological and geographical abnormalities" that could still get tourists to pay. [...] So easily

predicted these "villages" suddenly existed right next to very swank tourist lodges and camps. "Maasai villages" which in their original form never existed longer than the rains which fell on them for a single season, suddenly were in place for decades. (Heck, 2011, https://africaanswerman.com/vicious-village-visit/)

This is a contradictory discursive space: visits to sites such as Maasai villages in Kenya (where warriors perform wedding or hunting dances, introduce audiences to stereotyped Maa language practices and sell exotic souvenirs) produce essentialising narratives on authenticity and allochrony, and they also – often at the same time – trigger ironic performances that aim at unmasking and mocking the seemingly orientalist and inadequate representations of the VILLAGE (see Storch, this volume).

Heck's anecdotal texts suggest that these villages, dances and invented traditions need the tourist gaze (Urry, 2002) in order to make sense. This gaze is contradictory, too: gazing at commodified places and practices, and commodifying them at the same time. It needs the Other, and it creates the Other. Concepts of LOST CULTURE and LOCAL KNOWLEDGE are tourist magnets, and by displaying aspects of forgotten and traditional lives, tourists are confronted with the yesterday, with the Other from back then and the Other of today, who gives the tourist the sentiment of being a part of history. 'Tradition,' being a critically discussed term in academia, guarantees the interest of tourists. For this reason, 'traditional' dancers, like those in the 'Maasai show' (Figure 1.5), or elsewhere, such as the Tjapukai dancers in a museum in Cairns in Australia (Figure 1.6) perform in an out-of-space and out-of-time context what tourists seem to wish to see.

Urry classifies such sites of banal globalisation (Thurlow & Jaworski, 2011) in terms of three dichotomies 'whether they are an object of the romantic or collective tourist gaze; whether they are historical or modern; and whether they are presented as authentic or inauthentic' (Urry, 2002: 94), arguing, however, that this characterisation is quite simple and must be seen in a far more complex context.

Actually, successful tourist sites are design and architecture masterpieces that offer anything wanted by their visitors, from TRADITION and HISTORY to AUTHENTICITY. An example is a museum dedicated to community tourism and aboriginal culture, found in Cairns, Australia (otherwise known as a starting point for exploration of the Great Barrier Reef and as such visited by tourists from all over the globe). As the 'traditional Aborigines' are not to be seen in this place, an interesting form of a site comprising characteristics of the historical, authentic and romanticised is found in the museum. The Tjapukai Cultural Centre which advertises itself with the slogan 'discover the world's oldest living culture,' offers insights into all topics that tourists may connect with Aboriginal culture. It was not initiated by the community itself but by North American

Figure 1.5 Maasai dancers performing a wedding dance in a hotel in Diani, Kenya (photo A. Mietzner)

theatre and amusement park professionals; yet it is the only heritage museum devoted to local aboriginal culture (and language) around and seems to exist largely unchallenged and uncritiqued.

In the museum, besides being introduced to the knowledge of boomerang throwing, spear throwing and food use, the visitors are pelted with language fragments making them feel close to the history and tradition of Aboriginal culture. Although, according to Bob Dixon, the

Figure 1.6 Tjapukai dances in a museum in Cairns, Australia (photo A. Mietzner)

Tjapukai language is hardly spoken in Cairns today (Dixon, 2015), but its words play an important role in the performances of the Tjapukai museum guides.

While performing the Aboriginal culture in impressive light and dance shows, the accompanying English explanations are permanently interrupted by the Tjapukai translation of whatever was just mentioned: lexical items as interactive artefacts, thrown in by the other performers. Even though commodification of language and its dislocation in global capitalism are the two fundamental principles of selling 'language' in tourism, the obtrusive and inflationary presentation of Tjapukai words during the dance performances may be seen as a form of corporeal politics (Henry, 2000) in order to gain agency, revitalise identity and participate in representations of cultural authenticity. The young guides of the museum, who are members of contemporary Australian society, transform themselves into actors of an imaginary ancestral culture and language and use what some might call 'broken English' and others 'Aboriginal English' to explain the past. As we happened to talk to one of the guides outside of the museum, the 'broken English' was gone and the young woman turned out to be a graduate with a degree in performing arts, speaking English as most of the Australians around do. Neither she nor her colleagues really came from Northern Queensland, but they were professional entertainers who had studied Dixon's and other linguists' work in order to become a bit familiar with the languages that once existed there. In their performances, language is exhibited almost as a word list with the most important nouns that should be remembered and stored for posterity.

Figure 1.7 Website of the Tjapukai Cultural Centre

Not only is the 'lost language' presented to the visitors, but the equally 'lost' 'traditional' life of the Tjapukai was offered, to be experienced in exercises of spear throwing (Figure 1.8), boomerang throwing, lessons in fruit usage and didgeridoo playing (Figure 1.9). Authenticity here is presented as a form of invented tradition (Ranger & Hobsbawm, 1983) – the didgeridoo was only introduced to Australia's tropical north in the 20th century, and Aboriginal music today would equally be techno or country music, with a larger variety of instruments used.

When doing 'fieldwork' at the Tjapukai Cultural Centre and other such sites, we certainly enjoyed the experience. It was nice to throw a boomerang and to talk to the artist who, in his leisure time, composed contemporary musical pieces for the didgeridoo. And while speaking to the different players at these sites, we became part of the tourist site – unintended and impalpable. The construction of the 'researcher' has no meaning at the tourist site, it seems; we turn into those for whom these non-places and non-histories are scripted and become immersed in them. What we gain, though, are new insights into what we are actually *also doing*, as researchers in our linguistic fields: we perform, experience and embody, and because this is so, we come up finally with our *small stories* – anecdotes that typically are told during coffee breaks at conferences and in leisure time, but that contain much depth and truth (Storch, 2017).

Figure 1.8 Spear throwing at the Tjapukai Cultural Centre (photo A. Mietzner)

Figure 1.9 Didgeridoo performance at the Tjapukai Cultural Centre (photo A. Mietzner)

This is why this volume is dedicated to studies that are about the sociolinguistics of tourism as much as about performativity of the researchers themselves. The linguistic entanglements and representations with which this book is concerned are not simply those of other people (and research objects), but ultimately our own. Language in tourism settings helps to construct Self and Other, mark the differences between different players, constructs binaries and stereotypes, and – in all its fluidity – constantly gets commodified in various ways; yet, all this does not simply happen to those whose grasp at tourism is turned into a topic in the various contributions to this volume. All these processes, and all the meaning-making also happens to those who observe and write. This is reflected in a form of deep reading of her own photography output while exploring linguistic landscapes in Jamaica by Christiane M. Bongartz, who asks about the person behind the lens: who produces these images, and why? What landscaping is this – a search for the diverse and multilingual in order to highlight the postcolonial and the fluid of the exotic site, perhaps? The critical analysis of her own writing and photography leads to reflections on language ideologies and concepts of place and signs. It seems as if representation and reproduction are practices and dynamics that also need to be put into focus here.

Luís Cronopio's contribution highlights precisely this; his text on backpacking performances is a performance itself – an empirical contribution, as he calls it that frames the empirical as experience and embodiment. The critical thinker and researcher here is part of a performance and is interchangeable in all places where tourism takes place: backpacking, Cronopio suggests, is a globalised form of travelling. The backpack, however, in his text, is much more than a globalised accessory – it sets a stage which turns place into non-place, talk into non-talk.

Yet, the commodified place does speak. In Tawona Sitholé's poem *cape coast caper*, the walls of the Cape Coast Castle in Ghana, which now is a tourist site where the tourist guides' performances can be consumed, resonate with names that must be left behind when one enters. Truth, it seems, is in the lost name and the ever-repeated sounds of the environment (waves, spirits), but other things – those that we, the researchers like to make sense of – are noise: *if there is one thing / about this place / it's the noise / the many many volumes / of history.* Alison Phipps, in a reply to Sitholé's text at the end of this volume, asks for the voices that can be heard: *which ghost are you?* she ends her text with, and after having read the poem, one wants to answer immediately. This is not simply about historical experiences and voices from the past, but about the horror of now. It is easy to make the connection, these poems suggest, between forced migrations then, and today. The refugees leaving the coasts of Africa today may know a different truth about such sites and places.

And of course, sites of interest that are located there, where we travel in order to experience the authentic and real can be multilayered and complex. The tourist site in Sara Zavaree's study on heritage tourism in Iran is the island of Hormoz, where travellers come to watch sand art and spiritual ritual practices. The *Zār* spirits evoked there tell of complex entanglements of time and place: they come from far and relate to experiences of former displacement and subjugation. Spiritual concepts of translocality are at the basis of the performances and practices of *Zār* as public display in Iran. Yet, the place is never arbitrary: *Zār* spirits and *jinn* live in the hills and caves of Hormoz, a place that is avoided by locals but not by tourists, who do not believe in 'supernatural beings'.

The ways in which tourists try to control a place that is otherwise difficult and where practice is located that is deemed difficult practice is the focus of Angelika Mietzner's study on tourists and their cameras. At the places of the poor and needy, in visits to project sites, she looks at how the researcher and the pro-poor tourist take a snapshot. Depending on the kind of tourism, the camera can be used not only as a commodity to preserve moments but also as an important instrument in order to erect a barrier between themselves and the Other. Here, cameras and smartphones help to control emotional moments and keep unwanted ghosts at bay.

In her contribution on heritage tourism in Jamaica, Anne Storch reflects upon the texts and images she came across after a visit to a Jamaican village founded by German migrants. What unfolds is a freak show: these Others are playing unbecoming roles in the tourism play, being ridiculed and deformed. Tourism, this contribution suggests, is also the consumption of the text production that surrounds practices of travel. And these texts are a difficult heritage.

A creative and playful form of text production and language use in tourism settings is found in Manila (Philippines), where language among tourist guides can be seen as a collection of multimodal resources rather than simple linguistic units. This is in the focus of the work on postcolonial performativity in the Philippine heritage tourism industry by Raymund Vitorio. Here, language is seen as a semiotic resource in the context of political struggle and rehabilitation of history. Multilingualism there has become a resource for those who construct new or different ideologies.

The same might be said about multilingual practices of tourism workers in Kenya. The question of how practices and knowledge concerning tourism language are transmitted is explained in detail in the chapter on 'The Hakuna Matata Swahili' by Nico Nassenstein. He offers insights into a grammatically and lexically playfully reduced form of Swahili, which is used by Kenyan tourism workers with tourists and serves to transfer tourists in and out of the context of the holiday situation. He describes the intentions of the tourism workers and their sources of knowledge as well as their strategies of establishing contacts and profiting from them. Here, communicative patterns which are continuously adapted to the changing forms of tourism are unveiled as resulting in rather inhospitable communicative events.

In his afterword, Adam Jaworski correlates the various arguments and approaches offered by the chapters of the volume with the current strands of sociolinguistic research on tourism. There is space for agency and stance that both linguists and poets can make use of, he suggests: 'The legacy of colonialism and the economic disparities that underpin tourism from Global North to Global South do not remain unchallenged.'

Even though there is considerable interest in sociolinguistic research in uncovering inequalities, injustice and struggle as discussed by Jaworski, the sociolinguistics of tourism is not situated in a 'balanced' setting. As the contributions assembled in this volume suggest, the sociolinguistics of tourism remains a northern project, in spite of its interest in postcolonial contexts and the placement of players in the South. This is not surprising, keeping in mind that there is a continuity here, reflecting northern perspectives and epistemologies. An important aspect of the sociolinguistics of tourism is, however, that it could be seen as a framework in which the construction of language and the entanglements between participants in a globalised yet postcolonial world can be analysed. There is an annihilation of language-as-orderly-structure in these touristic scenarios, and also – at a closer look – a distortion of the figure of the researcher. What remains of language as a separate code, and of the academic discipline as a bubble that exists beneath the banal daily life? What we seem to get here are wonderful new old things: words that are reused as spoils, practices that are dynamically made to fit in ever-new contexts and settings, new architecture that evokes the past. What would it be like to write a grammar or some other kind of enregistered text on tourism language and its sites? This seems to be an impossible thought, almost, with everything changing all the time. Yet, language and culture are dynamic practices anyway that do not exist well in the disciplinary cages that were built for them – standardising, archiving and controlling them. Dislocation and brokenness might not be so bad and dangerous after all. Perhaps, we want to suggest, we need to learn again to trust in the power of a story, instead of deconstructing it.

References

Andrews, H. (ed.) (2014) *Tourism and Violence*. New York, NY: Routledge.
Behrend, H. (2013) *Resurrecting Cannibals*. Woodbridge: James Currey.
Blackwood, R., Lanza, E. and Woldemariam, H. (eds) (2016) *Negotiating and Contesting Identities in Linguistic Landscapes*. London: Bloomsbury.
Dixon. R.M.W. (2015) *Edible Gender, Mother-in-Law Style, and Other Grammatical Wonders*. Oxford: Oxford University Press.
Heller, M., Jaworski, A. and Thurlow, C. (2014) Introduction: Sociolinguistics and tourism – mobilities, markets, multilingualism. *Journal of Sociolinguistics* 18 (4), 425–458.
Heller, M., Pujolar, J. and Duchêne, A. (2014) Linguistic commodification in tourism. *Journal of Sociolinguistics* 18 (4), 539–566.
Henry, R. (2000) Dancing into being: The Tjapukai Aboriginal Cultural Park and the Laura Dance Festival. In R. Henry, F. Magowan and D. Murray (eds) The Politics of Dance. Special Issue 12, *The Australian Journal of Anthropology* 11 (3), 322–332.
Hunt, N.R. (2015) *The Nervous State*. Durham, NC: Duke University Press.
Jaworski, A. and Pritchard, A. (eds) (2005) *Discourse, Communication, and Tourism*. Clevedon: Channel View Publications.
Lezra, E. (2014) *The Colonial Art of Demonizing Others*. London: Routledge.
Lipsitz, G. (2014) Decolonizing the work of art in an age of mass destruction. Foreword of E. Lezra, *The Colonial Art of Demonizing Others* (pp. vii–xii). London: Routledge.
Nassenstein, N. (2016) Mombasa's Swahili-Based 'Coasti Slang' in a super-diverse space: Languages in contact on the beach. *African Study Monographs* 37 (3), 117–143.
Phipps, A. (2007) *Learning the Arts of Survival. Languaging, Tourism, Life*. Clevedon: Channel View Publications.
Ranger, T.O. and Hobsbawm, E. (1983) *The Invention of Tradition*. Cambridge: Cambridge University Press.

Roque, R. (2015) Mimesis and colonialism: Emerging perspectives on a shared history. *History Compass* 13 (4), 201–211.
Ruf, F.J. (2007) *Bewildered Travel*. Charlottesville, VA: University of Virginia Press.
Schneider, E. (2016) Grassroots Englishes in tourism interactions. *English Today* 32 (3), 2–10.
Storch, A. (2017) Small stories. *The Mouth* 2, 97–117.
Storch., A. and Nassenstein, N. (forthcoming) Balamane. Variations on a ground. In I.H. Warnke and E. Erbe (eds) *Macht im Widerspruch*.
Thurlow, C. and Jaworski, A. (2010) *Tourism Discourse: The Language of Global Mobility*. Basingstoke: Palgrave Macmillan.
Thurlow, C. and Jaworski, A. (2011) Tourism discourse: Languages and banal globalization. *Applied Linguistics Review* 2, 285–312.
Urry, J. (2002) *The Tourist Gaze*. London: Sage.

Web Addresses

Heck, J. (2011) Vicious village visit. [Blog] *Africa Answerman*. Available at: https://africaanswerman.com/vicious-village-visit/ [Accessed 15 December 2018].
The Pharaonic Village at http://www.pharaonicvillage.com/
Tjapukai Cultural Centre at http://www.tjapukai.com.au/

2 Transformations of the 'Tourist Gaze': Landscaping and the Linguist behind the Lens

Christiane M. Bongartz

Much has been said about the role of the linguistic researcher in the field – as hunter-gatherers, staying aloof from the community surrounding us, we document and sort linguistic data to compile grammar books, or we immerse ourselves as participant-observers, again with the purpose of compilation and categorisation. Storch (2017) comments on the burden shared by these approaches: the power of selection lies with the researcher, and the outcomes are frequently tainted by inherent prescriptivism, however well-intentioned and 'descriptive' the individual researcher might feel about their methodology. What is strange to observe is that the issue of personal accountability rarely is explicitly addressed: how will research products be made use of, for example, to serve as norms in educational contexts? What sort of control does the researcher have over future (unintended) use? (cf. (Bongartz *et al.*, 2015). In part, this is certainly due to the demands of the scientific method and its claim of objectivity. While quantitative and qualitative research methods get taught in linguistic graduate programs, there is no systematic instruction to examine and reveal personal dispositions and motivations, even though it is obvious enough and has been variously addressed that linguistic researchers often act from the luxury of privilege afforded by an education in the Global North.

Epistemology has a way of convincing us of innocence: looking upon the world to uncover language, such is the promise, cannot harm, and its results will prove enlightening with respect to the role of language, be it in its development, its use, or its dynamicity. These ideas, I have found in my own experience, help us think of linguistics as somehow 'good,' and our researcher identities can be built quite strongly on this core idea. Thus, when we invade a new research context, we do not first and foremost consider how our presence might affect these contexts; after all, we are just looking. In this, being a linguistic field worker and/or data collector is a bit like being a tourist – we expect to be welcome, and we are propelled by the idea that good things are to come. Also, and this turns out to be quite crucial, we can leave when our mission (enjoyment/data collection) has been fulfilled. Linguists and tourists, to put it differently, show up by their own choice in contexts of their own choice to turn their gaze onto these contexts for the purpose of reflection: an ideal experience entails a perfect match between their mission and its reflection in local circumstance.

'It no fair fi a discriminate gainst fi wi owna people through dem talk Jamaican' – this claim made to the Jamaican parliament by the linguist Hubert Devonish in 2002 captures an instance where a linguist, because of long-term immersion in a local context, can achieve actualisation of linguistic ideas of human rights; the efforts made by Devonish and his colleagues at the University of the West Indies at Mona have indeed since inspired bilingual programs in Patwa, the Creole that is the native language to most Jamaicans, and English, the language of schooling, of higher education, of administration, of power (cf. Devonish & Carpenter, 2007). Another linguist, Fred Cassidy (1961), enabled this effort 60 years ago when he developed a phoneme-to-grapheme transposition for Patwa. I took a picture of the transliteration table at Devonish's office when I was visiting Jamaica in 2015 (Figure 2.1).

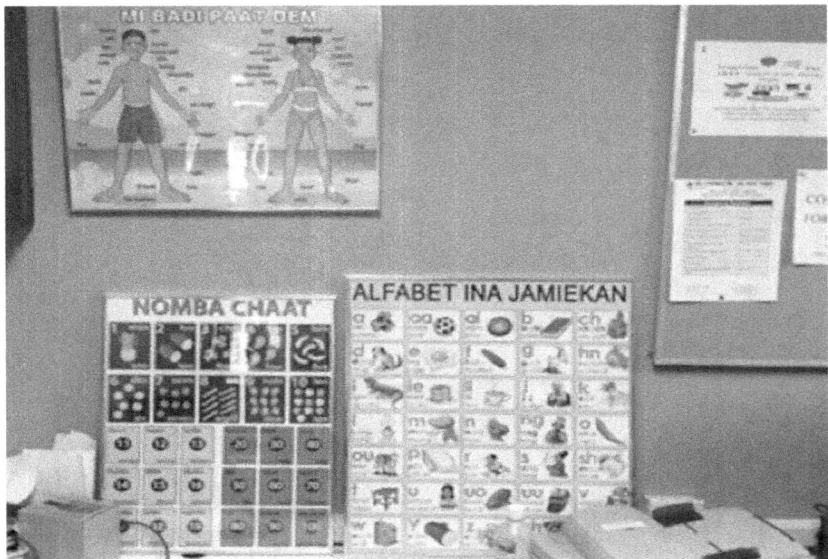

Figure 2.1 Writing in Patwa (University of the West Indies at Mona, photo CMB)

The photo belongs to a series that I compiled, in what was initially an effort to engage in linguistic landscaping. I have stored them in a separate directory of the eponymous title, which involved sorting out the photos belonging there from others taken while in Jamaica but not belonging there. Linguistic landscaping, in this case, became a separatist effort – discerning the linguistic from the non-linguistic. Number charts and the Jamaican alphabet visualise something I value: bilingual and biliterate education and the means to provide it. Turning my linguist gaze onto these artefacts I found reflection of my values.

On another occasion, a shop sign in Kingston attracted my attention, and I took a picture because of the creative use of the possessive in the English on display, and the lexical variation on 'wedding gown' (Figure 2.2). Again, the attraction is best viewed as a reflection – in this case, of my interest in the degree of independence Jamaican English has gained of the British Standard that is taught in schools there. In linguistic terms, such independence is desirable: '[...] spelling choices can shed light on whether speakers understand Creole to be a dialect within the larger system of English or a separate language system' (Hinrichs & White-Sustaíta, 2011: 47), varieties of English today are indicators of development, no longer labelled as 'shortfall varieties' (van Coetsem, 1992) and hence bleached perhaps of their colonial roots.

Figure 2.2 Shop sign in Kingston (photo CMB)

Another picture in this series combines use of English, this time in the standard variety including capitalisation conventions, with the locale of instruction: at this school in Mooretown, a Maroon town nestled in the hills near Portland, all children have the ability and obligation to learn, illustrated by a happy community in the wall painting, and somewhat incongruously disturbed in its message delivery by administrative signage (Figure 2.3). In this case, the combination of the coloniser language English with a moral imperative and colonial imagery prompted my interest.

Figure 2.3 School in Mooretown (photo CMB)

Another example I want to give here of the reflective nature of my linguist gaze is a picture I took at the grocery store, displaying expectations of appropriate attire both in handwritten but also in printed mode, thus perhaps reinforcing the message (Figure 2.4). This photo is but one example of several where English is used to instruct about appropriateness, all with the heading 'Notice' – no talking, no firearms; literacy in the service of silently controlling public behaviour. The attractor in this case was the juxtaposition of the somewhat inept rendering of the message in handwriting – with a mix of capital and regular lettering – and the printed, more elaborate flyer with the same message and further detail.

At an emergency room in Kingston I detected another rendering of the use of English to specify rules of expected behaviour; this time, the attractor was also that of juxtaposition, but of a different kind (Figure 2.5). As patients are queuing for their doctor's visit, signage is on display on a gate that serves as a physical separator of access, and a guard is present to ensure compliance – the ensemble of which reminded me of the procedure required when visiting a prison.

22 Language and Tourism in Postcolonial Settings

Figure 2.4 *No shirt, no shoes, no service* announcement at grocery store (photo CMB)

Figure 2.5 Emergency room and clinic access (photo CMB)

Unencumbered by linguistic concerns and motivations, friends of mine visited Jamaica close to my travel dates. Having been previously disappointed as tourists to the Dominican Republic, where they had felt sequestered in their hotel complex and had found the staff standoffish and not very welcoming, they thoroughly enjoyed their stay near Negril. As evidence of their great enjoyment – and hence the successful reflection of their tourist expectations – they sent me a photo via a messaging app (Figure 2.6).

Figure 2.6 Salesman near Negril (Private collection)

To them, being able to use English (and not Spanish, a language they do not speak), made it possible to relate to Jamaicans, whom they found friendly and engaging, and they described with joy the freedom of the experience, the laid-back nature of their encounters, the viewing of Bob Marley's golden LPs, the general well-being during their stay. In fact, they have since spent another vacation in Jamaica, bonded with their Jamaican butler, and sponsored him when he had a financial emergency. Upon contemplation, what is perhaps most striking about how their photo captures experience is its interactive character: an actual person is present, a black Jamaican peddling his wares, and a white index finger pointing to the product on display. Compare here my own engagement with the herbal experience of Jamaica (Figure 2.7).

Figure 2.7 Cover of a commissioned national report on marijuana consumption (photo CMB)

Certainly, I also took pictures involving people during my stay – but my linguistic gaze always stayed focused on the written word, on externalised language and its manifestations. While at first sight this might not necessarily imply a difference of experience in terms of encounters with local people, my photo brings to light an essential property of the enterprise of linguistic landscaping; that is, the absence of people from the pictures documenting literate language. Written text has variously been characterised as 'decontextualised'; might one thus define linguistic landscaping as an attempt at context-free re-contextualizstion? Sebba (2010: 73) observes that 'the linguistic landscapes paradigm has evolved rapidly and while it has a number of key names associated with it, it currently has no clear orthodoxy or theoretical core.' In other words, the activities under the umbrella of linguistic landscaping have not been reined in by set rules; however, a strong tacit agreement exists that the documentation of linguistically relevant languaging does not require the presence of people.

My friends, who share with me a history of extensive training in Marxism, political economy, and anti-imperialist philosophy, engaged with islanders in transactions and interactions that they found personally rewarding and that they documented, with pictures, via messaging, and with postings to social media. For them, the postcolonial tourist experience on the island was enjoyable; even though they deplored the violence that characterises the streets of Kingston and the obvious traces of poverty, they felt that people were open-minded, cheerful and extremely personable. As for my own experience, when comparing notes back home, it occurred to me that even during the handful of days I had spent in Jamaica as 'just a tourist' after the end of the period designated as field work, I had always stayed strangely removed from what I was experiencing. A young guy at the beach went spearfishing one day and prepared a meal for us; a victim of colonialism, he had to use his day off from lifeguarding to further pander services to tourists, I thought. But what if he enjoyed spearfishing? And cooking? The dialectic coexistence of facets of experience was not available to me; doing linguistic landscaping had put me under a kind of self-imposed moral obligation to not engage fully with what I was doing.

Linguistic landscapes, then, do not just curiously lack people in how they get documented; they also reveal nothing about the person who is doing the documentation. When taking my photos, I was guided by linguistic assumptions positing a separateness of the coloniser language English and the local language Patwa. Even though I was rooting for the role of Patwa, my viewing or better, my reading, was informed by the separation. Yes, I did find that written English was often employed to direct public behaviour (cf. Bongartz & Storch, 2016); but, as one reviewer pointed out, how is this different in Jamaica than in any other place using public signs? Because the research methodology did not require it, I did not question my role behind the camera. I did question all sorts of things, of course, my privilege in travelling to Jamaica for research, the nature of privilege in general, my interest in colonial footprints manifest in today's language use. Overall, I expected that colonialism would be tied up with suffering and disenfranchisement – and I was guided by this attitude when choosing what to take a picture of.

Differences in attitude, then, reflect differences in motivation; my friends and I, sharing an educated, critical European background, found our expectations filtered through the glasses we were already wearing. It is not at all my intention here to detract from the joys to be had as a tourist, but there is a commonality in the tourist and the linguist perspective that is of its own importance in postcolonial viewing; the freedom to choose. Consider how Zygmunt Baumann (1996) divides the postcolonial world into heroes and victims of postmodernity; in this view, tourists and linguists alike rank highly on the social scale: 'We are all plotted on a continuum stretched between the poles of the "perfect tourist" and the "vagabond beyond remedy" – and our respective places between the poles are plotted according to the degree of freedom we possess in choosing our life.' Associated with this freedom of choice is the kind of insulation brought to one's gaze, like mine as a linguistic field worker:

> the tourists keep distance, and bar the distance from shrinking into proximity. It is as if each of them was enclosed in a bubble with tightly controlled osmosis; only such things as the occupant of the bubble admits may leak in, only such things as he or she allows to go, may seep out. Inside the bubble the tourist may feel safe; whatever the pulling power of the outside, however sticky or voracious the world outside may be, the tourist is protected. (Baumann, 1996)

Choosing one's role in a postcolonial setting thus has an effect on one's interpretation of the experience. Fully expectant of ruination (Storch, this volume), my own view turned to ruined language. In recent critical discourse, my landscaping activities might draw scrutiny as a form of appropriation; coming in as an outsider, I chose to see according to my categories, all from my well-intentioned educated stance, but still indebted to the kind of privilege which is a root cause of that which it seeks to remedy (cf. Todd, 2009). My viewing, made possible despite a lack of experience with Caribbean travel or people from the region, brings about just that, my perspective, my reflection in the other, my freedom of choice. And as this may be an unavoidable subjectivity inherent in the travelling experience, it may prove epistemologically helpful to work on bringing out the moral disposition behind this intellectual attitude; separating standard language from vernacular is my chosen business, but it also gives me further defining power, about correctness, about degree of ruination of linguistic repertoires brought about by language contact.

It becomes very clear that viewer attitude shapes viewers' findings; preconceived notions about places in the post-colony are widely held in the Global North, but they may not at all coincide with views held locally, something the poet Derek Walcott pointed to when characterising his own Caribbean upbringing as 'benign':

> Now someone may say, "How can you talk like that; when the background of that is slavery, exploitation and stuff like that?" In my personal experience, I never went through any punishment as a colonial. As a matter of fact, the opposite happened. What I felt as a colonial young man or boy was that I was part of this Civis Brittanicae or sum idea, you know, we're all one; New Zealand, Egypt, you know, one-seventh of the world, and so on. (Walcott, 1988: 5)

To Walcott, there are special opportunities offered to those educated in the tradition of the British Empire; in that, he emphasises the role of his personal experience. However, in appreciation of his own individual history, he has also come to value ruination of what used to be – in fact, mixing of people, values and languages leads to the energising climate of places like Port of Spain (St. Lucia):

> every culture, every continent of the world is represented in that one city. And not just as a sort of detritus of slavery or indenture – actively represented by the Hindu religion, by Moslem religion, by Chinese, Indian, Syrian, Lebanese, white, black…There's a concept, rather, of how people can look at it as a bastardization. Some people can look and say, "Oh, well, Africa has lost its dignity because it's all mixed up with China; and China has lost its identity." But what is the identity? The identity is in the very fulfillment of criss-crossing of those various cultures within one very compact city…something is bound to ferment that is very, very fertile. (Walcott, 1988: 7–8)

Walcott's cultural optimism stands in relief to stereotypes that look back rather than ahead, and while one may observe that his upbringing represented a form of privilege, it enabled him to see the full potential of change, and it freed him of conservatism – which ultimately provides the root of his creativity as a poet.

Linguistically speaking, fertility has traditionally inspired mixed reactions. Diagnosed by Sapir (1921) as a drift inherent in language, but in reality a dynamism that emerges whenever people from diverse linguistic backgrounds encounter each other, language change proves unsettling to many. Literacy and codification of linguistic standards serve as means of preservation, and education as a generational transmitter of what was agreed upon in the past. Of course, linguists become aware of the tension between preservation and change during their training; however, because of the micro-focus of some of our work, we can be easily blinded with respect to the role we take in setting up the rigid boundaries that set apart educated elites from the rest of the world. This leads to a form of paradox that has attracted little attention so far (cf. Bongartz *et al.*, 2015): linguists are doing what they consider descriptive work, but they have next to no influence on how these descriptions are to be made use of.

How does this relate to my personal experience as linguistic landscaper? In the end, I did not create the landscapes, but the photos I took bear witness to a complex interaction of what was there to be seen and my intentions, motivations and beliefs that all informed the choices I made. Separating out standard English from the Patwa, in this sense, is linguistic viewing, but a viewing inspired by habits, training and values, something that became apparent in the comparison of experience with my tourist friends. The difference in role led to a difference of experience, but it is also connected to what one might call a difference in mission; a tourist leaves the vacation site to return to other roles, a field-working linguist becomes a writing linguist, and in the writing, owing to traditional academic style, the personal usually disappears. Linguists in particular are missing out on the opportunity of self-criticism, not in the strict Marxist-Leninist origin of this enterprise, but in terms of an epistemology that acknowledges its own situatedness. It is not 'bad' to distinguish non-standard forms from standard ones; but it is unenlightened to not reflect on the contextualisation of one's efforts.

Certainly, there are examples of commentary on the researcher self in the literature. In an essay on 'grassroots English,' Schneider (2016: 9), for example, remarks, 'When writing this I admit I cannot avoid a feeling of uneasiness, since in a way I am exploiting my privilege and individual good luck of being an academic from an affluent country who can afford to travel to those places and enjoys the support of the locals in their respective functions.' Such statements may be the starting point of a reformed approach to researcher privilege and the power of making choices. It would seem that such a reform would also increase the potential impact of linguistic landscaping as a research methodology – instead of providing de-peopled static documentation of literary artefacts, one could envision the accompaniment of shop signs with pictures of people visiting shops and conversations with these visitors.

Rich embedding of linguistic landscapes, something that has been done in previous work, would then coincide with an expected commentary on the researcher persona and the complexity of experience that presented itself during the viewing. Storch (2017: 115) provides an instructive example when reflecting on her exploration of the touristscape on the island of Mallorca:

> Accepting what others take us for allows us to step into the background, to move aside, and to stop controlling the non-place of 'the field.' [...] we can experience how it feels to be labelled, placed, and explained because the experience puts us to some extent in the same position as those we seek to describe and understand in our research efforts. (my translation)

Linguistic landscaping is but one way of documenting the interplay of various linguistic and writing systems in a given location. In educational and sociolinguistic parlance, notions such as 'code switching' have largely been abandoned because switching implies separateness. Speakers are said to have various repertoires that they can choose to engage in, resulting in an on-line stream of translanguaging in which togetherness rather than separateness is key. Such views have helped shape critical discourse about the inherent monolingualism of postcolonial education systems and attitudes held about language. Translatability and separateness of linguistic systems, in this view, are simply artefacts of the monolingual episteme, commodified to serve the needs of the GILT complex (Globalisation, Internationalisation, Localisation, and Translation, cf.

Cadieux (2002)) – something that Gramling (2016), for example, puts into focus. Chow (2014: 29) describes monolingualism as 'less the exclusive sign of imposition by political force or cunning than [...] the promise of the singular, a promise that remains open-ended and thus messianic in character.'

A monolingualist stance then is easy to adopt because it is the underlying default in educational systems and in the study of linguistic variation. In the attempt to classify, linguists seek to sort out messiness; when English as a coloniser language comes into contact with local languages, the resulting mix may come out as a Patwa, but then this Patwa is its own category and can coexist with a standard English that may have changed a bit and have adopted local flavour – but messiness is avoided and order restored. Still, translation from linguistic description into educational curricula is always subject to a renewed exposure to monolingualism, one language, codified, correct and 'better' than the alternatives; to be kept pure and without improper use of lexis and grammar. This is most evident when socially motivated change occurs, like the now common gender-neutral singular 'they/their' in English: such a change would expose the French language to 'deadly danger', as purist language politicians have recently pointed out (McAuley, 2017).

Linguistic ideologies such as monolingualism can be quite powerful in that they are also secret; that is, they are hidden even from those pursuing well-intentioned linguistic description. My experience behind the lens in Jamaica illustrates a form of self-imposed censorship whose roots took effort to reveal. It is one thing to enrich description by revealing contextualisation and authorial disposition, but what is it exactly that shapes the identity of the linguist? As it turns out, tools of self-examination are readily available as we struggle globally with the colonial partitions that still shape the world of today. Deumert (2017), as a case in point, explains current political events in Germany in terms of the systematic failure of (West) Germany to deal with its own colonialism and coincident attitudes:

> [...] colonial revisionism and a deep-seated racism that never went away, because its roots – located in the grammar of colonial rule – were made invisible, the memory was erased. Yet, like anything that has been repressed, the violence of colonialism does not simply disappear because we don't talk about it.

Notions such as 'white privilege' and 'white guilt' are all pervasive in today's political discourse, especially in the Global North. There is immediate linguistic fallout in ongoing debates – how is dialogue even possible given the prevalence of racism? Many have found political correctness lacking in authenticity – how, then, can we communicate?

Communication, we seem to discover, is not something that primarily should involve speaking. Concepts such as 'deep listening' are not intended to silence us or to impose censorship, but they lead us to doubt what it is that we are seeing, are doing, and are judging. Are we justified in our judgments? What makes it so?

A new kind of viewer-inclusive linguistic landscaping is hence conceivable, one more reflective of role and impact and contextual circumstance. *Es gibt nichts gutes im schlechten* – nothing good can exist in what is bad, this may be a necessary reminder of why self-reflection belongs with description as a matter of course.[1] The 'reflexive turn' (Clifford & Marcus, 1986) is, at least in some areas of linguistics, an episteme worth (re-)visiting, perhaps by considering the body of work devoted to 'decolonising anthropology' (Harrison, 1991). Gramling (2017) refers to our times as the 'linguacene', an extension of the preceding 'anthropocence' – an aptly thought-out name in that it covers the power language and linguistic choices have achieved. No one can be a global player without access to prestigious linguistic repertoires, most often English now, but possibly also Chinese or Russian or Portuguese in the future. Elites in capitalism have always been aware of this, compare the global network of expensive international schools that follow excellent practices in bilingual education while national debates still focus on 'one language – one country – one culture'; that outdated and dangerous Herderian triad.

Reflection on one's researcher identity requires taking a deliberate stance; what is my contribution and how will it be useful? More importantly, how might it be used and by whom to what purpose? Walcott (2015: 12) is aware of the power differential inherent in language choice when he observes:

> You know, there's an inherent superiority in English that says, any other language is really not up to it. Most empires have that, right? But if you have a sort of democratic approach to speech, right, not arrogance but a democratic approach to speech – you don't really listen to other people's languages because you think you're speaking the proper way. So, if you hear Spanish, you think immediately of saying, "Well, it's an inferior people. They don't really talk English." And so you call them Spics.

Slurs referring to Hispanic speakers in the United States are indicative of 'tuning out' – they are a form of anti-listening, and this is how they are increasingly seen by those seeking freedom from existing linguistic patterns. 'We are all hurt by systems of colonization,' states a flyer by the US-based movement 'Idle no more – Decolonizing our activism' (2017). Participants actively seek to build authentic alliances and to honor indigenous traditions without appropriating their cultures [...] To heal from the historical trauma, you must first understand how colonization has impacted indigenous people. By acknowledging our collective past and focusing on the present healing often leads participants to become aware of historical barriers that can be removed effectively in a safe and comfortable environment (Idle No More).

In this context, debates about racism and one's own implication with what is a racist system has given white liberals pause; in linguistic circles, the issue of racism and how one might be implicated by it by being gainfully (albeit often precariously) employed by the institutions of such a system has proven hard to face. In general, it is left to the individual and hence not part of training in graduate schools or in research methodology courses to determine the roles and general purpose of one's research activities. Often driven by the need to reach the next stage of qualification, to finish a dissertation or to apply successfully for another grant, junior researchers may not be able to gauge the scope of what goes on when turning the linguist gaze onto other people's linguistic behaviour. Even for me, a tenured Marxist explorer of linguistic landscapes, it was easy to make choices based on what I thought was expected in the chosen framework – a choice I could look at the very least as neutral; I was doing no harm.

There are unfolding discourses especially in the Trump-era United States that seek to teach us or let us experience the nature of privilege so that something might be done about it. Efforts range from workshops to talks and publications that help reveal that which is hidden:

> White people have the privilege to interact with the social and political structures of our society as individuals. You are "you," I am "one of them." Whites are often not directly affected by racial oppression even in their own community, so what does not affect them locally has little chance of affecting them regionally or nationally. They have no need, nor often any real desire, to think in terms of a group. They are supported by the system, and so are mostly unaffected by it. (Metta, 2015: 2)

This kind of listening may be hard to do, but it can prove instructive and ultimately revolutionise our seeing. In the end, the issue is not how I might feel better about my activities in the field. The issue is how I might actually be able to avoid doing more harm than good, and then to see how something good might be accomplished. Deep listening and the tools of non-violent communication (cf. Rosenberg, 2001) will assume a deeper relevance once self-criticism is practiced not as the moral obligation an individual might self-impose, but because as linguists we are in fact part of a group, and while we may feel powerless and worry about continued employment and the next grant, we are in positions of power. What we see and why we take notice matters, and it is harmful not to acknowledge this.

It would, of course, be naive to assume that this kind of change can be affected easily. For one thing, it may be too easy to agree to the general line of argumentation to then actually bring about change in how we publish and how we review papers. For another, there is always backlash to be expected. Take, as an example, a critique in another academic discipline of algebra and geometry as perpetuators of 'unearned privilege':

> On many levels, mathematics itself operates as Whiteness. Who gets credit for doing and developing mathematics, who is capable in mathematics, and who is seen as part of the mathematical community is generally viewed as White. (Gutierrez, 2017: 11)

On Facebook, where the article reporting on Gutierrez's observations was shared, this drew a commentary where the poster rejects this kind of reckoning with colonial bias:

> In fact, it's part the all-too-common, anti-rationalist narrative university campuses are swimming in these days thanks to the ceaseless efforts of post-modernist, neo-marxist faculty and junior bolshevik students. (anonymised, commentator known to me)

In popular culture, the disbelief and disinclination of those that are holding privilege to engage in self-criticism for the sake of a decolonised epistemology has found a reflection in movies or TV shows like *Dear White People*; they visualise, inform, and also frame dramatically the fact that access to white-dominant elite education is fraught with problems and cannot be simply thought of as fair access via fair academic competition. One of the problems of decolonisation is certainly language: what are our discourses like, and how can we even communicate effectively, given the historical divide rooted in colonialism and imperialist exploitation informing today's world order?

My Jamaican experience and my taking for granted my role and my choices behind the camera (or smartphone screen), in this sense, merit reflection beyond the personal. Choice-making is an expression of privilege, and this privilege simply exists; that is, it is not a matter of interpretation, but a matter of material analysis (cf. Hale & Stephen, 2013). The notion of 'white guilt', recently explored by Mietzner (2017) as part of a stance-based linguistic effort investigating tourism, is only partially helpful because of the negative and sometimes even flippant connotations it invokes. Its basic weakness – and one that it shares with the conversation in general about decolonisation – is its rootedness in 'morality', and morality is a matter of belief and interpretation. However, execution of privilege goes beyond individual ethics; crucially, it is a political matter and ought to be construed as such in order to be handled rationally. Neither brow beating nor self-accusation will be effective tools of decolonisation, but as much as the moral and the political are separate categories, my landscaping choices are not 'linguistic' choices alone, they are also personal ones. In this sense, the personal is political, and in withholding information from the reader on why my choices were made and who I am as the chooser, I am offering a perspective that perpetuates a colonial division: a point of view that separates researchers from those that get exposed by our research as users of language to be categorised by us researchers for our own reasons in our own debates – othering in perfection.

Self-imposed standards of objectivity adhere to a research tradition that has long claimed exclusive use of the adjective 'scientific'. However, this adjective in particular is what Freud would have called an 'enigmatic signifier'; fraught with the promising semantics of neutrality, it fails to deliver on the promise, and that is what makes it attractive. Why should we lament the coincidence of the personal and the professional? Increasingly, social media foster immediacy of discourse, such as in the #metoo campaign which is a form of public transcontextual grappling with sexual transgression. It is thus increasingly through language of the personal via Facebook or Twitter that opinion is expressed and shaped, and 'science' and 'objectivity' are not going to save us at the thin line of division between the factual and the fake. Language is the vehicle, always, and we ought to take a good look at it. Gramling (2017: 1) observes in this context that

> the scientific principle of the anthropocene since the 1980s has strongly favored the idea of human activities, actions, and impacts and has been relatively uninterested in the discourses and languages that frame, perform, and translate those activities.

The 21st century, according to Gramling, poses problems of complexity that put language itself on centre stage; machine-based automatic translation exposes us to the corporate interests that are providing the funding for the automation, and this ultimately causes loss of transparency of meaning-making. In the 'linguacene', as Gramling aptly refers to our times, discourse and ownership of language can be expected to incend multilingual political resistance. My previous observations about linguistic landscaping find a reflection here from another angle in the strong emphasis Gramling puts on the need to take language personally.

A radical way of linguistic ownership is, of course, the writing of poetry, and poets like Derek Walcott are keenly aware of the intimate relationship of language and power, and of the masked and secret properties shaping these. Walcott (2015: 10) makes a connection between 'language of the empire' and listening (Walcott, 2015: 12); listening with a 'colonial ear' instigates judgment, thus speakers become *spics*. This attitude of dismissal derives from assumed superiority but is masked by populist speech (Walcott, 2015: 10):

> That here, the man who gets up and says, "We're not gonna take any nonsense," or x, or y, does not speak like a dictator. [...] He speaks with the monosyllables of American averageness, but he's still carrying the same force.

While power should avail itself of polysyllables of power, populist 'mediocrity of monosyllables' serves as a masking device.

Potential for change and resistance, then, would lie in the unmasking of the hidden power structures, making it an obvious first step to listen rather than to judge; in fact, in the debate about white privilege, deep listening has variously been proposed as the only effective and respectful first aid to be applied in a world that is shaped by colonial ruination and its outfall (Bongartz & Buschfeld, 2017). While it may be straightforward to imagine doing so, it is perhaps less clear what deep listening might mean, on an individual basis, but it proves particularly challenging when applied to specific listening opportunities. Reframing my linguistic landscaping endeavour in Jamaica as one of deep listening immediately brings to the forefront the absence of listening space in making my choices. Because I was 'doing being a linguist,' I was applying what I thought I knew, and claiming the right to be doing so. It is perhaps the habitual absence of listening, or, to put it more succinctly, the practice of listening without listening deeply, that has led to the estrangement of linguist from language proper; the need to classify and label becomes self-defeating, or, as Storch and Faraclas (2017) have noted

> Linguistics is now becoming more and more of a conservative patriarchal 'science', an exclusivist, expert-driven discipline, which is about claiming power, upholding standards, enforcing discipline, and domesticating what is written and said in its name. There is less space, it seems, for hospitality in linguistics, for opening the field to other ideas about language, and for sharing resources.

This is not the place to offer a full-fledged criticism of current linguistic practice; colourful and creative efforts are well on their way into mainstream practices. My efforts at introspection of motive are not solely owned by me, of course, and what I am suggesting here, the inclusion of the viewer into the viewing of linguistic landscapes and resultant academic writing, is ultimately a practice of point of view. While long shunned as not scientific or not rigid or not verifiable, subjectivity turns out to be a crucial component of listening. Seemingly contradictory, awareness of self comes with respect of other; in my case, it is not the observation of 'married gowns' that change but the evaluation and integration of what that observation entails. Such practice, even though it might be suspect of navel gazing, is a prerequisite for taking a deliberate stance and awareness of responsibility of how the outcome of my research might be contextualised and used in circumstances beyond my control.

Walcott points to the difficulty of finding his voice as a poet, voice as 'an inner thing that makes me speak, I hope, the way I would write; totally, not just in terms of vocabulary.' Finding one's personal voice is a lifetime effort and requires that the poet 'get to hear his own voice without affectation.' Situated in time, voice-finding then constitutes an effort and may involve changes; something that we can draw lessons from in linguistic writing. Why should we follow the same moulds time and again because they have been established by way of a canon? How can we account for things we learn as linguistic practitioners as we move through our professional development?

Asking such questions does not entail a call for radical subjectivity; for my own personal linguistic writing, it is beginning to involve attention to more open-ended writing practices such as the reflexive essay. Franzen (2017) reminds of the role of such an essay as a mirror as he comments on a published piece of his that 'reflected an angry bird-loving misfit who thinks he's smarter than the crowd. That character may be me, but it's not the whole me, and a better essay would have reflected that.' Following this spirit of situatedness and hermeneutic hindsight, I can reflect now on the choices I have made when doing linguistic landscaping in Jamaica. There is not either the tourist experience or the linguistic experience; and thinking about my motivation for choosing the written language to be documented for my project encourages me to unveil my stance, to the reader, but ultimately also to myself. Me, linguist, landscaper and person with the privilege to choose – these may just be the ingredients that will enable a deeper listening and aid in making linguistics more hospitable, at least for this individual linguist.

Note

(1) I wish to thank an anonymous reviewer for their very helpful contextualisation of my impressionistic account and to the residents of 'Somewhere West' for sharing their insights during our research stay on Jamaica.

References

Baumann, Z. (1996) *Tourists and Vagabonds: Heroes and Victims of Postmodernity.* Vienna: Reihe Politikwissenschaft / Institut für Höhere Studien, Abt. Politikwissenschaft 30.

Bongartz, C.M. and Buschfeld, S. (2017) Observations about the descriptive paradox: Postcolonial linguistics and its struggles with defining power. Paper delivered at the GSSC Biannual Conference, 22 June.

Bongartz, C.M., Deumert, A., Hollington, A. and Storch, A. (2015) 'Unmaking language' – the role of linguistics in removing diversity. Volkswagen Application.

Bongartz, C.M. and Storch, A. (2016) Making sense of the noisy. *Critical Multilingualism Studies* 4, 2.

Cadieux, P. (2002) Feeling GILTy: Defining the terms Globalization, Internationalization, Localization, and Translation. *Language International: The Business Resource for a Multilingual Age* 14 (3), 22–25.

Cassidy, F. (1961) *Jamaica Talk*. London: Macmillan.

Clifford, J. and Marcus, G. (eds) (1986) *Writing Culture: The Poetics and Politics of Ethnography*. Berkeley, CA: University of California Press.

van Coetsem, F. (1992) The interaction between dialect and standard language, and the question of language internationalization. In J.A. van Leuvensteijn and J.B. Berns (eds) *Dialect and Standard Language in the English, Dutch, German and Norwegian Language Areas = Dialekt und Standardsprache* (pp. 15–70). Amsterdam: North-Holland.

Devonish, H. and Carpenter, K. (2007) Bilingual education in Creole situations: The Jamaican case. *Society for Caribbean Linguistics*, Occasional Paper No. 35 (February), 1–48.

Franzen, J. (2017) Is it too late to save the world? *The Guardian*, 4 November.

Gramling, D. (2017) Translating culture in the linguacene: On the politics of large-scale impact of cross-linguistic data retrieval. Paper delivered at AILA – World Congress of Applied Linguistics, 25 July.

Gramling, D. (2016) *The Invention of Monolingualism*. London: Bloomsbury.

Gutierrez, R. (2017) Challenges in mathematics teacher education from a (mostly) constructivist perspective. In S. Kastberg, A. Tyminski, A. Lischka and W. Sanchez (eds) *Building Support for Scholarly Practices in Mathematics Method* (pp. 11–38). Charlotte, NC: Information Age Publishing.

Hale, L. and Stephen, F. (eds) (2013) *Otros Saberes: Collaborative Research on Indigenous and Afro-Descendant Cultural Politics*. Santa Fe, NM: School for Advanced Research Press.

Harrison, F. (ed.) (1991) *Decolonizing Anthropology: Moving Further Toward an Anthropology for Liberation*. Washington, D.C.: American Anthropological Association.

Hinrichs, L. and White-Sustaíta, J. (2011) Global Englishes and the sociolinguistics of spelling a study of Jamaican blog and email writing. *English World-Wide* 32 (1), 46–73.

Idle No More http://www.idlenomore.ca (accessed November 20)

McAuley, J. (2017) Gatekeepers say gender-neutral pronouns pose 'deadly danger' for the French language. *The Washington Post*, 27 October.

Metta, J. (2015) I, racist. *The Huffington Post*. US edition, 10 July.

Mietzner, A. (2017) Mein Ballermann – eine hervorragende Fernbeziehung. (My 'Ballermann' – an outstanding long-distance relationship). *The Mouth* 2, 34–45.

Rosenberg, M. (2001) *Nonviolent Communication: A Language of Compassion*. Encinitas, CA: Puddledancer Press.

Sapir, E. (1921) *Language: An Introduction to the Study of Speech*. New York, NY: Harcourt.

Schneider, E. (2016) Grassoots Englishes in tourism interactions. *English Today* 32 (3), 2–10.

Sebba, M. (2010) Discourses in transit. In A. Jaworski and C. Thurlow (eds) *Semiotic Landscapes: Language, Image, Space* (pp. 59–76). London: Continuum.

Storch, A. and Faraclas, N. (2017) *Hospitable Linguistics*. Residency Project Announcement, Ouarzazate/Morocco, 26–31 August 2018.

Storch, A. (2017) Small stories. *The Mouth* 2, 98–117.

Todd, S. (2009) *Toward an Imperfect Education*. London: Paradigm.

Web Addresses

Chow, R. (2014) Interview. *Columbia University Press Blog*. Accessed 25 September 2015. http://www.cupblog.org/?p=14707

Comment on Facebook (2017) accessed 20 November 2018 by CMB.

Deumert, A. (2017) Colonial amnesia, the rise of the right and everyday racism. *Diggit Magazine*, 28 October. https://www.diggitmagazine.com/column/colonial-amnesia-rise-right-and-everyday-racism. Accessed 6 February 2019.

Idle No More – Decolonizing our activism (2017). Accessed 20 November 20. www.idlenomore.ca

Walcott, D. (1988/2015) A conversation with the Caribbean-born writer. In B. Moyers, *A World of Ideas*, November 1, 1988. Interview transcript accessed on 20 November 2017. www.billmoyers.com

3 Backpacking Performances: An Empirical Contribution

Luís Cronopio

> They cross boundaries, not as invaders conquering territory, but as passersby accumulating nothing, and collecting nothing but perishables – impressions and stories.
> Dean MacCannell

Warm-up

The understanding of tourism goes beyond the explanation of a formal rational thought. The experience of living, in our case, of backpacking, is extremely personal. The inferences and hypotheses rely on the emotions of the researcher and in the interpretation of others' gestures, words, emotions. Observation itself affects the subject. The observer and the observed are not two separate entities; they belong to a system where the whole is greater than the sum of its parts. It is in the midst of this interaction that ideas are developed. But what fosters these ideas is the feelings one experiences. We cannot scan the brains of others to know what they are feeling or thinking, and the answers we draw from direct questions can be a source of biased information. This forms the basis of Malinowski's anthropological methodology: do not exclusively accept what people say about the meaning of social events they participate in, but rather see for yourself what appears to be your and their *realities*.

During the time I was backpacking, I became aware of my feeling towards other backpackers: it was disgust. But where does it come from, this disgust? It is as if someone would come to *steal* my moment of *brotherhood* with the local community, or as if my *neighbor* would reveal that myth of authenticity. If like me, others feel disgust, even hatred, towards other tourists, then we do not travel for the sake of a holiday. We travel to impress ourselves. For one or two weeks, we dress up with a new *local* identity, we play the part of someone we are not and someone we want to be. It is like a lie we are not conscious of. Don't tell anyone. It is our little secret.

Whether the traveller books a flight while lying down on a comfortable sofa or sitting on a chair at a tourist agency, they decide, in that moment, to initiate a journey, a predetermined schedule of time and space, a promise offering them a rest from the stress of work life. The *sine qua non* of tourism is the illusion of happiness, and yet, there seems to be something else that drives the traveller to leave home. In order to be able to research the issue of tourism, in particular the backpacking movement, we need to reduce the social event to a social fact. By drawing these borders, we start to build an enclosed setting in which the performance of the traveller follows predetermined actions just like in the production of a theatrical play. We might be lacking in dramatic intentionality, but we abound with the quantity of tourist encounters. First, we need a setting, a stage.

At the beginning of the 20th century, the Irish dramatist Sean O'Casey stated that 'all the world's a stage and most of us are desperately unrehearsed.' What he meant by desperation is the difficulty we have in making sense of our lives, in understanding the roles we play. Almost one hundred years later, the anthropologist Marc Augé (1995: 85) states in *Non-places: Introduction to an Anthropology of Supermodernity*:

> Space, as frequentation of *places* rather than a place, stems in effect from a double movement: the traveller's movement, of course, but also a parallel movement of the landscapes which he catches only in partial glimpses, a series of "snapshots" piled hurriedly into his memory and, literally, recomposed in the account he gives of them, the sequencing slides in the commentary he imposes on his entourage when he returns. Travel (something the ethnologist mistrusts to the point of "hatred") constructs a fictional between gaze and landscape. (1995: 85)

A parallel here can be drawn with a comparison between the concepts of house and home. The *house* as the architectural structure, the walls, the objects within a space; and *home*, without a definite article, as the place where the immaterial qualities of human beings come together, where a dialogical interaction *takes place*. When we enjoy the company of others, when we share with them moments of joy and of monotony, of smiles and tears, we have a home in the world. The latter conceptualisations *scream* to blend into each other. Territoriality and geographic spatiality assume secondary or less important roles in the backpacking scenario. But Augé's words echo in our heads and we can no longer see the world as it once was: everywhere, whenever, becomes a non-place.[1]

Once we have a home, a stage, we need a plot and a script. The plot is what we see (or what we don't see), what cultural studies aim to give meaning to. Let us close our eyes for a while and imagine a colonial landscape from the past. What we see is the *European* walking from enclave to enclave, with pockets filled with money and good intentions – these are the same *islands* where our grandparents played their games. The latter have remained almost unaltered, because we are, 'regardless of personal views – malicious or benign – incapable of thinking about or acting in the Orient independent of Orientalism' (Barrett, 2009: 29).

The script is a juxtaposition of what we idealise of the authentic experiences to come and the acceptance of their subjectivity. It all comes to the capitalist system: our script. One explanation for this issue is given by the chief propagator of 19th century anarchism, Michael Bakunin (1871: 1–2). He comments:

> Since neither property nor capital produces anything when not fertilized by labor – that means the power and the right to live by exploiting the work of someone else, [...] let us suppose that this economic relationship between exploiter and exploited is altogether legitimate, that is the inevitable consequence, the product of an eternal, indestructible social law, yet still it will always be true that exploitation precludes brotherhood and equality. It goes without saying that it precludes economic equality.[2]

However, this relationship between exploiter and exploited assumes different forms and often it is messy and unstable. In daily interactions, the coloniser turns into the exploited in a matter of seconds, as he adapts his language to deal with the power he feels he no longer owns. These encounters often reveal the status each of us feels when confronting the Other, conveyed by our social self-awareness and/or by our economic situation. It is the latter we now examine. As mentioned before, work life is the conducting wire that permits the backpacker an excuse to travel. This *leisure is non-work for the sake of work* and *it is done on account of some product or output that the worker (or, more often, somebody else) gets out of it* (Black, 2009). So, are we just working *machines,* and a holiday is just a resetting of the hardware and an update of the software? What *really* urges us to travel?

Whether as short-term holiday or long-lasting journey, tourism seems to be the escape from and search for liberation, what Wilson and Richards (2008) call, a *suspension of reality*. The backpacker has the intention of abandoning the materiality of daily life consumption or, at least, to reduce it. And yet, inside the wallet on the side-pocket of the bag lies a card. It is the credit card which allows the pseudo-experience of abandonment and creates another paradox to live with. In our anonymity, we join others, we get along with other backpackers and locals; however, this moment of togetherness is much more individual than communal, we keep our solitude, we lend some of our time and we try to glorify the best of our memories. We try to impress others from a safe distance. Meanwhile, we are also collecting. We are looking for a story to tell, sorting out from the performances of togetherness, which of them is worthy of becoming a memory. During the process of *sorting out*, we meet the Other, who we imagined to be, not exactly like she *actually* is. We become disappointed when we realise *she* is a person like us, not just a myth. It is in this moment that the Other vanishes. We tolerate this, but we do not accept it. And we start searching an-Other. Moreover, this process is never completely sealed. It is permeable and interchangeable, an ongoing interplay of words, silences and symbolic actions. What once was widely accepted as strange and perhaps subversive, becomes normative.

Rehearsal

> Not only the construction of a tourist "class conflict" but also backpacking's subcultural roots in hippie culture come shining through. (Welk, 2004: 84)

Before we explore backpacking acting further, we need a dramaturgy.

The reason we engage in performing a backpacker's social identity becomes apparent when we look at the fashion, the styling of backpackers. It is not a coincidence that the clothes worn by a majority of backpackers resemble the styles of the hippie movement, which reached an apogee in the late 1960s and early 1970s. During this period, the youth saw an opportunity to break down a conservative past, to confront their parents' conformity with a socio-political system. In many ways, it was the fear of a nuclear world war brought on by the Americans and Russians, an awareness of civil rights and the dream of equality, the threads which made the sewing of this fabric of confrontation possible. The *youth* we refer to, however, do not constitute the entire category of young people. As Seaton (2014: 154) writes: 'Those who would reject middle-class comforts had to come from comfortable backgrounds; the have-nots of society had no material luxuries to rebel against.'

Based on exotic bohemian notions, the clothes and styling of these rebels aimed to break the conventions of the time: monochromes were replaced by polychromes; loose hair was preferred instead of tight hairstyles, gendered styles got mixed; fabrics representing other cultures such as Native American, African, Asian and South American were incorporated. Hippie fashion became the symbol of an identity.

Another important feature of the hippie counterculture was the widespread use of drugs. The word 'drugs' is embedded in controversy and a simplified definition borrowed from the medical sciences seems to be the clearest, namely that a drug is a product inducing side-effects. There was also disagreement over the word 'drugs' at that time as well. In terms of a definition, it is essential to understand the polarity between the clashing forces:

> We're talking about doing revolution, attack on all fronts, political, educational, religious, cultural, even business…and dope is part of that revolution, and if you fear dope (Dope, not DRUGS – alcohol is a drug, pot is dope; nicotine is a drug, acid is DOPE; DRUGS turn you off, dull your senses, give you strength to face another day in Death America, DOPE turns you on, heightens sensory awareness, sometimes twists them out of

shape and you experience that too, gives you vision and clarity, necessary to create Life from Death) if you fear DOPE more than you fear Richard Nixon and his Machines Men of Death, then you have indeed sold out and bought in [...] the difference between stupor and ecstasy is the difference between Jack Daniels and Orange Sunshine, between Pentagon and Woodstock [...] we all have to make our choices. (Coffin [1969] cited in Miller [2012])

Although our parents (the youth of the 1960s and 1970s) had the intention of bringing about an egalitarian society – to attack on all fronts – it seems they fell into the same trap as we do now as backpackers: we say that we do one thing, but we end up doing another. Peter Welk (2004) refers to the absence of a mission when drawing a comparison between hippies and backpackers, namely that their actions are only true in form but not in content. Furthermore, we are content with our lives and we use drugs, not to achieve objective states of perception, 'we don't want the sky, we take drugs to control ourselves better, to be able to work better, to understand ourselves and to understand the others, to enjoy' (Escohotado, 2003: 1). Do we want to know what is behind the horizon?

Whether 'dope' was used as a means of understanding and of coping with the evils of American culture, or as a religious experience, or as an awareness of nature and one's unity with it, or as a sexual experience, or to heighten intimacy, interpersonal interaction and cooperation, or as a neutral tool (like an 'active placebo' where the effect is substantially supplied by the user), or just for fun and as something that makes us feel good, or for therapeutic use, or creativity enhancement, it is of less importance when we bring backpackers into the equation (Miller, 2012: 10–19). What is evident is that backpackers adopt not only the hippie-like styles, but also the speech used fifty years ago, which they can only imagine and, reinvent. Today's backpackers 'like to wander off the "beaten track", and may seek apparently unorthodox mystical, drug-enhanced and other counter-cultural experiences' (Edensor, 2001: 74).

Act and Applause

Act 1

Our hashish stories, their qualities and politics fade away. Mr. L felt he could be honest with me, as when you sit at a bar, order a handful of whiskies and share your deepest secrets with the old man sitting next to you: performance sprinkled with psychoanalysis or vice-versa, Schechner meets Freud.

Mr. L took a deep breath:

My parents are very rich, I was born rich. I still am. In my early twenties, I used to hang around with other rich kids. We were finishing our Bachelors in Madrid in one of the following, finance, economics or business. The typical cliché: we were to make our parents happy, and happier, if later, we would take over their businesses. Anyway...

That was a crazy time. We were fools, we felt free. In a few months we became real junkies, and we attended our classes, we wore our ties and, most important, we always had cocaine in our pockets. We sniffed *houses*! I surely spent half a million euros those years. We tried all drugs one can imagine. For a time, we did Calvin Kleins (C for cocaine and K for ketamine). We were the kings of the road, we had this feeling of having everything under control, of having everything done and we had no pains. Some days we were totally down, extremely depressive, suicidal tendencies, but then there was cocaine again...

I could sense sorrow in his eyes and in his voice.

He added

'One day I woke up in a hospital and since then only THC, alcohol and ibuprofen. For five years, I have been travelling around the world with the jewellery I make.'

I did not know how to act. I felt that Derrida was wrong: I did not feel he was performing a text. I shook his hand and thanked him for sharing his story. He thanked me for listening. I wanted to roll a joint and he stopped me:

'Roll your normal cigarette and we will add a drop of cannabis oil. It is really good, it cures even Parkinson's.'

Act 2

On the sofa nearby, sat Ms E., a Swiss woman with sad green eyes. She was reading a travel guide written in German, I noticed. Ms Z. climbed the stairs to the rooftop, and was about to finish the welcome tour of the hostel with Mr A. She was impressed by the place, as everyone was, I think. She turned her body without moving from the place where she was, to look at the corners:

'It is awesome here!'

I thought, America, Donald Trump, fried bacon.

I tried to get up but I could not. My leg was numb.

Ms Z. stayed at the terrace, quietly greeted everyone, and in silence pointed with her right hand to a place to sit by the Swiss woman.

She had just arrived from Agadir, a city she found amazing and similar to Miami. I sat with my feet laying on the corner of the small table; two ashtrays, tobacco in a pack bearing a sentence written in Spanish: *Fumar mata* (Smoking kills), rolling paper, a pen, a bag full of dried dates, an oily page of an Arabic newspaper filled with the bones of fried fish, a bottle of water and a glass, almost empty, of orange juice. The numbness in my left leg was gone. I had the Portuguese edition of a novel by Ben Jelloun on my lap, and pretended I was reading. I was not quite pretending but I had been on the same page for fifteen minutes. I was listening to others' conversations. It was more interesting than the book, which started majestically and then in the middle became poetry written in sentences.

Ms Z: 'I'm originally from Houston, Texas.'

Green eyes blinking with joy: 'Just like Beyoncé!'

Ms Z: 'Yes, like all the single ladiessss.' – Shook her boot, they laughed together and high-fived their empathy.

Act 3

She stopped speaking. The weight of silence, this *in-between* triggers the plot-discourses to come, both the scenario and the script. The next seconds build upon other seconds. We looked at each other and smiled nervously, as if it was something in the air to be grabbed, imagining a cool set for the next act: those beautiful words with which to win her over.

Silence.

More silence.

First signs of discomfort: what would be the right question to ask; deep breathing and a fast pulse.

I wanted to talk about the weather. I could not. It would be very suspicious.

I had just finished a cigarette and I was about to roll another.

More silence: she was also nervous.

The silence was becoming unbearable. I thought about leaving without saying a word.

Kevin broke the silence. Thank you, Kevin. He commented on the question of why so many butchers become pimps: 'I imagine,' he said, 'a tired butcher, sawing bones, cutting meat all his life, deciding on a change of profession. "I am done with the dead meat business, I am going to be a pimp."' We burst into tears with laughter.

Act 4

We were sharing the same room. He refused to say his name. 'Call me Norway', he said. Some days later, I asked him about drug experiences. He told me about his ayahuasca encounter in Mexico:

'I need no more ayahuasca. Now, I just need to embody what I had felt, what I have seen.'

Act 5

Outside of our island, language is fragmentary. A chicken has just been killed in the alley, in front of onions and zucchini and tomatoes, in front of everyone, blood drops on a plastic container; there is a huge amount of dust and feathers, the remains of the bird's struggle. I think I am the only one who is disgusted. Two merchants discuss prices and they are about to have a fight, then they shake hands and kiss each other, I must be lost in translation. Flies visit a hanging pieces of meat, and once in a while, the butcher beats the flesh with a whip. The teenage boys look like Cristiano Ronaldo or Messi – the cristiano-ronaldinisation of societies; super-modernity fabricates not only non-places but also non-cristiano-ronaldos. I realise that I have been paying double the price for bread. A man with no arms looks at me, begging with his eyes, I put a coin in the pocket of his vest. I love the fish market: I buy the fish, I pay five dirhams to a man to clean it and in the restaurant nearby they grill it. I think I am paying more than the Moroccans do. I wish my daughter was here, I think I am Israel and my daughter is Palestine[3]: power relations performance. I want to buy a tajine for nine guests, a multicoloured Moroccan floor seating and a black *djellaba*. The souvenir is to the tourist as a paleontologist is to fossils, but not the other way around: through the souvenir, the tourist becomes a living fossil. The idea of collecting items conveys the idea of materialisation of memory and can define both initial and final ideations of the exotic. I want to keep passions at bay, I laugh alone by the pot, I eat wonderful pastry, fried doughnuts for two dirhams. A young woman flirts with me, I flirt back because I know it ends there, I drink a tea and say *sucre-shuea*; in Morocco, tea is served together with stones of white sugar the size of packs of cigarettes, I think about diabetes in Morocco. I play soccer at the beach, the wind blows strong, I scored one goal and made four assists. A woman carries two plastic bags full of bananas, I wonder if she sells banana cakes or dried bananas. I bargain with the tailor but he does not blink, men gather in the patio in front of the tailor's shop. It is the second-hand market, the people. The items, bicycles, washing-machines, tables, lamps, are shown in a circle round. I imagine a woman presenting the next round of a boxing fight. The bids are made loudly, it is an auction. I think it is a way to reveal the day-to-day secrecy of conducting business. I am searching for fried octopus but today I cannot find it. I read a graffiti sentence on a wall, I do not know what it means. I see a beautiful paper collage on a wall: it is of a poor man sitting staring at me, just beside him is a scene from the first movie about the Syrian war, a building in ruins. Two real men built a wooden house in front of it. There are sentences in French and Arabic written; I think they are protesting the occupation of that place. They must have had houses there and were kicked out for a movie set or a five-star hotel. Not far from there is the set for some episodes of *Game of Thrones*. The surf instructor of the hostel received 300 euros per day as a extra for the movie because his face showed up on the screen. Had it not appeared, he would have received 150 euros. We walk through the red-light district: it is full of garbage, the stoned-paved streets are full of shit, it smells horrible, I wonder how someone can have sex in this place. I love the vegetables in Morocco, their taste is intense. The streets are narrowing; we have arrived back at the starting point.

Aftermath

This era of megacities, hyper-reality, super-modernity and other superlatives has led to another prefix: it is the time of hypo-meaningfulness of conversations. However, these dialogues are not hermetic. Do we mean what we say? Do we listen? After listening to myself and others for a while, the idea of the non-place of Marc Augé popped into my head and I imagined a non-language or a non-speech or a non-discourse, something you cannot categorise well but which is worthy of having its own title, or is it life, an interacting life that I wasn't aware of before, a non-togetherness? The hostel is a stage, we are the actors and our apparent meaningful intimate discourses are the script. This *non-togetherness* in a place far from home seems to be the way that we perform *intimacy* in terms of giving meaning to our memories and aggrandising our importance in a touristic setting. I feel that I have found what it means to be the ultimate traveller, and no one else's experience can beat the one I have chosen to have. This is the source of disgust. And yet, we project on to others the disgust we feel towards ourselves, because we need to fly away to become what we want to become: a better version of ourselves.

Understanding tourism seems an impossible task; it envelops the whole world, the I, the us, the Other and the others. So where can we start? Do backpackers have colonialist intentions? Moreover, a particular question is crying out for an answer: As tourists, why do we recreate dramas from the past, whether as a bohemian or as a hippie or as a European colonialist? What are the structural psychological forces influencing the formation of ideas and their consolidation into short-term or long-term beliefs? Said's corpus on Orientalism provides a socio-psychological answer to this question: Europeans and the West have, through recent human history, shaped ideations of the exotic, referring to the Other as a deviant, excessive, mysterious, less trustworthy, less human; they have done so in the name of religion, ultimately, to possess the Other's riches.

What categorisations try to bring to light, can, at the same time, disrupt. Often, we do not accept the stereotype others use to categorise us. And we wish we could meet halfway. In 1968, the year when the civil rights movement reached its apogee, many believed they could build a perfect society. In a way, they had changed societal morals in the name of an egalitarian world. But that *mission* which Peter Welk (2004) refers to, was more an effect of the search for inner well-being, than it was its cause. Apparently, today's backpackers try to re-enact this – more than less homogeneous – identity. It looks like an easy role to play: you buy a plane ticket, you dress up and you talk about things you would not dare talk about to your boss. In this sense, you are reinventing the hippie; it is the hippie movement 2.0. The particularity now is that we do not claim to change the world. We pack some belongings, we stuff them in our backpacks and we move to another reality because we feel the urge to do so. Because industry urges us to do so. And yet, we search for a new home, with our *houses* on our back, because we feel something isn't right, like a pebble inside our shoe. The dream of abandonment of materiality is conveyed by the backpack itself. The backpack fits like a glove, it symbolises that wish for the immaterial. We walk, we search for *nothing but perishables* (MacCannell, 1992), with that pebble still inside the shoe.

What I imagine is that, in a mystical way and as a primal instinct, backpackers and other wanderers want to purge capitalism from their bloodstreams, from their guts. This profit-oriented *ethos* has not yet attacked our DNA. Furthermore, the limits of the backpacking stages we step into configure a possibility. It is the possibility of communication, the possibility for more self-awareness and the acceptance of the Other as a sister or brother, whether she or he is a backpacker or a local or even our neighbor. What we need is the perfect audience, those people who will embody the artistic direction of our plays. Now, we just need to rewrite our plays, think critically about the disgust we feel and, hopefully, remove that pebble from our shoe, turning it into a piece of art.

Notes

(1) Non-place or nonplace is a neologism coined by the French anthropologist Marc Augé to refer to anthropological spaces of transience where the human beings remain anonymous and that do not hold enough significance to be regarded as "places". Examples of non-places would be motorways, hotel rooms, airports and shopping malls. The term was introduced by Marc Augé in his work *Non-Places: Introduction to an Anthropology of Supermodernity*. The perception of a space like a non-place, however, is strictly subjective: each of us in his or her own way can see the same place as a non-place, or as a crossroads of human relations. For instance, a shopping mall is not a non-place for a person who works there every day. Accessed on 8th of March 2018 on Wikipedia.

(2) Bakunin, Michael (1871) The Capitalist System; retrieved on 13 February 2009 from an excerpt of *The Knouto-Germanic Empire and the Social Revolution* and included in *The Complete Works of Michael Bakunin* under the title 'Fragment'. Parts of the text were originally translated into English by G.P. Maximoff for his anthology of Bakunin's writings, with missing paragraphs translated by Jeff Stein from the Spanish edition, Diego Abad de Santillan, trans. (Buenos Aires, 1926) vol. III, pp. 181–196, The Anarchist Library, Anticopyright. Accessed on 15 January 2018.

(3) "There's no country on Earth that would tolerate missiles raining down on its citizens from outside its borders," said President Obama. When he made this perfectly sensible statement he was not thinking of the Palestinians in Gaza, helpless victims of Israeli bombs and missiles in some cases dropped or fired by F-16 fighters or Apache helicopters manufactured in the US. For years now, there have been the same shortcomings in accounts of events in Palestine. First, the tendency to repeat the half-true tale in which the "terrorism" of the besieged justifies the besiegers' "response". Then, the granting of impunity to a belligerent with overwhelming military superiority, a belligerent that claims to be the victim just before a further escalation. (…) Lastly, the stressing of the democratic character of Israel, although its government includes a racist, extreme right wing, represented in the cabinet by the foreign minister." Halimi, Serge: *Back to Gaza again*, Le Monde Diplomatique, December 2012.

References

Augé, M. (1995) *Non-Places: Introduction to an Anthropology of Supermodernity*. London: Verso.

Barrett, S. (2009) *Anthropology: A Student's Guide to Theory and Method*. Toronto: University of Toronto Press.

Edensor, T. (2001) Performing tourism, staging tourism: (Re)producing tourist space and practice. *Tourist Studies* 1 (1), 59–81.

MacCannell, D. (1992) *Empty Meeting Grounds: The Tourist Papers*. New York, NY: Routledge.

Miller, T. (2012) *The Hippies and American Values*. Knoxville, TN: University of Tennessee Press.

Richards, G. and Wilson, J. (2008) Suspending reality: An exploration of enclaves and the backpacker experience. *Current Issues in Tourism* 11 (2), 187–202.

Schechner, R. (1985) *Between Theater and Anthropology*. Philadelphia, PA: University of Pennsylvania Press.

Seaton, C.T. (2014) *Hippie Homesteaders: Arts, Crafts, Music and Living on the Land in West Virginia*. Morgantown, WV: West Virginia University Press.

Welk, P. (2004) The beaten track: Anti-tourism as an element of backpacker identity construction. In G. Richards and J. Wilson (eds) *The Global Nomad: Backpacker Travel in Theory and Practice* (pp. 77–91). Clevedon: Channel View Publications.

Web Addresses

Black, B. (2009) The abolition of work. The Anarchist Library, Anti-Copyright., accessed on 21 October 2017. www.primitivism.com

Escohotado, A: Advices from a psychedelic grandfather in interviews (Juan Rendón) my translation from Spanish, accessed on 6 January 2018. www.escohotado.org

4 'We Have Our Own Africans': Public Displays of Zār in Iran

Sara Zavaree

Introduction

Hormoz Island is one of the most beautiful places I have seen. Located eight kilometres off the Iranian Coast of the Arabic/Persian Gulf, the island is covered by colourful sedimentary rock and volcanic material. The bizarre rock formations and the island's many colours make it look like god has attended an amateur painting class. On stormy days, the waves wash away red sand from the shore and create the impression of a bleeding sea. The population of 6000 inhabitants is concentrated in Hormoz Town on the northern shore, living from fishing during the unbearable heat of the summers and increasingly from tourism during the pleasant winters. Quite a few young men make an additional income in the vibrant smuggling business with the Emirates. However, if you lack the right connections with local authorities you might end up being shot by water police. Sometimes the visitor stumbles on bizarre things at shore, like an occasional aubergine or a t-shirt, hastily thrown overboard by smugglers escaping the water police. As a distant reminder of the island's geopolitical position, these otherworldly objects spend some time at the pristine beaches streaked with silvery sand glittering in the sun.

Until recently, Zār spirits, jinn and other supernatural beings used to live in the rocky hills and salty caves. The locals avoided these places, especially at night, as you might step on a spirit and provoke its rage. The visitors did not mind. So, with the tourists climbing into the caves and around the hills, most of the spirits have left. Not yet a mainstream tourist destination but with the first hotel in construction, it is safe to assume that Hormoz will develop a similar tourist economy as the neighbouring island Qeshm. For now, Hormoz remains an insider tip, popular with day visitors from the mainland, young independent travellers from Iran's urban centres and increasingly among European adventure-seeking globetrotters. Here they can camp in the less accessible beaches, unharassed by the moral police, and avoid wearing the hijab. Now and then, smugglers back from Dubai stop by to leave some cans of beer. Every year around February, a Sand Carpet Festival takes place. Young artists from Tehran are invited to Hormoz and create a carpet from the island's coloured sand. The festival is accompanied by a folkloristic cultural programme with music and dances from the South. It was here that I accidentally happened to witness a public ceremony of Zār.

Actually, I was just killing time. In 2014/15, I was doing field research on slavery and spirit possession in Hormoz and waiting to attend a ritual that was delayed for a few days. There used to be a level of secrecy surrounding the ceremonies, so it surprised me to see the public performance at the festival. The spirit possession practice of Zār is closely connected to slavery, the slave trade and maritime interconnections over the Indian Ocean and the Gulf. Travelling spirits called winds (*bad*) enter a person's body, cause disease and discomfort and demand a ritual for their satisfaction. A healing practice at its core, the ritual involves music, movements, fragrant oils and incense, an animal sacrifice and the drinking of its blood. Through polyrhythmic drumming and antiphonal singing the spirits are invited to come down. Then the patient and the other participants fall into trance. Spiritual experts, called *mama Zār* and *baba Zār* communicate in their respective languages (i.e. Arabic, Urdu, Swahili) with the trouble-causing wind: 'What is your name?', 'Where are you from?', 'Why are you harming this poor soul?', 'What do you want?' Then the terms of appeasement are negotiated. When the language of the wind is unknown, translators are engaged or signs are used. The presence of both *mama* and *baba* was crucial in the communities I encountered. The spirits involved in Zār have outspoken ethnic (i.e. Arab, Indian or African), religious (Muslim or kafir) and gender (male or female) identities and distinguished characters. The identities of the human practitioners, in contrast, are not precisely assignable. Zār is known in the Southern Iranian provinces of Khuzestan, Bushehr, Hormozgan and Sistan-Baluchistan and is largely associated with their Black population. Behnaz Mirzai has coined the term *Afro-Iranians* for Iranians of African descent, an academic label inspired by Anglo-American discursive conceptualisations. She states nevertheless that 'local people perceive themselves as fully Iranian and reject any outside attachments' (Mirzai, 2014: 353). Indeed, for most of my interlocutors the articulation of an Iranian identity was very important. Keeping this in mind, this form of external designation is problematic and has raised some controversy among Iranian-American academics (e.g. Baghoolizadeh, 2015). So, in absence of better terminology, I use the term *Black Iranian*, as I often encountered self-identifications like: '*man ye iranie siapust hastam*' – 'I am a black-skinned Iranian'. However, not every person I spoke with who was externally designated as Black would want to be called this way. The history of Black Iranians is strongly connected with the history of slavery (e.g. Afshar, 2000; Cacchioli, 2008; Hopper, 2010; Mirzai, 2017; Ricks, 1988, 2001). Although it is important to note that a notable number of Africans migrated to the Gulf as sailors, merchants, carpenters and more, the experience of slavery is ingrained in the lives of the majority of African migrants and their descendants. It is particularly due to Behnaz Mirzai that the subject of slavery in Iran has been brought to our attention. The practice of Zār is depicted by Mirzai as a means for Black Iranians to preserve an *African* identity, while gradually being assimilated or integrated into Iranian society. She further states: 'members of integrated communities were not segregated or discriminated against on the basis of race (as in the Americas); instead, they lived in parallel, self-sufficient communities' (Mirzai, 2014: 363). Such peripheral representation disguises the complexity of Zār on the one hand and ignores the discrimination and marginalisation which Black people face on the other. Still in many locations in the south, inter-marriage is a societal hybris. Lacking the resources that are historically connected to class background, economic and social mobility is paved with difficulties. And last but not least, many Black Iranians face blatant racism through racist comments on their appearance, through segregated seating in community events like weddings and so on.

The term Zār itself bears multiple meanings: the illness induced by spirits, a certain category of spirits and the possession practice as a whole (Boddy, 1989). Zārs roots remain obscure, though an Ethiopian origin is plausible (Natvig, 1987). Variations of the practice are found in a wide range of regions in the Middle East, Northern and Eastern Africa (e.g. Bilkhair Khalifa, 2006; Kahle, 1912; Kenyon, 2015; Larsen, 2008; Leslau, 1964; Lewis *et al.*, 1991). In the case of Iran, Zār has been given little attention by Western academics, but it is increasingly evolving into a pop cultural trope. Gholam Hossein Sa'edi's (1967) seminal monography, *Ahl'e hava*, remains, to date, the most comprehensive contribution to the study of Zār. Other pioneering studies were done by Riyahi (1977) and Modaressi (1968). In the last two decades, however, publications on Zār have risen exponentially within and outside of Iran (e.g. Beeman, 2015; Darwishi, 1997; Dejgani, 2014; Mirzai, 2002; Khosronejad, 2013; Mianji & Semnani, 2015; Moghaddam, 2012; Sharifian, 2004). The new interest in Zār certainly results also from a globally recognised artistic output and has prompted increased media production: in various documentaries (e.g. Heidari, 2013; Mirzai, 2007; Squillacciotti & Insom, 2017; Varahram, 2014), photographic compilations (e.g. Ehsaei, 2016; Khosronejad, 2017) and blog articles (e.g. Baghoolozadeh, 2012; D'Amour, 2016; Hassanzadeh Ajiri, 2016) Black Iranians and their cultural practices are subjected to a global gaze. Notably in the form of fusion, music artists from the south have integrated Zār elements into their repertoires. Saied Shanbezadeh (2011) and Mohsen Sharifian (2014) both released albums with interpretations of Zār songs or *African* musical motives. In September 2014, a Zār International Music and Dance Festival took place in Istanbul. The Iranian Film Festival in Munich in July 2017 had 'AFRO-Iran' as its thematical focus, with talks and book readings on the subject matter.[1] Hassan Ravande, working at *ershad*[2] in Tehran and literary scholar Ali Rezai from Bandar Abbas have both written theatre plays centring on mythical elements, including Zār.

Spectacle (and) Ritual

The increase of international attention coincides with a decrease of the rituals themselves. An observation of almost all of my interlocutors was that Zār is disappearing. 'There used to be two to three ceremonies every week,' said an elderly man from Bandar Abbas, 'now people do not believe anymore.' The disappearance of Zār in Iran is certainly related to repression and criminalisation during changing political regimes in the course of the last century. The Shah's attempts at modernising and 'westernising' society led to phases of prohibition of Zār in the 1960s and 1970s. And immediately after the Islamic Revolution of 1979, when all form of music was banned, practitioners were not able to perform the rituals. Religious authorities objected (and to some extent still do) to elements of Zār like the drinking of blood as un-Islamic. Also advances in and the availability of medicine, conditions of modern labour and many other factors have transformed the ways people handle questions of sickness and health. Various scholars confirm the observation of a marked decrease of Zār. Mirzai (2017: 288) says, 'Although some are still practiced today, genuine Zār ceremonies are rarely witnessed.' Pedram Khosronejad (2013: 135) makes a similar claim:

> Today the only official way that zar healers and their groups can perform and show their activities with the permission of the state and local governors is in the guise of folkloristic music festivals.

In addition, Edward Alpers (2003: 33) states that '[s]ince the Iranian Revolution there are some indications that a certain level of commercialisation of regional folk culture is occurring.'

Indeed, from a rather secretive, private performance, accessed by the initialised members of the community only, Zār is gradually shifting to public display. The Oxford dictionary defines display with 'putting (something) in a prominent place in order that it may readily be seen'. In the context of Zār rituals, public display exhibits a ritual with the purpose of placing it out on view, making it evident. Following Richard Schechner (2006), I view performance as

> a 'broad spectrum' or 'continuum' of human actions ranging from ritual, play [...] the enactment of social, professional, gender, race, and class roles, and onto healing (from shamanism to surgery), the media, and the internet. (Schechner, 2006: 2)

In this reading, performance and display appear not on opposing ends but share the same interface, in constant interplay, in, as Henry Bergson (2012 [1911]) has put it, 'a *movement* between action and representation'.

I have encountered three different types of public displays: (1) in theatres on stage in the context of folklore festivals or shows, (2) at festive events outdoors (like the one I witnessed in Hormoz), as the supporting program of festivals or weddings and (3) on site at the spiritual experts' own ritual location (i.e. their house) documented by a film crew. While in all three cases, permission from authorities is required, in the case of the first two, the performances are particularly subject to restrictions. The performances are situated in theatre format, on stage, with the audience sitting on chairs or surrounding the practitioners in circles with an immovable viewing direction. Other than participating in antiphonal singing and clapping, the audience's role is reduced to that of passive consumption. Zār practitioners are hired to perform at folklore festivals, sanctioned by the government, that are predominantly attended by middle-class, well-educated and urban multitudes. Consequently, contact to government institutions and invitations to festivals has turned into another resource in economic competition between rivalling Zār communities. *Mama Zār*, female spiritual experts do not act on stage. If women appear at all they perform as background singers.

The emphasis of vanishing on the one hand and *commercialisation* and *folklorisation*, the loss of the *genuine* and *original* on the other is mirrored in various other locales of trance and possession practice. Jannice Boddy remarks that her interlocutors in Sudan do not practice Zār anymore because it is viewed as un-Islamic by the government.[3] Susan Kenyon (2015), who has done research in a different part of Sudan, states that due to increased Wahabi influence, Zār leaders were beaten and imprisoned in the 1990s. But after 2000 that seems not to be the case anymore and she has observed a renewed interest in Zār, especially in the form of folklore. A similar development is recognisable for Bori in Northern Nigeria. Since the introduction of Sharia law at the end of the 1990s, strictly restricted to the eyes of the ordained, rituals or elements of the ritual are now performed as cultural displays in official events in the northern cities. These kinds of performances were described by a local practitioner as 'secular', in contrast to the real Bori in the rural areas. A participant of Zār rituals in Cairo claimed Zār had lost its spiritual power. He himself has a middle class and academic background and started attending Zār rituals after he became interested in Sufism. As in Nigeria, 'original' and 'real' rituals would not be found in the city, he said, but rather in the rural areas. We do not need to look far to witness this development, but just across the Gulf at Dubai, where spiritual performances are displayed in annual festivals and tourist quarters (Hopper, 2014: 344).

An Iranian musician I interviewed prior to the field research predicted that I would encounter both real rituals and ones I would have to pay for.

I was not interested in the *fake* ones, leaving aside the fact that I could not afford them. I wanted to see the *real* Zār. By audience and practitioners alike, public displays are understood as non-spiritual and artificial, based on semantic differentiations of authentic versus folkloristic, secret versus staged, public versus private. Guy Debord's essay 'La Société du spectacle' (1967) has been seminal for our understanding of the spectacle, paving the way to the theory of the simulacrum (Frederico, 2011). From an anticapitalistic point of view, Debord articulated a critique on the division between image and reality and also consumerism and media-centricity. Society is in a constant search for the authentic, but reality is being replaced by images, which then become reality. Historically, theatre and performance were termed different acts, but increasingly theatre was seen as a subcategory of performance (Cull, 2012: 2). In studies on spirit possession the spectacle, theatre, drama and dramatisation have been modes of articulation. Various scholars carry theatre in their publication titles or within their texts when elaborating on spirit possession (e.g. Basu, 2000; Constanides, 1972; Giles, 1995). Paul Stoller (1989) structures the introduction of people and spirits in his book *Fusion of Worlds* as in a stage play. In the section *personae*, he lists people (from the social world) and spirits (from the spirit world).[4] In the liminality of the spiritual ritual, the boundaries of reality and imagination become blurry and opaque. The re-enactment of the Other leads to liberation by means of imitation, performing a mimetic relation to alterity (Taussig, 1993) and interpreting the Other by mimesis (Kramer, 1987). However, the interpretation of mimesis as a means of acquiring the power of the Other, of the (colonial) oppressor, as an agentive strategy of subversion, is insufficient. Rey Chow calls the sound imitation of city noises in a radio drama 'auditory simulacra' (Chow, 2014: 112). The Zār ritual can likewise be interpreted as the simulacrum of experience, a visual, auditory and tactile interaction of a distant, contested past with contemporary concerns.[5]

The rituals I encountered in Southern Iran seemed to me to be social catalysts. Within the arena of the initiated, among relatives, neighbours and friends, social conflicts were addressed and resolved. During the trance, spirits demand reconciliation between in-laws. Or a woman's extensive crying is interpreted by community members as being severe marital problems. Due to an overall observance of Islamic law (no drinking of blood) or fire hazard safety rules (no burning of incense), some elements of Zār are missing on the public stage. If we consider the utilisation of objects in ritual (i.e. blood or incense) as a means of crossing the boundaries to transcendence, to create communication with the spirit world and oblige them to act or not to act in a specific way, then their absence might alter the balance and composition of the ritual. The same occurs with the concurrent presence of other mediating objects as lights, microphones and cameras. A *mama Zār* from Bandar Abbas who has centred in many documentaries and films told me about the strangeness of all the cables and wires in her living room. Where there is plenty of filming and photographing in public displays, any form of visual documentation is usually strictly forbidden in private rituals. Then there is the complex of gender and the public sphere. Women traditionally work as spiritual experts in Iran, yet they are restricted from taking centre stage in theatres or public events. They do not fall into trance and if at all present, they wear the *borghe*, common public attire for South Iranian women that hides the face but is not worn in private Zār rituals. Overall, public displays lack the frenzy and ecstasy evoked in Zār, they seem tamed and reduced, as if the spirits intend to keep up appearances.

The ritual as theatre is a public image often deployed by practitioners themselves to represent Zār as harmless entertainment and as unthreatening to Islam and social order. A historical case that has been described by Kapteijns and Spaulding (1994) is particularly interesting here. In 1926 Aden/Yemen, British colonial authorities prohibited Zār after complaints of the local elite on the grounds of being un-Islamic and disturbing the public order. In a perennial legal battle, Zār women practitioners tried to lift the prohibition, inter alia by labelling themselves as 'Zār theatrical women', a label that functions as protection against legal repression until today. A female spiritual expert from Bandar Abbas also hinted at the fact that public performances help against criminalisation. She and her crew went to Tehran, the capital, and 'proved that what she does is correct', namely, that her power is real. The public display thus not only protects one from prosecution but is also a strategy to negotiate a given social order in an acceptable way. Martin Zillinger speaks in the context of Moroccan trance rituals of *graduated publics*. Building on Jürgen Habermas's (1962) discussion of *Öffentlichkeit* as publicity, the process of making things public, and Talal Asad's (2003) conceptualisations of the domestic, semi-public and public, Zillinger argues that mediating trance into public realms needs to be graduated:

> at times it is elaborated and worked on secretly, hidden from the attention of a wider public; at times it is negotiated within the "ritual intimacy" shared by fellow acolytes of a certain cult; and at other times it is celebrated in the streets or staged for the broadest audience possible.

The hidden, the intimate and the public appear as cornerstones on a continuum of publicity production. Conceptualising degrees of publicity can help to order and to name different forms of rituals without reproducing the normative binaries of real and staged.

The Tourist-Researcher

For a better understanding of the dynamic relationship between the hidden and the public, let us go back to Hormoz Island and take a closer look at the little sand carpet festival. The festival grounds are located outside town at one of the wider sandy beaches. For the duration of a week, a crowd of volunteering young artists from Tehran creates a carpet from the coloured rocks and sand. Following a controversial debate on environmental conversation – the island's natural beauty is at hazard as souvenir-hunting tourists destroy the crystalline rock formations – this year's organisers decided to restrict themselves to the widely available red sand only. The accompanying cultural programme entailed a solo concert of *ney'amune* (a wooden flute), a gypsy dance and flute play that is usually performed at weddings, a sword dance, initially known as Arab Bedouin dance, but now a very popular and entertainment show around the Gulf, and the aforementioned public display of Zār. It was dark, when the Zār performance happened. Day-visitors from the mainland and most spectators from Hormoz town had gone home, but a few local young men with their own means of transport stayed on site. The festival organisers shushed them down every time they were too much carried away by the music and clapped their hands too enthusiastically. Present were also the artists and the travellers, the latter unwashed and unkempt from weeks of wild camping. Several times I heard the locals wrinkle their noses at the 'dirty hippies'. After the performance, the main Zār performer stayed to answer questions and was encircled by the highly enthusiastic, attentive crowd that I would label as young, well-educated and urban, politically and culturally interested and critical of the government. Among the travellers were four German globetrotters (to one of them I was surprisingly acquainted) and someone from Japan. Most of them were barely veiled, in t-shirts and short trousers, feeling safe in the darkness and the companionship of like-minded fellows. I became chatty and talked to the travellers about the 'real' Zār ceremony I was going to attend. Some begged me to take them with me, but I insisted that I could not disclose the location, as it was an exclusive, invite-only kind of event (or at least I felt that way). It was the third and last day of the ceremony when they suddenly appeared. It turned out that they had somehow convinced my research companion to show them the place. Two other outsiders were attending. Wealthy ladies from Tehran on an educational trip, guests of renowned artist Ahmad Nadelian, who resides on the island during the mild winters and who hosts international visitors in his art centre.[6] As usual, all of us were rigorously instructed not to film or to take photographs. The Tehran ladies walked right to the centre of the arena, not sitting down as is expected from participants, but stretching their mobile phone in any direction an audio record seemed promising. Later they complained a lot that they were not allowed to take pictures. Some of the young travellers were wearing black, a prohibited colour during the ritual. One of them was shaking his head rhythmically to the music. Movement is a common signifier for the presence of spirits, and so he had to involuntarily endure a pot of incense being held under his nose for quite some time: the *baba Zār* was inviting his spirit to come down. When I asked one of the young women afterwards how she liked the ceremony, she said she was disappointed. She had heard so much about Zār but had expected more from it. In accordance to the semantic differentiation, she had expected a deeper spiritual experience.

I felt bewildered by this kind of attitude. I found it rude. I had prepared cautiously for the rituals, had learnt by heart all the rules and restrictions, had even bought a pretty chador, a full-body veil, and it had taken me some time to learn how to wear it. I had tried hard to be discreet and not to disturb. But like the outsiders who walked in, I was looking for the genuine. How could the ritual be genuine to begin with? I changed it through my presence. Latest when a ritual is described in text, it becomes public, no longer hidden. My own part in the publicity of Zār was no different to that of the tourist in quest for authenticity. To understand the expectations of the tourist-researcher, it might be useful to recur to a seminal text in trance research: Michel Leiris' *L'Afrique fantôme* (1934). After attending a Zār ritual in Gondar, he reflected on exoticisation through anthropology and the complicity of anthropology with European colonialism. But writing about the ritual also functions as a form of therapy, as catharsis, as a therapeutic dealing with alterity. In Irene Albers' interpretation

> this corresponds to Leiris's own retrospective studies of the zar cult as a cathartic externalization of alterity and as a theatre of alterity. In his failed search for a truly sacral, authentically primitive or salutary ritual, Leiris above all discovered one particular ritual: writing, 'poésie'. (Albers, 2008: 271)

Not only the anthropologist is in quest of a therapeutic experience. The tourist, the journalist, the artist seeks the same. Therapy operates as an exercise in (political) escapism. Those urban, middle-class, non-conforming youths object to societal norms. They act and perform resistance. Could the popularity of Zār be an expression of political dissent, possibly a disagreement with hegemonic Islamic dogma?

Under the pressures of cultural censorship, many Iranian artists feel the need to emigrate to the West. In exile, they are influenced by the world music industry and global discourses on cultural diversity and the African diaspora. Narratives of opposition to Islam are formed by deploying exotic motives from 'outsiders', namely, a Western perspective. As Susan Kenyon (2015) has stated for Sudan, Zār remains popular not *despite*, but *because* of the rigidity of global reformist Islam. In *Not a Native Speaker* Rey Chow (2014) retells a mourning ceremony in China in the 1930s written in a novel by Ba Jin. She puts the novel in the context of a *political wish* for change and modernisation. Against this background, the description of the mourning and other rituals amounts to something of an exotic ethnographic find, whereupon an indigenous custom receives the spotlight not for the significance it carries in its conventional context, but rather for a displaced kind of effect – as an absurd drama seen with fresh – that is, foreignized – eyes. (Chow, 2014: 63)

I believe that public displays of Zār also need to be understood in the greater context of a generation longing for political change. Close-knit to this question is the othering of the *African*, as spiritual, authentic and real.

Referencing *Africa*

The title phrase of this paper – 'We have our own Africans' – is taken from an interview I had with an Iranian musician in exile. I met him before one of his concerts in Germany. The statement was meant rather as a joke. He was referring to the fact that a new generation of curious musicians has been rediscovering the musical heritage of the South. 'We do not have to look at Africa to get inspiration' he said, 'We have our own Africans'. The recent discovery of Africans in Iran has an aftertaste of exoticisation and reproduction of racist stereotypes. According to film director Farhad Varahram, the narrative of the Black was invented by intellectuals. Blacks would imitate African dances on YouTube to please Western desire for exoticism. So, what we see in the performances is imitation instead of originality. Varahram is internationally known for ethnographic films on cultural subjects. One of his films, *Siahan-e jonoobe Iran* (the Blacks of Southern Iran) (2014), has been presented at various festivals inside and outside Iran. The protagonists in the film hardly speak. The only time we hear their voices is when they say their names which indicate a slave origin. After spending around one year of research in the South, he is convinced that 'the Blacks' do not remember anything, that they do not have any knowledge of their African past. Remarkably, most contributions on Black Iranians employ visual media to materialise their 'African-ness' phenotypically.

The agitation around the African-ness appears to be quite new, the racial marking of Black-ness, the construction of Blacks as the internal Other, however, is not. There is a long-standing tradition of Black employment as professional entertainers. As *motrebin* (singer) Black Iranians still sing and perform at weddings or funerals. Traditional theatre genres of *Ru Howzi* and *Siah-bazi* centre on the Black figure. *Ru howzi* (lit. up the pool) was a humouristic theatre where a wooden stage was placed on the family home's courtyard pool and addressed domestic issues. *Siah-Bazi* (lit. playing Black) covered more political subjects and was performed in public places like the coffeehouse or the theatre (e.g. Beyza'i, 1965; Floor, 2005). Historically, performers in *Ru*

Howsy and *Siah Bazi* were Africans or Black Iranians. Later they were replaced by blackface actors who mimicked downgrading stereotypes of Black-ness with servile attitude and funny accents. Similar to *Haji Firouz*, a blackface slave and important figure of *nowrooz* (New Year celebration), they embody ambiguity. The slave cannot leave the fixed societal frame of serving the master, as cruel and immoral the latter might be portrayed. At the same time, the slave enjoys the freedom of the fool or the harlequin to openly address and criticise (political) authority. Racist practices like blackface and the genre of *siah-bazi* are increasingly under scrutiny outside Iran – particularly in Iranian-American communities (e.g. Shirazi, 2016). Nevertheless, the recursive emphasis of the African element indicates a concept of Africa as primal and rife with old magic. Fed by contemporary imaginations, these discursive notions of Africa do not always rely on tradition. Saied Shanbezadeh, the aforementioned musician, puts on ripped clothes on stage and performs dances that are supposed to remind one of slavery and the slave experience. So, the performance turns into a performative language to process and articulate the past and construct heritage and memory. Furthermore, the influx of scholars, journalists, artists, tourists and other interested crowds visiting Southern Iran in quest of the 'African-ness' amidst Iranian society has had certainly a reciprocal influence on the self-perception and representation of Black Iranians and the practitioners of Zār.

Reza Olabandari, offspring of a long line of Zār practitioners, told me that the youth request the elders for permission to film and record the rituals. They seek to prevail the songs and the ways from being forgotten. He is part of a younger generation of Black Iranians that is actively engaging with their family's past. He says:

> The past is always forming identity. Some are offended when they are called "Black". This is because of today's society. Everyone knows the Black as someone who has been a victim of injustice, who always needed an *arbab* [master] above him and who was in the lowest rung of society. This past is painful for them. But I believe this is the wrong attitude. My identity is whether I want or not Black. I am proud about that [...] I have culture. They say about Africa that there is no culture. But Africa has culture [...] Zār is a souvenir that the Blacks brought with themselves.

For Olabandari, performing Zār is an active way of integrating the notion of Africa into his own personal narrative. Africa appears here as a reference point for longing and desire. Of (painful) memories and pride. Since Sa'edi (1967), we know that within the cosmology of Zār the spirits associated with Africa or of African languages are dangerous and difficult to tame. But also, powerful and prestigious for those who master their operation. And this is still very much in place today. One of my interlocutors carries a wind, a Zār spirit, which speaks a language no one knows. It has been diagnosed African by spiritual experts. She told me that African-speaking spirits are higher in hierarchy and more respected within the community. African spirits speaking African languages are an integral element of Zār cosmology. Swahili songs, memorised over generations and partially forgotten in the course of time, are found in the musical repertoire. 'African-ness' is performed during rituals through exaggerated ecstatic dance and mimicking African languages, notably Swahili. Command of Swahili mimicry is particularly prestigious. Mastering the performativity of 'African-ness' marks spiritual authority and thus is a desired resource among possession practitioners. In the same time, referencing Africa is evident in other localities. Richard Jankowsky (2010) highlights linguistic practices of Stambeli communities which utilise Hausa words. In Morocco, Zillinger (2013) has observed among Sufi brotherhoods of the zawiya that the expression 'our Africa' is indexed as 'real trance' and Sufi practices associated not with economic profit but with true sacredness. In his enlightening paper on *Linguistic Evidence of Bantu Origins of the Sidis of India*, Abdulaziz Lodhi (2008) argues that the use of Swahili serves as a marker for a perceived African heritage:

> Sidi cultural societies have been participating internationally with their Muslim Sufi song and dance and their renewed contacts with East Africa have increased slightly the number of Bantu words in their language use, such as Swahili greetings, emphasising their East African heritage and misconceiving Swahili as their ancestral language. (Lodhi, 2008: 30)

So, it is not only the Iranian intellectual and cultural elites that construct their own Africans in order to distance themselves from the Islamic Regime and participate in global discourses of exoticism, but also some Black Iranians create the single story of their African heritage in order to position themselves in relation to slavery and to retell their family story on their own terms. An important framework for this positioning is Zār.

Memory and Erasure

In a different reading, Zār transgresses the dichotomies of authentic versus commercial, real versus staged. Zār is not disappearing but is rather a very resilient and dynamic means of acting and reacting on (global) transformations. Naturally, these transformations are not free of conflict. The integration of Zār practices into global commercial markets and their representation in movies and music albums has created certain controversy. For instance, the mixing of Shia mourning music (*azadari*) with elements of Zār by internationally known musicians is viewed critically in their hometowns. As I was walking in the footsteps of many other researchers, filmmakers and musicians, I often encountered criticism on the outcome of their research. Actually, condemnation and critique were expressed on every single publications or albums which I mentioned.

Practitioners complained that the depiction of *their* songs and rituals was not correct. However, complaint was raised also from other ends, as visitors of Zār performances were disappointed by the lack of intensity and deep spirituality they were expecting.

The display (and modification) of the Zār practice is also discussed in terms of commercial gain. Who is profiting economically from and – hereby touching the complex question of cultural appropriation – who owns Zār? The main performer in the public display I witnessed in Hormoz was a White Iranian. During his childhood he became acquainted with Zār in his neighbourhood and got hooked. He has recorded many CDs with Zār music and is regarded as an expert. Artists, among them many Black Iranians, profit from the global attention, also economically and they take artistic liberties to fusion different musical genre. Zār communities profit too. They can generate additional income through shows, fame and prestige. And reframing Zār as harmless theatre and folklore protects from criminalisation and prosecution. And last but not least, also governmental institutions benefit, as they can control the practices. On Qeshm Island, the biggest island in the Gulf, where tourism is much more evolved than on Hormoz, Zār is now performed for paying audiences. The events, overseen and promoted by the authorities, are part of a stage programme that entails all kinds of heritage from the South. The regulation of the (international) presentation of Zār is in line with the construction of a specific narrative of the 'multi-ethnic nation'. The government sponsors some events that take the form of folklore. According to Mirzai, '[t]heir performance and music are considered part of the cultural heritage of Iran' (Mirzai, 2014: 367). It is quite remarkable that rituals that are common in a diversity of different locations around the world are considered national heritage. We observe structurally similar processes in other locales: in Egypt, for instance, public Zār performances are promoted on a weekly basis by the Egyptian Center for Culture and Arts as *Egyptian* heritage in need of safeguarding.[7]

When rituals are reformulated into national heritage, the question remains which other stories become suppressed. De Jong and Rowlands (2007) speak in this context of heritage technologies. In their dissemination of heritage politics in Africa, they conclude that Africa is mainly associated with authentic intangible heritage formations:

> UNESCO policy in Africa has resulted in an opposition between tangible and intangible heritage, which has privileged the idea of an authentic Africa as performative rather than monumental. UNESCO and other agencies promote technologies for producing pasts and futures, by which we mean archives, artefacts, ritual practices, performances, and material spaces. [T]hese technologies affect individual projects of self-realization, and in particular the intangible nature of performative culture and everyday practices [...] Therefore, we need to explore the issue of which

memories are privileged and which are repressed through heritage politics. (De Jong & Rowlands, 2007: 15)

Reformulating Zār as national heritage opens the possibility of regulation. Regulation of the frame, the form but also the specific version of history that aligns with current politics. At the same time, other encodements within Zār are obscured or even erased, namely the implications of slavery and of marginalisation.

Notes

(1) Cf. http://cinema-iran.de/programm/mittwoch-18-uhr-ausstellungseroeffnung-afro-iran/ (accessed 30 November 2017).
(2) The ershad organisation is part of the Ministry of Culture and also responsible for censorship.
(3) Personal correspondence, February 2017.
(4) Remarkably, European people are not part of the *personae* but are appreciated in the acknowledgements.
(5) Thanks to Anne Storch for sharing this thought.
(6) For further information on Nadelian and the art center cf. riverart.net/hormoz/nature/index.htm (accessed 30 November 2017).
(7) Cf. http://www.egyptmusic.org/ (accessed 30 November 2017).

References

Afshar, H. (2000) Age, gender and slavery in and out of the Persian harem: A different story. *Ethnic and Racial Studies* 23 (5), 905–916.
Albers, I. (2008) Mimesis and alterity: Michel Leiris's ethnography and poetics of spirit possession. *French Studies: A Quarterly Review* 62 (3), 271–289.
Alpers, E. (2003) The African diaspora in the Indian Ocean: A comparative perspective. In S.d.S. Jayasuriya and R. Pankhurst (eds) *The African Diaspora in the Indian Ocean* (pp. 19–50). New York, NY: Africa World Press.
Asad, T. (2003) *Formations of the Secular: Christianity, Islam, Modernity*. Stanford, CA: Stanford University Press.
Basu, H. (2000) Theatre of memory: Performances of ritual kinship of the African diaspora in Sindh / Pakistan. In M. Böck and A. Rao (eds) *Culture, Creation, and Procreation: Concepts of Kinship in South Asian Practice* (pp. 243–270). New York, NY: Berghahn Books.
Beeman, W. (2015) The zar in the Persian Gulf: Performative dimension. *Anthropology of the Contemporary Middle East and Central Eurasia* 3 (1), 1–12.
Bergson, H. (2012) *Matter and Memory*. Dover Philosophical Classics. Newburyport: Dover Publications (original work published 1911).
Beyza'i, B. (1965) *Namāyesh dar Iran: bā shast taṣvir wa ṭarh wa yek wāzanāme (Theater in Iran: With sixty pictures and one play)*. Tehran: Kawiyan.
Bilkhair Khalifa, A. (2006) African influence on culture and music in Dubai. *International Social Science Journal* 58 (188), 227–235.
Boddy, J.P. (1989) *Wombs and Alien Spirits: Women, Men, and the Zar Cult in Northern Sudan*. Wisconsin: University of Wisconsin.
Cacchioli, N. (2008) Fugitive slaves, asylum and manumission in Iran (1851–1913). *Cultural Interactions created by the Slave Trade in the Arab-Muslim World*. Paris: UNESCO.

Chow, R. (2014) *Not Like a Native Speaker: On Languaging as a Postcolonial Experience*. New York, NY: Columbia University Press.
Constantinides, P.M. (1972) Sickness and the spirits: A study of the zaar spirit-possession cult in the Northern Sudan. PhD thesis, University of London.
Cull, L. (2012) *Theatres of Immanence: Deleuze and the Ethics of Performance*. Basingstoke: Palgrave Macmillan.
Darwishi, M. (1997) *Ayina wa Awaz (Ritual and Song)*. Tehran: Waḥid-i Musiqi-i Hauza-i Hunari-i Sazman-i Tabligat-i Islami.
de Jong, F. and Rowlands, M.J. (eds) (2007) *Reclaiming Heritage: Alternative Imaginaries of Memory in West Africa*. Publications of the Institute of Archaeology, University College London. Walnut Creek, CA: Left Coast Press.
Debord, G. (1967) *La Société du spectacle (The Society of the Spectacle)*. Paris: Buchet/Castel.
Dejgani, F. (2014) *Djenzadegan dar Joonoobe Iran (the Jinn-possessed in Southern Iran)*. Rafsandjan: Sourme.
Ehsaei, M. (2016) *Afro-Iran*. Heidelberg: Kehrer Verlag.
Floor, W.M. (2005) *The History of Theater in Iran*. Washington, D.C.: Mage.
Frederico, C. (2011) Debord: From spectacle to simulacrum. *MATRIZes* 4 (1), 179–191.
Giles, L. (1995) Sociocultural change and spirit possession on the Swahili coast of East Africa. *Anthropological Quarterly* 68 (2), 89–106.
Habermas, J. (1962) *Strukturwandel der Öffentlichkeit: Untersuchungen zu einer Kategorie der Bürgerlichen Gesellschaft (Structural Transformation of Publicity: Studies on a Categorie of the Bourgeois Society)*. Neuwied: Luchterhand.
Hopper, M. (2010) Globalization and the economics of african slavery in arabia in the age of empire. *Journal of African Development* 12, 156–184.
Hopper, M. (2014) The African presence in Arabia. In L. Potter (ed.) *The Persian Gulf in Modern Times: People, Ports, and History*. Basingstoke: Palgrave.
Jankowsky, R.C. (2010) *Stambeli: Music, Trance, and Alterity in Tunisia*. Chicago studies in Ethnomusicology. Chicago, IL: University of Chicago Press.
Kahle, P. (1912) Zar-Beschwörungen in Ägypten: Mit einer Tafel (Zar incantations in Egypt: With a tableau). *Der Islam* 3, 1–41.
Kapteijns, L. and Spaulding, J. (1994) Women of the zar and middle class sensibilities in colonial Aden, 1923-1932. *Sudanic Africa* 5, 7–38.
Kenyon, S.M. (2015) *Spirits and Slaves in Central Sudan: The Red Wind of Sennar*. Contemporary anthropology of religion. Basingstoke: Palgrave Macmillan.
Khosronejad, P. (2013) The people of the air: Healing and spirit possession. In T. Zarcone and A. Hobart (eds) *Shamanism and Islam: Sufism, Healing Rituals and Spirits in the Muslim World* (pp. 131–167). London: Tauris.
Khosronejad, P. (2017) *Qajar African Nannies: African Slaves and Aristocratic Babies*. Visual studies of modern Iran no. 1. Stillwater, Oklahoma.
Kramer, F. (1987) *Der rote Fes: Über Besessenheit und Kunst in Afrika (The Red Fes: on Possession and Art in Africa)*. Die weiße Reihe. Frankfurt am Main: Athenäum.
Larsen, K. (2008) *Where Humans and Spirits meet: The Politics of Rituals and identified Spirits in Zanzibar*. Social identities 5. New York, NY: Berghahn Books.
Leiris, M. (1934) *L'Afrique fantôme (Phantom Africa)*. Paris: Gallimard.
Leslau, W. (1964) *Ethiopian Argots*. The Hague: Mouton.
Lewis, L.M., El Safi, A. and Hurreiz, S.H.A. (eds) (1991) *Women's Medicine: The Zar-Bori Cult in Africa and Beyond*. International African seminars new ser., no. 5. Edinburgh: Edinburgh University Press for the International African Institute.
Lodhi, A.Y. (2008) Linguistic evidence of bantu origins of the sidis of India. In K.K. Prasad (ed.) *TADIA, the African Diaspora in Asia: Explorations on a Less Known Fact*. Papers presented at the First International Conference on TADIA in Panaji, Goa, held during January 2006, 1. print (pp. 301–313). Bangalore: Jana Jagrati Prakashana.

Mianji, F. and Semnani, Y. (2015) Zār spirit possession in Iran and African countries: Group distress, culture-bound syndrome or cultural concept of distress? *Iranian Journal of Psychiatry* 4 (10), 225–232.

Mirzai, B. (2002) African presence in Iran: Identity and its reconstruction in the 19th and 20th centuries. *Outre-Mers: Revue d'Histoire* 89 (2), 229–246.

Mirzai, B. (2014) Identity transformations of African communities in Iran. In L. Potter (ed.) *The Persian Gulf in Modern Times: People, Ports, and History* (pp. 351–376). Basingstoke: Palgrave Macmillan.

Mirzai, B. (2017) *A History of Slavery and Emancipation in Iran, 1800-1929*. Austin, TX: University of Texas Press.

Modaressi, T. (1968) The Zar Cult in South Iran. In R.H. Prince and R.M. Bucke (eds) *Trance and Possession States* (pp. 149–155). Montreal: R. M. Bucke Memorial Society.

Moghadam, M.S. (2012) Zar believes and practices in Bandar Abbas and Queshm Island in Iran. *Anthropology of the Middle East* 7 (2), 19–38.

Natvig, R. (1987) Oromos, slaves, and the zar spirits: A contribution to the history of the zar cult. *The International Journal of African Historical Studies* 20 (4), 669–689.

Ricks, T. (1988) Slaves and slave traders in the Persian Gulf, 18th and 19th century: An assessment. *Slavery & Abolition* 9 (3), 60–70.

Ricks, T. (2001) Slaves and slave trading in Shi'i Iran, AD 1500–1900. *Journal of Asian and African Studies* 36 (4), 407–418.

Riyahi, A. (1977) *Zar va Bad va Baluch (Zar and Wind and Baluchi)*. Tehran: Ketabkhane Tahwari.

Sa'edi, G.H. (1967) *Ahl-e Hava (Descending from Air)*. Tehran: Intisharat-i Muassasah-i Mutalaat va Tahqiqat-i Ijtimai.

Schechner, R. (2006) *Performance Studies: An Introduction* (2nd edn). New York, NY: Routledge.

Shanbezadeh, S. (2011) *Zar: Jazz and Music from South Iran*. With Ensemble Shanbezadeh and Mathieu Donarier Trio.

Sharifian, M. (2004) *Ahl-e zamin: Musiqi wa auham dar jazira-e Kharg (Descending from Earth: Music and Ritual on Kharg Island)* (2nd edn). Tehran: Markaz-e Nashr wa Taḥqiqat-e Qalam-Ashna.

Sharifian, M. (2014) *Dingue Marrow: Bushehr Fusion Music*.

Stoller, P. (1989) *Fusion of the Worlds: An Ethnography of Possession among the Songhay of Niger*. Chicago, IL: Univ. of Chicago Press.

Taussig, M.T. (1993) *Mimesis and Alterity: A Particular History of the Senses*. New York, NY: Routledge.

Varahram, F. (2014) *Siahan-e jonoobe Iran (Blacks in Southern Iran)*.

Zillinger, M. (2013) *Die Trance, das Blut, die Kamera: Trance-Medien und Neue Medien im marokkanischen Sufismus (The Trance, the Blood, and the Camera: Trance-Media and new Media in Moroccan Sufism)*. Bielefeld: Transcript-Verlag.

Zillinger, M. (2017) Graduated publics: Mediating trance in the age of technical reproduction. *Current Anthropology* 58, 41–55.

Web Addresses

Baghoolizadeh, B. (2012) The Afro-Iranian community: beyond Haji Firuz blackface, the slave trade, and Bandari music. Ajam Media Collective, accessed 30 November 2017. http://ajammc.com/2012/06/20/the-afro-iranian-community-beyond-haji-firuz-blackface-slavery-bandari-music/

Baghoolizadeh, B. (2015) Picturing the other: Race and Afro-Iranians in documentary photography. Ajam Media Collective, accessed 30 November 2017.https://ajammc.

com/2015/07/20/picturing-them-vs-us-race-and-afro-iranians-in-documentary-photography/
Cinema Iran (2017) Festival program, accessed 30 November 2017.http://cinema-iran.de/programm/mittwoch-18-uhr-ausstellungseroeffnung-afro-iran/
D'Amour, J. (2016) 'We are Iranians': Rediscovering the history of African slavery in Iran, accessed 30 November 2017. http://www.middleeasteye.net/in-depth/features/they-are-iranian-discovering-african-history-and-slavery-iran-970665328.
Egyptian Center for Culture and Arts Makan (2017) We have a Dream, accessed 30 November 2017. http://www.egyptmusic.org/
Hassanzadeh Ajiri, D. (2017) The face of African slavery in Qajar Iran – in pictures. *The Guardian*, accessed 30 November 2017. https://www.theguardian.com/world/iran-blog/2016/jan/14/african-slavery-in-qajar-iran-in-photos
Nadelian, A. (2017) Personal Website, accessed 30 November 2017. http://www.riverart.net/nadalian/index.htm
Shirazi, M. (2016) A review of tarabname, or, why are Iranian-Americans laughing at blackface in 2016. *Ajam Media Collective*, accessed 30 November 2017. https://ajammc.com/2016/12/07/why-are-iranian-americans-laughing-at-blackface-in-2016/

Documentaries

Heidari, K. (2013) *Dingomaro*.
Mirzai, B. (2007) *Afro-Iranian Lifes*.
Squillacciotti, G. and Insom, C. (2017) *Archipelago*.

5 Cameras as Barriers of Understanding: Reflections on a Philanthropic Journey to Kenya

Angelika Mietzner

Introduction

Philanthropy and a fear of contact may at first seem incompatible concepts, as philanthropy is a form of tourism that is often seen as a very personal way of helping people in less affluent countries (Hall & Raymond, 2008). Yet as can be found in a special form of philanthropic tourism – the philanthropic journey – this special reserve indeed exists and is often combated with the building of invisible protective barriers between oneself and the other.

The various forms of philanthropic tourism are just as manifold as is tourism itself. The form discussed in this paper is the philanthropic journey that I define as a journey which lasts the duration of a regular holiday period, is organised by or together with a non-governmental organisation and which intends to show people where or how they can help, as well as where they can donate before, during and even after the journey.

This article came about through the long-term observation of four philanthropic journeys to Kenya offered by a German organisation. The participants in all four journeys displayed a similarly excessive practice when it came to the use of their cameras, even though the reason for their journeys would have led one to believe that social interaction and personal contact should be the central aspect of these encounters.

Philanthropic journeys, as with voluntourism (Callanan & Thomas, 2005), are often seen as mutually beneficial forms of tourism, with the locals benefiting from the tourists in the form of long-term support by the organisation, and with the visitors benefiting in their personal development. In contrast to pro-poor tourism,[1] voluntourism is said to have nothing to do with foreign currency or the rendition of services within the community. This also holds true for philanthropic journeys. Yet, the mutual benefit of philanthropic journeys seems to be neocolonial or imperialistic, with the visitors coming to experience whether the effort they put into the organisation in Europe reaches the poor, while the locals have to demonstrate their well-being and gratitude towards the donors; the result being that power inequalities are systematically raised and performed (McBride et al., 2006).

The exact demarcations of the definitions in the literature overlap and blur somehow, this is even more so for the definition of the so-called philanthropic journey, which I will position within the edu-tourism and within philanthropic tourism. The philanthropic journey conveys not only some knowledge of history and the culture of the respective country, but also knowledge of the fate and the use of the money collected and donated in the participant's home country.

In this chapter, I will first present insights into the development of tourism in Tiwi, the place where the philanthropic journeys took place and the background of the journeys. This is necessary in order to understand the immense dependence of the Tiwi population on aid from abroad in association with the work of *Asante e.V.*, the German organisation. Afterwards, several encounters within the journeys will be introduced in order to embed the use of cameras during these encounters in the academic discourse of photography in tourism.

Development of Tourism and its Implication on the Population of Tiwi

The place that will be taken as an example for the destination of a philanthropic journey is an area that has been immensely influenced by tourism for decades. Tiwi and the adjacent Diani are districts located in Kenya, south of Mombasa on the Indian Ocean. Kenya is known for its beaches, and after having been discovered and enjoyed by British settlers for recreation purposes, Germans and Italians started choosing Kenya as their holiday destination after Kenya's independence in 1963. The economic activities of the tourism sector were initiated either by the government or by Europeans (Akama, 1996: 145). Since then, tourism has increased tremendously (Sindiga, 1999: 73). In contrast to wildlife tourism, the Kenyan government did not have plans to build a tourism industry on the coast. People living along the coast simply started small-scale entrepreneurships. As start-up capital was not planned for by the government, Kenyans were forced into temporary unlicensed kiosks or shops while the Kenyan Indians and Europeans inhabited the official shops (Sindiga, 1999). In fact, approximately only two to five percent of tourism receipts reach the local population (Akama, 1996: 149). But what can be seen among the Digo population (Mijikenda/Bantu) living in Diani and Tiwi is a very passive type of behaviour in relation to personal responsibility, especially regarding education. Berman (2017) traces this form of passivity back to the former communal forms of reciprocal aid and solidarity within the community which disappeared in the 1970s when tourism in the area increased and brought salaried positions in hotels. But as neither the state nor other institutions became engaged in developing the region, the growth in population went hand in hand with unemployment and poverty. These forms of communal support formerly available were *harambee*, *utsi* and *mweria*, involving the whole village (*utsi*, *harambee*) or only a small group of people (*mweria*) who benefit from others but in return participated in other forms of communal aid (Berman, 2017: 68ff).

The massive presence of expatriates and tourists who wished to assist the local populations led to a form of dependence:

> [T]he tourism-dependent economy of Diani, as it developed over the past fifty years, is unable to sustain the African Kenyan community that surrounds it. The case of Diani documents that failed, lacking, and ineffective planning and infrastructure development resulted in the economic precarity of the local community, which in turn led to the creation of a pervasive culture of charity. In Diani, charity fills the gap that was created through the disappearance of communal forms of support but, arguably, also contributed to their disappearance. Although charitable actions address needs that were previously attended to through various forms of communal social action and also tackle new areas of need and want. They differ from utsi and mweria in terms of notions of accountability and reciprocity, which are key elements in creating not only coeval relations, but also sustainable forms of social and economic action. (Berman, 2017: 77)

In Tiwi, as well as in Dini, European-led or supported schools and kindergartens are popping up like mushrooms. One of the schools is the Kristina Academy, founded with the help of the German organisation *Asante e.V.*[2] in 2003 which organises social journeys called *Patenreisen* (sponsor's journey) to Kenya in order to offer transparency to the interested sponsors.

The Philanthropic Journeys of Asante e.V.[3]

Philanthropic travel – whether in the case of voluntourism, philanthropic journeys or pro-poor tourism – are highly controversial when it comes to the traveller's actual intention. It is often said that these journeys are purely egocentric, that they are made under the guise of altruism;[4] that subjective impressions of tourist settings and their analysis result in a dualistic construction of the self and the other (Galani-Moutafi, 1999: 206) as wild versus civilised, poor versus rich and – especially in the context of philanthropic tourism – hungry versus satisfied.

Taking one example from many, the internet platform *Make a Difference*[5] offers journeys worldwide in cooperation with humanitarian organisations. Here, the viewing of a local organisation is embedded in a journey beside the other typical aspects of a trip like safaris, beach trips and city viewing. They begin on the front page of their website with a proverb from Africa saying, 'The one who visits others shall open his eyes and not his mouth' and continue with their promise to 'build bridges between experience and responsibility, give and take, wealth and poverty, luxury and a down-to-earth awareness.'[6]

These shibboleths very clearly display a background of social travel, already implying that the place where one comes from is experienced and wealthy, and that the people visited clearly need help. Even more meaningful is the proverb, which reflects the visitor's wordlessness towards the visited people, already named as 'the other'. The tourism industry has the power to position the other in a different time (Fabian, 2002 [1983]) and, as is seen here, also in another space of moral and social distance with the intention of increasing the will to help and donate. This wordlessness is compensated through the 'eye of the tourist', namely the camera. It plays an important role in encounters of extreme differences, not only to catch the moment, but also in order to build safe boundaries. The eye/camera of the tourist is a means with which to transport the other's voice with various intentions. One intention of the participants of social journeys certainly is to illustrate back home how poor the other is, and to raise money or the interest of the people back home in order to support the project in the future. The other aspect seems to revolve around capturing the moment for stirring memories of the journey and the emotions bound to them back at home.

Through the aspect of gazing and taking pictures yet not talking, a very interesting aspect of speaking for the other arises: social journey travellers tend to speak on behalf of the other who, in their opinion, has no potential to express himself and who is rather a subaltern, in the sense of Spivak (1988), compared to a human with a voice and a choice.

These aspects of othering and positioning the exotic other in the centre of the journey, as well as the construction of invisible walls with the help of cameras will be the focus of the following encounters which took place during the philanthropic journeys of *Asante e.V.*

Formation, Background and Realisation

The journeys offered by *Asante e.V.* were planned to be conducted in a yearly cycle in order to enable donors, members and sponsors of the organisation to travel to Kenya for two weeks. All tourists participating in the philanthropic journeys have a high interest in the project. The tour includes a one-week cultural programme with a focus on school education in Kenya through several school visits, attending church on a Sunday, a bush tour on foot, a visit to the organisation's self-help women's project, a visit to the heritage site 'Fort Jesus' in Mombasa and a 'meet the sponsor' day. A second week is left open for a free choice of activities during which safaris are offered. The idea and the realisation of the *Patenreisen* of *Asante e.V.* arose out of a certain need. The organisation, which was founded in 2003, currently has 415 members.[7] Furthermore, through the organisation, 714 children are sponsored by Germans in the organisation's own primary academy as well as in public primary and secondary schools. Over the years of sponsoring, sponsors had developed quite a one-sided relationships with their sponsored children and were unsatisfied with the fact that these children had not tried to contact them. *Asante e.V.* therefore organised a yearly 'letter to the sponsor' in which the child normally writes what she/he is doing and what is going on at home (see Figure 5.1). A current photo of the child is also put into the envelope.

Figure 5.1 A letter to the sponsor (photo AM)

Over the years, some of the sponsors went on holiday to Kenya and wanted to see their sponsored children, whose development they had been monitoring through the letters to the sponsor. This led to diverse problems, including disturbances in classes during school time, taking pictures unasked on school grounds and distributing sweets, but it also led to cultural problems, such as the sponsor's misunderstanding of statements made by the child or the child's relatives.

As *Asante e.V.* wanted to give sponsors the chance to visit their sponsored children, and at the same time to understand their culture and social background, and to gain insights into the lives and living conditions of the children, a social journey was offered. These social journeys were supposed to establish cross-cultural understanding but also a stable relationship between the sponsor and the child in order to secure financial support for the child's education. *Asante e.V.* is in tune here with a small number of NGOs who offer trips wherein small groups of tourists are brought to project sites.

The Germans' Intention for Participating in the Social Journey

The tourists eagerly accepted the chance for a social journey because most had never been to Africa and were afraid of visiting the continent for the first time all by themselves. With the personal mentoring and care of the two organisers, the German chairlady and the founder of the organisation in Kenya, they were eager to take this step. Often, tourists travelling with social journeys choose this opportunity out of convenience because they don't have to worry about transport or other practical aspects (Salazar, 2004: 97). *Asante e.V.* tourists were not only searching for a new experience or collecting as many destinations as possible (Salazar, 2004: 97), but they were extremely keen on getting closer to the culture and the local people, as they were already involved in the project. This can also be seen in a later *Asante e.V.* social journeys of through which some of the participants repeated the tour. The highlight of the journey was the opportunity to meet the sponsored children, whom some had been financing for many years.

Statistics

This article draws its knowledge and data from four journeys that were undertaken in the years 2010 (22 participants), 2011 (17 participants), 2013 (18 participants) and 2016 (13 participants). In total, seventy people joined the four journeys. In 2012, no journey was planned. The decreasing number of participants and the missing journeys in 2014 and 2015 trace back to the outbreak of Ebola in West Africa in September 2014 and the two attacks by the al-Shabaab terrorists in April 2015 at the University of Garissa where 147 people, mostly students, were killed, and to September 2013 in the Westgate Mall in Nairobi where hostages were

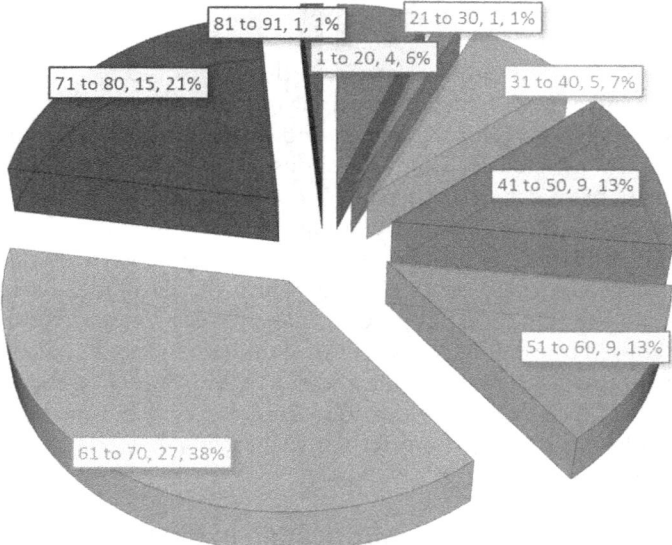

Figure 5.2 Participants as per age; n = 71

taken and 67 people killed. The 2013 journey took place a month before the terrorist attack in Nairobi and thus it didn't have any effect on the already booked journey of that year.

Figure 5.2 shows the age distribution of the participants. Almost half are between 51 and 70 years of age, 64% are female. The younger ones (under 20) are children who accompanied their parents during the journey.

The Encounters and the Performance of Tourists and Locals

The encounters between the journey participants of the journey and the Kenyan recipients of the donations were organised in order to enable exchange and interaction between both parties.

First Encounter – The Welcome

The first meeting between guests and hosts normally takes place on the school compound of Kristina Academy in Tiwi, where enough space is provided for the sixty women of a self-help handcraft women project (one section of the organisation) to sing, dance and welcome the guests. The place for this first encounter is chosen due to the relaxed atmosphere on the compound, in order to allay the guests' fear of the unknown.

In the first few minutes, the opposite of what is intended by the meeting occurs. The two groups (tourists and locals) stand face to face and gaze at each other. The women start to sing and perform; meanwhile,

Figure 5.3 The welcome (photo AM)

the guests take out their cameras. The organisers of the journey arranged the chairs for the visitors and the stage for the performers in the way that Kenyan welcomes are normally held. The visitors are given no chance to interact with the women by, for example, joining them in their dancing or singing. The cameras set up a border and turn the first meeting into an objectification.

Second Encounter – The Food Distribution for Orphans

Food distribution is a part of the journey's agenda that is very positively experienced by the German participants. In this subproject of the organisation, orphaned children and very poor children receive a fixed amount of food every second week. They come to the distribution with their carers or their parents. The distribution is organised by the Kenyan staff of *Asante e.V*. The so-called 'orphan feeding' came about in response to some cases where parents were deceased. The orphans' relatives approached the head of the organisation, requesting help in order to care for all the siblings and to avoid having to split them up by sending them singly to other relatives or friends. This idea of not separating orphaned siblings is one of the most favoured projects of German sponsors, and the participants are keen to take part in the food distribution for one day.

The idea behind this is that the guests can see how the distribution, for which they have collected or donated in Germany, is conducted, and they can come into closer contact with the people. Already on the first journey in 2011, it became clear that the sponsors and the locals couldn't connect due to reserve of both parties. Many of the Kenyan parents and carers and the German travellers didn't know English, making conversation complicated. But neither the tourists nor the locals dared to approach the other and instead gazed at each other or – on the part of the tourists – started taking photographs.

The organisers were able to ease the situation by asking the tourists to help distribute the food. The tourists could start small conversations

Figure 5.4 Hosts and guests are too shy to converse with each other (photo AM)

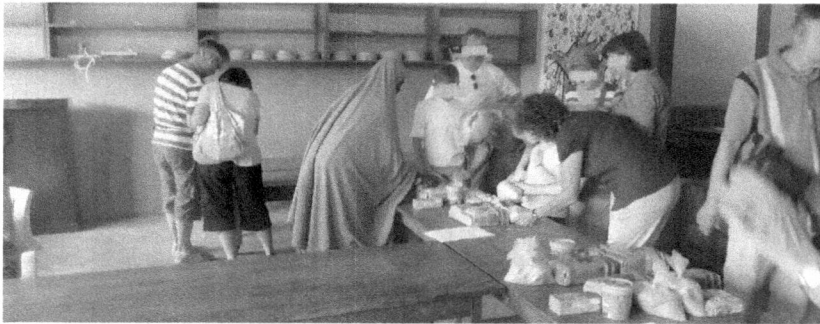

Figure 5.5 Participants of the journey distributing food (photo AM)

like 'how many rations?', and the recipients could answer. Not uncommon were the words, thank you, *asante*[8] and you are welcome, *karibu* with which both parties seemed to feel more comfortable. They found themselves in the structure of neocolonial power inequalities, but it was nevertheless the structure they seemed to feel comfortable with. In all of the journeys it was interesting to see that even if the tourist was extremely aware of power inequalities, he/she had no problem with the role of being a donor.

Third Encounter – The Bush Tour

The bush tour on foot is a much-favoured part of the philanthropic journey. It is offered because it allows the guests to walk through the Tiwi area, which otherwise is not possible for individual tourists, due to crime. During the tour, the guests visit locations where they can see how the locals prepare food or make handicrafts like roasting cashew nuts, weaving baskets or cooking manioc.

Cameras as Barriers of Understanding 75

Figure 5.6 Visiting, discussing and photographing the house of a needy family (photo AM)

Each year, one stop is made at the house of one of the women from the self-help project who is in need and who urgently requires help to get her house repaired. This stop is made because the participants of the philanthropic journey really care about the people in Tiwi and are willing to help them financially. In all three philanthropic journeys undertaken, the participants collected money after the excursion in order to repair or even build a new house for the woman they had been visited.

Yet although the inhabitants of the house are around and willing to answer the guests' questions, they are not the centre of the visitors' concerns, who mainly want to see the rotten house and the poor interior. The urge to continuously take photos creates invisible walls which make a personal interaction impossible.

This encounter is a very touching moment for many of the participants, as it shows the extreme need of the poor in Tiwi. The photos are used by the participants back home in Germany to show and transmit the

Figure 5.7 The group of 2010 inspecting the house of Mama M, which had been built by *Asante e.V.* shortly before (photo AM)

desperate situation of many people in Tiwi. It is thus not astonishing that a participant, who had joined the tour a second time, mentioned that the house visited in 2010 was in much worse condition than the house visited in 2011. He was disappointed that the photos which he had expected to take would not be as dramatic as the year before.

Fourth Encounter – Meet the Sponsor

An agenda item which is particularly looked forward to by the guests is the day when they meet the children whom they have been sponsoring at the school.

This day has already been a topic of discussion during the preparation for the journey in Germany when the participants of the trip ask the organisers what they should buy as a present for their sponsored child, whether they should buy presents for the relatives, what the boys and girls need, and other details, for example, the size of clothing or shoes, likes and dislikes of Kenyan children. On each of the journeys, meeting the sponsored child is the most emotional event of the whole tour. When the tourists are picked up at their hotel, they are equipped with presents for their sponsored children, the children's siblings and other relatives who might join the meeting. Their feelings of excitement and anticipation, but also worries concerning language barriers are shared among the visitors. Many of these worries and concerns have been discussed in the preparation phase of the journey.

For the meeting, seating arrangements are prepared so that each sponsor and their sponsored child, together with the family, have time to talk to each other. Where language is a problem from the side of the sponsor or the child and the family, a translator is provided.

This encounter stands in stark contrast to the other meetings, as it is the only very personal and extremely emotional one. Although there are problems with shyness and sometimes with keeping the conversation going, a common denominator – the child – creates a situation

Figure 5.8 Meeting of sponsors and sponsored family (photo AM)

where there is shared interest and knowledge, and makes it possible to sit together and feel comfortable. Presents are mutually exchanged, and the hosts, who normally give Lesos (a traditional garment), as a present, wrap the guests in the Kangas. The guests take some pictures, at the end of the day, together with their sponsored child.

The Discourse of Photography in Philanthropic Tourism

As the pictures from the encounters show, cameras are a steady companion of the tourist. 'Most tourists feel compelled to put a camera between themselves and whatever is remarkable they encounter' states Susan Sontag (1977: 9 f.). Often the parallel use of a camera and a video camera can be observed. The analysis of photography in situations such as that described previously offers new perspectives for the discourse on philanthropic tourism and photography. As each tourist type can be characterised by the different kinds of photos they are taking, (Chalfen, 1979: 438), philanthropic tourists can be characterised by unintentionally seeking to erect a barrier, a wall between them and the locals. Stylianou-Lambert (2012: 1819), referring to the work of Sontag (1977) and Graburn (1989), notices that

> [t]he camera functions as a filter, or even better, a transparent wall which separates the known from the unknown and thus offers a sense of control and security.

This contradicts the purpose the traveller has connected to this journey. The highly emotional involvement during this trip combined with the cultural shock as well as the awareness that the exotic other, who before seemed to be in a far way, unknown place and is suddenly a part of one's reality, creates insecurity and fear.

The philanthropic journeys of *Asante e.V.* reveals a new concept of photography in tourism. Photography in this kind of highly emotional tourism is different from photography in other tourism settings. In this case, it functions as a tool with which to distance oneself from the emotional experience that is anticipated. On these trips, the expectations of what one will see are defined in advance. The focus is on the poverty and the powerlessness of the locals, the reasons why the Germans are engaged in collecting money back home. It is for this reason that pictures need to be taken during the journey, it is to meet the expectations back home. The locals must appear needy in the photos in order to generate donations; thus, their outer appearance must meet German expectations of how the needy other looks. Houses without electricity and running water are a must in order to transmit the idea that help from outside is necessary. The same holds true for their outer appearance. Untraditional clothing, meaning any clothing other than typical Kanga, are often left out of photographs. Likewise, the condition of the clothing is important, and spoiled or ripped Kangas or skirts are often central in the photographs. This representation corresponds to a postcolonial theory according to which people in non-Western countries are mostly photographed without an indicator of development (Price, 2009).

The representation of locals in photography depends upon the level of emotionality. The more emotions are connected with the journey and one's own input, the more impossible an interplay between the locals and the visitors seems to be, and the more the local can be defined as a *touree*, a subject defined by the tourist (Scarles, 2013). The travellers often portray the locals in certain situations and display them as the exotic other. This kind of exoticising contributes to the retention of the tourist gaze (Urry, 2002) and seems to play an important role in the photography of the philanthropic journeys. In these encounters, it is not so much the production of aesthetic photographs which matters, but the production and reproduction of poverty and need. Throughout the encounters, a wish to be in the photos has never been expressed by the tourist. For this reason, a self-portrait with a local, implying being a part of the picture, is not necessary or even desired.

Photographers normally play the agentive part in a photographing situation. Thus, the tourists, who seem to be the actors in the philanthropic encounter, through their status as donors – the visitors or the ones with power – play the privileged and agentive role. The locals scarcely have the opportunity to gain agency because the tourists demand to see the *real*, the exotic Other in desperate and poor surroundings. In a highly emotional journey, as is the sponsor's journey of *Asante e.V.*, which is conducted in order to monitor the success of one's own engagement in development aid, the stereotype of the poor locals is forcefully brought into the lens, and any aspect of progress is intentionally ignored.

As defined in postcolonial and tourism studies (Mellinger, 1994; Price, 2009; Urry, 2002), power relations between locals and tourists are created in photography, which is used as a tool of knowledge and power. In this sense, the question arises as to whether the photographers of this philanthropic journey can be analysed as passive consumers of places and reproducers of images or rather as active cultural producers who recreate spaces (Stylianou-Lambert, 2012: 1817 f). Indeed, they may not actually be cultural producers, but they intentionally and artfully create spaces which correlate with the intention of their journey, namely the abstract space of need for aid and assistance. This space is created for them by the organisation and the locals and is gratefully internalised for their photographs.

Nevertheless, it seems important to comment that the locals' agency is not completely lost and there is a benefit for the: all those who serve as the exotic other profit financially from the situation. The organisers of the journeys as well as the locals are aware that photographing the needy persons and situations is necessary in order to collect donations abroad. The display of poverty is the only means by which to raise funds.

In conclusion, a new perspective on photography in tourism can be found in the philanthropic journeys sector, where emotions have a higher role than in other journeys. Where in other settings cameras are used by tourists to artfully play with the here and now, in philanthropic journeys they are used to create barriers to distance the self from reality, poverty and integrity, thereby avoiding overly-emotional involvement.

Acknowledgements

I would like to thank Anne Storch for the wonderful cooperation and for sharing her thoughts and ideas on tourism with me, Nico Nassenstein for inspiring discussions and Penelope Allsobrook for proofreading and commenting on the article.

Notes

(1) A form that concerns the generation of net benefits from tourism in favour of the people in the poor country and applies to any kind of tourism, even if the non-poor also benefit (Harrison, 2008: 856).
(2) Asante e.V. Verein zur Förderung von Schulkindern in Tiwi, Kenia.
(3) e.V. is the abbreviation for *eingetragener Verein*, and it identifies organisations as registered societies.
(4) On 9 March 2017, the German radio channel *Deutschlandfunk* broadcasted from the tourist trade fair that took place in Berlin. The broadcast focused on voluntourism and introduced aspects of completely inhuman humanitarian aid during travelling. http://www.deutschlandfunk.de/anders-reisen-fuer-und- wider-von-voluntourismus. 772.de.html?dram:article_id=375901.
(5) https://www.makeadifference.de/.
(6) Wir bauen Brücken zwischen Erlebnis und Verantwortung, geben und nehmen, Reichtum und Armut, Luxus und Bodenständigkeit.
(7) Latest update of numbers in November 2017.
(8) Swahili for 'thank you'.

References

Akama, J.S. (1996) Western environmental values and nature-based tourism in Kenya. *Tourism Management* 17 (8), 567–574.
Berman, N. (2017) *Germans on the Kenyan Coast. Land, Charity, and Romance*. Indiana: Indiana University Press.
Callanan, M. and Thomas, S. (2005) Volunteer tourism – Deconstructing volunteer activities within a dynamic environment. In M. Novelli (ed.) *Niche Tourism: Contemporary Issues, Trends and Cases* (pp. 183–200). Oxford: Elsevier Butterworth Heinemann.
Chalfen, R. (1979) Photography's role in tourism: Some unexplored relationships. *Annals of Tourism Research* 6 (4), 435–447.
Fabian, J. (1983) *Time and the Other: How Anthropology Makes Its Object*. New York, NY: Columbia University Press; New Edition (2002).
Galani-Moutafi, V. (1999) The self and the other: Traveler, ethnographer, tourist. *Annals of Tourism Research* 27 (1), 203–224.

Graburn, N.H. (1989) Tourism: The sacred journey. In V.L. Smith (ed.) *Hosts and Guests: The Anthropology of Tourism* (pp. 21–36). Philadelphia, PA: University of Pennsylvania Press.

Hall, C.M. and Raymond, E.M. (2008) The development of cross-cultural (mis)understanding through volunteer tourism. *Journal of Sustainable Tourism* 16 (5), 530–543.

Harrison, D. (2008) Pro-poor tourism: A critique. *Third World Quarterly (Tourism and Development in the Global South)* 29 (5), 851–868.

McBride, A.M., Brav, J., Menon, N. and Sherradon, M. (2006) Limitations of civic service: Critical perspectives. *Community Development Journal* 41 (3), 307–320.

Mellinger, W.M. (1994) Towards a critical analysis of tourism representations. *Annals of Tourism Research* 21 (4), 756–779.

Price, D. (2009) Surveyors and surveyed: Photography out and about. In L. Wells (ed.) *Photography: A Critical Introduction* (pp. 65–112). Oxon: Routledge.

Salazar, N. (2004) Developmental tourists vs. developmental tourism: A case study. In A. Raj (ed.) *Tourism Behaviour, a Psychological Perspective* (pp. 85–107). New Delhi: Kanishka Publishers.

Scarles, C.E. (2013) The ethics of tourist photography: Tourists' experiences of photographing locals in Peru. *Environment and Planning D: Society and Space* 31 (5), 897–917.

Sindiga, I. (1999) *Tourism and African Development: Change and Challenge of Tourism in Kenya*. Hampshire: Ashgate Publishing.

Sontag, S. (1977) *On Photography*. New York, NY: Delta Books.

Spivak, G.C. (1988) Can the subaltern speak? In C. Nelson and L. Grossberg (eds) *Marxism and the Interpretation of Culture* (pp. 66–111). Chicago, IL: University of Illinois Press.

Stylianou-Lambert, T. (2012) Tourists with cameras: Reproducing or producing? *Annals of Tourism Research* 39 (4), 1817–1838.

Urry, J. (2002) *The Tourist Gaze* (2nd edn). London: Sage.

6 Heritage Tourism and the Freak Show: A Study on Names, Horror, Race and Gender

Anne Storch

Introduction: An Invitation to Quiet Places

In an advertisement for a holiday home posted on the Airbnb website, a moderate kind of paradise is offered. It is not about tropical tourism stereotypes, such as white sandy beaches and colourful Caribbean sights underscored by reggae tunes, but rather about the unison of the tropics – hills and the sun above them, and a beer at the end of a long day:

> Nestled in the lush Grange Hill of Westmoreland, Seaford Town. Steeped in History. Its lush rolling hill are a delight. Chillax on the verandah see the sunrise, see the sunset. Bathe in the wonderful ambiance of the sun. Sip cool Red Stripe Beer. (Airbnb website)

This text reveals, already after a brief second look, what the actual attraction of the location offered here might be: besides place names and the name of a beer brand, the only other word written with a capital letter is 'history'. History seems to be particular here, and a major reason for a visit.

Yet, history at this place is nothing to 'discover' or to be enchanted by; it is what makes this place difficult and its inhabitants being seen as different. Seaford Town, were the advertised holiday home is located, is one of the many Jamaican heritage sites (Jamaica National Heritage Trust), and not because of some outstanding historical building or commemorative site, but because of a particular form of discursive racialised marginalisation concerning many of its inhabitants.

Inscription into the Jamaican National Heritage Trust's list serves many purposes and making a place attractive as a heritage tourism site is one of the most important ones. Heritage tourism thereby is by no means a very recent phenomenon, as the touristic visit to 'the village' has over decades been part of the average shore leave programme, safari trip and ambitious sightseeing trip alike. The artificiality of tourism experiences here seems to have its counter piece in the form of an experience of reality, truth and the down-to-earth life of the indigenous other.

Yet, as the blogger and tour operator Jim Heck writes, the 'village visit' is probably the most viciously artificial aspect of prearranged and guided tours. The authenticity to be found there, he writes, is one of colonial exploitation, social injustice and postcolonial othering:

> The so-called "villages" that people claim to have experienced are impoverished groups of people who wish they were better off and in most cases are stuck in the worst of two worlds. [...] It is the identical situation to many impoverished communities in America — distressed villages in Appalachia or southwest Wisconsin. I'm infuriated that travelers will actually return from these visits, claiming to have experienced "the real Africa." (Africa/Answerman)

The blog continues with a description of a tour, to people who perform otherness and marginalisation in rather ironic ways: they appear as mock impersonations of the other, who comments on all the holes and cracks in the surface of this performance of past authenticities: '[...] we watched this poor kid trying desperately to start a fire rubbing two twigs, together. He looked up at me and said woefully, "*Zamani, Mzee, tuna kibiriti!*" Roughly translated, "A long time ago, *Mzee*, we used matches!"'.

Yet, anything will do. The village and the authentic heritage site serve their purpose well even when being performed sloppily. What makes the visit to villages noteworthy, in particular in the context of heritage tourism, is not perfection of an orchestration, as in a theme park, but the illusion of the messiness of real-life practices, whereby 'real-life' here refers to the ways of doing of the past: making fire without matches, watching lush greenery while being immersed in history. The imperfect performance and the simplicity of the experiences available in the village-as-heritage ('see the sunrise, see the sunset') are part of a form of othering that bases on the ideology of uninterrupted continuity and of history as a form of stagnation. The other here, I want to demonstrate in this contribution, is always objectified, as a persona of the past, undeveloped, still poor and photogenic in a primordial surrounding (Hall & Tucker, 2014).

Allochrony – the positioning of the other in another time (Fabian, 2002 [1983]) – is a strategy that affords power, and the tourism industry clearly is able to provide it. In this chapter, a closer look is taken at how othering and heritage tourism feed into each other on a discursive level. I claim that names, which in Seaford Town and beyond are presented as hailing from the far colonial past and are used as a discursive means in the construction of the village; the hinterland, class, race and heritage do the job of othering in a very particular way. This chapter offers an analysis of how such forms of othering contribute to presenting heritage sites as arenas of the freak show. I largely tell the story of the discursive racialisation and deformation of a group of people who share life in a village that is now a heritage tourism site, and by doing so I focus on travelogues, tourist guidebooks, blogs, newspaper articles and comments by travellers and other players. These texts do not only reflect practices of marginalisation and deprivation, they also provide a hegemonic concept of history (or, 'History', as in the previous Jamaican airbnb advertisement) as a heritage tourism construct.

Putting emphasis on the names needed in order to place the other in particular historical imagery involves thinking about ways of unmaking people and places and ways of ascribing community identity constructs. I argue, in line with Karin Tusting (2005: 53) 'that critical social linguistics offers a fruitful way of conceptualising the role of language within [a] situation, giving us better understandings of the relationships between language and other social processes, and between local interaction and broader social structures.' Yet, by focussing on *interaction outside the local*, on what others say and do, still other understandings of how language and society interact emerge, and these appear to be of particular significance for tourism and heritaging practices.

Naming as Unmaking

The social semiotics of naming and names in this chapter are seen as being crucial for an understanding of practices of othering and heritaging, especially in an approach informed by postcolonial theory and critical discourse analysis. Hence, while in the dominating research of names in European-American contexts (Nübling *et al.*, 2012), names appear to typically bear all the characteristics usually attributed to them in onomastics – as proper nouns they have no lexical meaning as such but designate the *individual* – in the previously colonised parts of the world, a different take on the study of names might be chosen (e.g. Anchimbe, 2011). Here, the focus on names is on their potential to transgress boundaries: they are words that have a Janus-faced quality, being used as a means to denote individual persons and at the same time functioning as (often derogatory) terms that express the notion of a sort or a type rather than a single, predefined referent – depending on who speaks to whom and in which context.

The important thing to look at, in the setting studied here, is how naming practices and specific terms focus on fragility and difference. This particular aspect naming in a colonial world has been quite early addressed in postcolonial theory. Frantz Fanon, as one of the major figures to theorise the relationship between exteriority (making a person available to his or her environment to be objectified, identified and seized), naming and racism, observed that while the (white) coloniser claims the right to have a personal name (without the need to share it with others) and to name others, the (black) colonised person doesn't possess the same power. This puts the colonised, according to Fanon's biographer and interpreter Lewis R. Gordon, in a situation of epistemic closure: 'Epistemic closure is a moment of presumably complete knowledge of a phenomenon. Such presumed knowledge closes off efforts at further enquiry. The result is what we shall call perverse anonymity. Anonymity literally means to be nameless' (Gordon, 2015: 49). The name of the colonised characterises its bearer as a generalisable member of a uniform group, a person about whom all is already known, and who may be called by any name given to him or her: *Negro* can be used as a personal name in such contexts, Fanon writes, as can be any other name, whatever source it derives from.

The postcolony as a field of onomastic enquiry considerably differs from other conceivable settings in which names could be studied insofar as it is fundamentally characterised by continued injustice and inequality (which Mbembe, 2001: 32 sees as a continuation of colonial practices). Names here become crucial tokens of class and power; they have very particular indexicalities of their own, as they undergo specific pragmatic changes depending on whom they denote, by whom they are given, and when they are called. In sociolinguistic contexts where experiences of enslavement and extreme marginalisation continue to play a role, such as in creole societies, in geographic areas such as the Black Atlantic, a name therefore is a highly ambiguous word.

The following sections all concentrate on names present in a village in Jamaica, which has a complex history of African, but also of European – here: German – diasporas. The tropical space in which the village of Seaford Town is located is, I argue, conceptualised as devouring and void of 'civilization' (Bongartz & Storch, 2016). The devouring power of the colonial void (Gordillo, 2013) is also at work when places and people are designated and turned into objects that can be listed and sorted: giving a name, Frantz Fanon writes, is not only unmaking places but even more so persons. His much celebrated analysis of what the colonial other is called also is an analysis of how the other is turned into an object that can be put into its place. Fanon recalls a little boy shouting, 'Look, a negro!': 'My body was given back to me sprawled out, distorted, recoloured, clad in mourning in that white winter day. The negro is an animal, the negro is bad, the negro is mean, the negro is ugly; look, a nigger' (1967: 113). The named other has no control over what he might be; he is turned into a frightening thing, an object that evokes pathological emotions – fear, rage, hate. Naming as turning people and places into undesirable matter is a strategy of maintaining control. Therefore, the colonial other 'cannot live a life of anonymity, etymologically, "without a name" or "nameless." Apparently, only whites have that wonderful capacity to live anonymously, thoughtlessly, to be ordinary *qua* human, to go unmarked and unnamed – in essence, to be white. They are like Clint Eastwood's white stock characters in his Western shoot-'em-up movies who come into town nameless and mysterious', as George Yancy (2012: 4) suggests.

Naming the other, in a postcolonial world, therefore needs to be seen as a particular historical practice, one that aims not at making a place, a person or a social group, but at objectifying them. What remains is rot, I suggest in accord with Ann Laura Stoler (2013): 'Names is for tombstones, baby!,' as they say in Fleming's *Live and Let Die* (Hamilton, 1973). The names in this contribution are imperial debris, piled upon other rubble: language as ruinous practice, naming as a continuing process of ruination. This requires seeing names not as structure but as action. They are, in this contribution, considered social ways of doing that make people 'strange', as freaks and ultimate others. The metaphor of ruination enables us to understand the presence of these ways of doing as a continuous phenomenon and a consequence of a catastrophe that still is of concern, in the sense of Walter Benjamin's comment on the philosophy of history as the history of the imperial catastrophe (1968: 257 f.).

A Name that Recalls the Past

In Franklin Schaffner's *Papillon* (1973), we see how Henri Charrière ('Papillon', played by Steve McQueen) and Dustin Hoffman as Louis Dega are taken to a penal colony in French Guaiana. With them are several dozen of unnamed men, emaciated and clad in rags, playing fellow deportees. They look like *real* inmates, as realistic as does the prison's reverend: we are tempted to assume that these men are not actors, but as local and real as the scenery around them – the jungle, the ruins, the mud, the hot humid air. None of these men is mentioned in the film's credits, which might make them even more real and authentic: just extras from around where the film was shot.

What is hard to guess though is that the men in the background had only been found after a long search. The film's production company had long tried to find men who would make credible inmates: miserable, half-starved and lacking white shiny teeth to smile with. Obviously, this proved to be not an easy task in the prosperous early 1970s, but eventually the casting team succeeded. They were told about a remote village in Jamaica's parish of Westmoreland, and found its population perfectly suited for the project. They hired as many of the men of Seaford Town as they could get, complete with their priest who even didn't have to change his wardrobe.

Until early 2017, a few laminated newspaper clippings and film stills made part of Seaford Town's heritage museum (which is now closed), and many older people around can still tell who was playing which role: the man operating the guillotine was Pater Francis, the poor guy just right behind Dustin Hoffman was one Mr Kameka, the man carrying a heavy load in the back was called Somers... The museum was not, however, a pilgrimage site for film buffs, even though *Papillon* has become a cult movie. Visitors to Seaford Town come for a very particular history.

Seaford Town was founded in 1835 by Charles Rose Ellis, Lord Seaford, a politician whose family had owned plantations in Jamaica since the 18th century. After the Slavery Abolition Act of 1833 had been put into effect, landowners such as Seaford not only faced a rather sudden shortage of labour force on their plantations, but also were confronted with the social consequences of the inhumanity under which most who lived on those plantations had to suffer. The social and psychological situation of the liberated slaves after centuries of bondage also is of concern to current discussions of Seaford Town's history:[1] oral history shared in the village focuses on examples of formerly enslaved people's revenge inflicted upon their former masters, on how communities lacked access to education and state institutions, and how families were weak and provided only insufficient care for children whose fathers until recently had not been permitted to act as family heads and husbands who would have some kind of control over their matrimonial relatives (Clay Groskopf and Fitzroy Chambers, pers. comm, 2017). The newly established settlement of Seaford Town was consequently established for two reasons – namely to settle supplementary

Figure 6.1 A monument to Pater Francis, fondly remembered as local historian, pillar of his community and a film extra (photo AS)

labourers and to provide a means to transmit metropolitan techniques of daily life practice to the liberated slaves (Curtin, 2010).

In many parts of early 19th century Germany, there were people who would readily migrate to engage in any possible work, to escape miserable living conditions, bad harvests and military service, and through a broker several hundred persons were made to leave their villages in Westphalia and around Bremen for Jamaica (Klieber, 1913). They were craftsmen and peasants, often without any land of their own, and were tempted by the promise that in Jamaica they would be given a plot of land with a house on it, tools in it and a weekly salary for their basic needs. Upon arrival, they soon realised that none of the promised implements and possessions existed, and that the land allocated to them was hard to till and didn't yield much (Hall, 1974). They faced forested hills of thick green nothingness and a downpour at each afternoon. It seemed that all that had changed was their geographical location, until the first settlers began to die. Malnutrition, hunger and tropical diseases took their toll. In the former museum of Seaford Town, but also in the stories told by its inhabitants, the horror of the passage and of the first years in those remote hills is present. The memories of starvation and disease, of fear and desperation, are part of a visit to the village, and they are seen as part of the heritage of the Germans, as well as poverty, Catholicism, living in cottages with basements (which are unusual elsewhere in Jamaica), and bearing German names (Hall, 1974; Orizio, 2000).

Those names of the original settlers remain present in the archived museum – Kameke, Kleinhans, Wedemeyer, Sauerländer, Eltermeyer, and they are still found on Seaford Town's graveyard and everywhere else in their anglicised forms as Kameka, Clinance, Wedemire, Sourlender, Eldemire and so forth. They provide a frequently referenced resource for the reconstruction of family histories and are often the only remaining link to the little towns around the cities of Münster and Bremen, where the ancestors once had come from. But these names are not the only ones that have been identified as evidence of German heritage. There is another term that is part of an entire class of words that leads a more concealed life. While proper nouns might be part of heritage research as well as grammatical description, and toponyms and ethnonyms are not only celebrated topics of linguistic typology and anthropological linguistics, but are also occasionally listed in lexicographic sources, nicknames and socially pejorative terms are something different. They are often problematic, racist, unwanted, politically incorrect linguistic material that is largely absent from average descriptive sources. However, there are numerous interesting exceptions. In their dictionary of Jamaican English, Cassidy and Le Page present the following entry (2002: 196):

German /jaaman/ – 1. A poor white.

Even if stereotyped expectations – Germans are not frequently poor at tourism destinations such as Jamaica – could be left unregarded, the term is unsettling. It refers to a state of exclusion and liminality in which the settlers remained over decades, if not generations, their isolation and their failure to become wealthy.

Cassidy and Le Page provide a helpful note on earlier documentation of the name:

> 1959 DeC West /jáaman/ – what the Negroes of Seaford Town call one of the Germans there; the German himself[2] would say /jarman/.

By 1959, the former ethnonym explicitly referred to the population of Seaford Town, and obviously it was of importance who used the term: there is a slight phonological difference here that marks autonymic and xenonymic usages. While the Patwa form of the name is marked for tone, a phonological feature that came into the Caribbean with the languages spoken by enslaved people from West and Central Africa (Devonish, 1989), the autonym is not marked for tone but retains the /r/. Obviously, by the time of its notation in the dictionary, the term encoded not only the meanings 'inhabitant of Seaford Town with German ancestry' and 'poor white', but also bore connotations, marked phonologically, of group-membership (or exclusion), socioracial positioning of the speaker, and place (where the term was used, referring to poor white people in general or just to a those living in Seaford Town, for example). Today, this seems to have become less relevant: these linguistic practices are no longer a marker of racialised difference in Seaford Town. In Riccardo Orizio's poetic account of Seaford Town, Tony Wedemeyer, an activist and Rastafarian is given a voice. He refers to other ways of naming difference: 'We have seventeen different definitions for seventeen different shades of skin, from white white to black black. Each shade has its own name: Quadroon, Quintroon, Octoroon, etc. And the destiny of each is pre-determined' (2000: 57).

Naming Race and Class

Those of the first German settlers who were able to leave moved on to northern America. The hundred-and-some Germans who remained at Seaford Town, however, learned to farm ginger, bananas, manioc and breadfruit. For years, they remained poor people who frequently depended on the help of the liberated slaves who lived around Seaford Town. Even though they shared economic strategies, lifestyles and poverty with the people around them, they seemed to strangely remain a closed group, white and unwilling to blend in. This is precisely the way in which they were represented in travelogues, guidebooks and newspaper articles on the Jamaican Germans that appeared from the 1980s onwards, when political change in Jamaica and elsewhere translated into an increase of interest in the colonial afterlife of race and class.

The then very popular German monthly journal *GEO* presented one of the first articles on Seaford Town in 1985, which offers rich photographic material that formed part of the exhibition in Seaford Town's heritage museum.³ Unbeknownst to the majority of the villagers who do not read German, the people of Seaford Town here are not *quadroons*, but white, and not just *jaamans* – poor whites – but degenerated poor whites:

> Something that travelers encountered in Seaford Town at the beginning of our century was supposed to hurt their national pride: there was an incoherent miserably poor mob of peaceful savages, who had endured in agony. Of those who had once emanated from the 'Olbers', only two were still alive by 1911. Not few of those with blue eyes and 'flaxen hair' however had to call the black landlords 'Massa' [...]. (Sasse & Drexel, 1985: 80)⁴

Misery here is accompanied by incest and perverted religious practice:

> Even half brothers and sisters went to the altar, and the church, fond of racial segregation, blessed the incestuous relationships. Fear of a hostile environment, perhaps also belief in white supremacy, in spite of their sick lives, forced the 'Germans' into reclusion. (Sasse & Drexel, 1985: 86)⁵

The people who have made Westmoreland their home, like so many others before and after them, are referred to as 'human driftwood' (Sasse & Drexel, 1985: 72 f.), forgotten Germans, who look weird on these images offered to us: piercing gazes, faces that resist to smile. At a time when the audiences of such articles were able to afford fashionable clothing, regular visits to a coiffeur and health care, these elderly people stood on their porches, thin-lipped mouths without dentures, and their appearances reminiscent of the traumatic poverty of the continental post-war years. The Germans in these photographs are presented as counter-images of the self, as images of colonial ruination.

The 'lost Germans' are framed in the same colonial discourse that postcolonial intellectuals such as Derek Walcott (2014) refer to when they deconstruct the tropical rainforest as an empty landscape. The language, skills, intellectual capacities and humanity of the Jamaican Germans, too, have been devoured by the tropical void: 'Among those who were left, even though largely isolated from their environment, all traditions and memories expired abruptly. [...] The social bonds of the community dissolved completely [...]'⁷ (Sasse & Drexel, 1985: 80). WHITE MAN, this suggests, will degenerate in the tropics, in all that BLACK surrounding, heat and humidity.

Alice Kameka mit einer Fotografie ihrer Ahnen – eine Rarität in Seaford Town. Denn die Erinnerung an die Vorfahren ist erloschen, ihre Sprache längst vergessen

Figure 6.2 Presenting the 'poor white' as uprooted and lacking (Sasse & Drexel, 1985: 76)[6]

Michael Taussig in his work on secrecy makes an important point: the dissolving tropics don't simply devour those northern 'traditions and memories', they transform them into secrets hidden underneath reality. Nothing here, however, exists without the Other, and the forests and hills around Seaford Town are only then resolutive when they surround people marked for northernness. Whatever there is that turns 'traditions and memories' into nothingness, we will not know; the *jaamans* have forgotten about it, and nobody else will be able to tell: 'For the secret is overdeterminedly southern. But at the risk of enormous and enormously-forgotten banality, note there can be no south without a north' (Taussig, 1999: 80).

As another genre of writing about such places, namely that of travel guides, reveals, dissolution also has a different connotation. The idea of a lost race in the tropics has some of its roots in the freak shows of the mid-19th century, reconciling the weird and noisy with the rationalism of the expeditions and discoveries: 'Most stories fabricated as part of exotic presentations were based on real contemporary events – scientific expeditions, colonial struggle, and general exploration of the non-Western world' (Bogdan, 1988: 122). While it was profitable for entertainers to make this link – to make a connection to the idea that expeditions resulted in a still better knowledge of the ultimate other – authenticity was not necessarily created by actually exhibiting people from the tropic voids, but by simply presenting otherness. The people who were exhibited as specimen of a lost race therefore often came from Europe or America, where they had been born with a deformed body part, had fallen victim to an accident, or else. And they served, as representatives of the abnormal, not as images of the proximate other but of the distant other, imagined as having lived in tropical rainforests where mankind was supposed to decay and assume a lesser human state.

This way of presenting otherness, and this discourse have not ended with the freak shows. The text archive of tourism in its contemporary neoliberal context provides insights into how the tropical void is portrayed as a space in which ruination goes on. By means of presenting the postcolonial other inhabiting these spaces as the lost, ruined and unknown, tourist guidebooks, travel journals and documentaries fill the gap the freak shows have left, in particular when they address heritage tourism and its practices. They continue to turn the ordinary into the abnormal, and the commentary sites of travel blogs reveal how persistent these constructions are. In a 1995 guidebook on Jamaica, Seaford Town is mentioned as follows:

> The white migration never amounted to much, but it left a few rural pockets with English and German names. The most noted of the racially German locations, Seaford Town in the parish of Westmoreland, still exists today – although migration in recent years has depleted its population. Moreover, nearly a century of in-breeding has sadly had a degenerative effect on the population of 200 or so residents, nearly all of whom have one of four family names: Somers, Eldermeyer, Wedermeyer or Kameka. Their ancestors had immigrated to Jamaica at the beckoning of a Prussian doctor, William Lemonius, settling on land provided by Lord Seaford. Those Germans who began intermarrying with Jamaican blacks in the 1930s contributed to a dilution of the number of whites living in the area. (Zach, 1995: 89)

This text adds other names given to the Germans: *freaks*, a term that encodes as a common noun abjection and resentment, but bears, in its postcolonial setting, indexicalities otherwise rather shared by names; it can serve as a word with which one may address and identify the other. What type of other might be referred to is detailed in the guidebook:

again, the text is supplemented by images of elderly, wispy people. These people are not just poor, without dentures, but lack intact genes; they are the product of inbreeding. Such representations of the LOST WHITE who are already partly devoured by the tropics have extremely racist connotations. Being white and poor at the same time is considered an impossibility that needs to be explained away, and addressing the degenerative consequences of inbreeding does the job. These Germans are, in other words, not poor because they are peasants, but because they have degenerated.

But the discourse is complex. Neither the tourists nor the writers of tourist guidebooks portray themselves as racist, but the people whom they describe are presented that way. This twist in many of these narratives attributes the responsibility for having failed to become rich to the 'lost Germans' themselves: hadn't they been so racist and therefore reluctant to marry 'Jamaican blacks', they wouldn't have fallen victim to such degeneration. A more recent report on Seaford Town reflects on such previously established certainties:

> When I first heard about Seaford Town, I was ambivalent. I had heard that the residents were white and wondered why they didn't want to mingle with dark-skinned Jamaicans after living there so long. I thought they practised inbreeding – after all, that's what I had been told! Additionally, I didn't see the sense in upholding 'German culture' after almost 200 years since the first group of Germans settled there. [...] Several residents told me that until the middle of the last century most of the German descendants didn't want to mingle with the inhabitants of dark complexion for racist reasons. Times have changed and nowadays, the new generation of school children and teenagers are all mixed. (Koch, 2014)

Race is a complex concept. The Germans who first settled in Seaford Town predominantly were Catholic, and their descendants continue to form one of the few Catholic communities in the country. And the historical practices surrounding the Westphalian migrants included marriage constraints with regards to religious denomination. In their new environment, where people either were Anglican protestant or not Christian at all, marriage outside the community was almost impossible even to imagine. Even though the community didn't receive visits by Catholic clergy before 1839 (Orizio, 2000: 83), there was no interruption of Catholic practices.

Marriage to their equally poor neighbours, the liberated slaves, wasn't possible for precisely these reasons, not so much on racist grounds. In a discussion on when and why the Germans stopped speaking German, Mrs Kameka, and elderly woman who looked after a creche next to the village museum, told me that she always had heard how much the Germans economically depended on the interaction with the liberated people around them. Sharing such close relationships with English- and Patwa-speaking neighbours made them change their linguistic behaviour rather quickly, she assumes, together with the experience of sharing those people's practices of daily life. Marriage to non-Catholics, however, was out of question among many.

Mrs Kameka's remark turns our gaze to another aspect of race, namely that of class. To her, there were no substantial differences between her ancestors and the liberated Jamaican slaves in terms of how they continued to experience poverty and leading lives controlled by others. The experience of the *jaamans* is not unique, though. Anthony C. Winkler, one of Jamaica's most celebrated literary voices, has made it one of the topics of his writing. In *Trust the Darkness*, he recalls growing up in Jamaica being white and poor: 'There was a paradox in being white and poor in Jamaica in the 1950s. Because we were white, people assumed that we were better off than we were' (2008: 160). Kim Robinson-Walcott, whose comment on Winkler's texts is an extremely insightful analysis of race and class in Jamaica, remarks: 'Being a white in a country where 92 percent of the population is black, but where whites still represent the upper echelons of society, produces a peculiar dilemma of privilege counterpoised by marginalization, of entitlement counterpoised by unbelonging' (2009: 114).

The influential work by Diane Austin-Broos highlights precisely that:

> Social class and color groupings jointly present the major issues of status that constitute a Jamaican sense of hierarchy. These groupings intersect and overlap. [...] How Jamaicans in different positions figure the issues of 'race' and 'class,' and whether and in what degree they are distinguished, could hardly illicit a simple model of one univocal discourse. (Austin-Broos, 1994: 214)

The point here is, Austin-Broos argues, that in spite of the absence of an univocal discourse, issues of colour and class are continuously brought together by ideas of heritable identity. Economic and cultural constraints 'make poverty the experience of the black majority' (1994: 230). The converse argument would then be that white people have heritable identities of being rich. This is precisely what makes Seaford Town a place that needs to be presented within the framework of a freak show: here whites are poor. As one user commented on Koch's article: 'I am from close by and this was the first place I went and saw a poor white, barefooted, drunk, dirty and illiterate, it was a real eye-opener that blacks and whites no real difference poor white, poor black they all exist on this earth.' The exhibition of WHITE POVERTY in a tropical tourism paradise, in posts, articles and in photographs, culminating in excessive naming, constructs a kind of ultimate other, who at the same time bears a heritable identity that provides a linkage between the other and the self. The other, living in the tropical void, is still the offspring of the self, the metropole, the normal. Like the two-headed lamb born in a stable nearby, this is otherness that exists at the edges of the metropole: the freak show is not simply a project of the production of exoticism, but of otherness, and of making the common 'strange'.

A Name and a Rope

The biosemiotics that are at work here are complex, as they don't just address current experiences of economic struggle and ideas about skin, but also heritable identity and attributed status. Winkler recalls, in *Going Home to Teach* (2006) that in postcolonial Jamaica, a white person was called *pork*, a name that elicits white, rich landowners as a now unwanted social class (Robinson-Walcott, 2009: 114). Seaford Town is not the home of people whose ancestors were wealthy landowners, but is a place that is portrayed as being haunted by memories of enslavement, of being put to work in a strange hostile environment until savings sufficed to leave – or to invest in a better plot of land.

The social disruptions created by these biosemiotics and historical practice translate into pain and hurt. When visiting Seaford Town, which is now placed on heritage tourism map in Jamaica (Brown, 2009; Jamaica National Heritage Trust), I first found it hard to meet a person who wanted to talk to me. People had experienced, I was told during my visit, so many defacing and humiliating presentations of themselves that they didn't want to talk with visitors very much. Fitzroy Chambers, who offers guided tours to the village museum, said: 'We are not Germans, we are Jamaicans. Out of many, one people: that applies to us.'

Sharing identity concepts of people whose ancestors were slaves and not landowners, and whose lives were controlled by others, has considerable consequences for how heritage is framed. And here, heritage is not just class and colour, but to a very large extent language. As in the various reports and postings on them, the Germans of Seaford Town are portrayed in a recent documentary as people who have lost their heritage: this is an extremely salient feature, as in terms of ideologies of race and class, white people cannot be poor and cannot lose their language. In *The Lost Story Of Seaford Town* (Ritter, 2015), solemn folk tunes accompany interviews with community members who talk about being 'pure German' without speaking the language. The significance of language is indicated not only in interview snippets, but also in the design of the film poster (Germantown Jamaica) which uses gothic letters that to me, watching the film at my German home, appear like a rather common strategy of constructing a commodifiable Germanness in globalised settings. David Ritter, the film's producer, recalls that he began the film project based on a desire to take a stance against misrepresentations and stereotyped images: 'I agree that there have been horrific representations of Seaford Town and its population and that is something I have also addressed often and have been working my best to combat' (Ritter, pers. comm., July 2018). Yet, he explains, this has been contested by many, in a discursive environment where ruination is ongoing for all.

In these representations, heritage imagined as something handed down from one generation to the other, within the community, is contested at least twice: first, the colour of the skin as heritable whiteness (Austin-Broos, 1994) cannot be accepted as heritage because of its association with ideas about inbreeding and degeneration discourses. Secondly, sharing ideas about a past enslavement with the 'black Jamaicans' requires also sharing a language. People in Seaford Town speak Patwa, marked as a local code by a few emblematic German words such as *Leberwurst, Puffer, Speck, Wurstkessel* (also see Müller, 1981). These words formed part of the exhibition in the museum, but as communal heritage and not markers of racialised difference.

Language, framed as a distant colonial, European, white heritage seems to have dissolved in the tropical void – like all other distant colonial, European, white culture. As a consequence of imperial ruination, it has become wreckage, and this is as what is presented in the many portrayals of Seaford Town. However, from the perspective of the *jaamans* there is no void; the colonial discourse on the dissolving tropics makes no sense here. At least, these rainforests are now a home, and have long ceased to threaten the materiality of heritage and memory. As Orizio (2000: 91) writes, people even keep the maps and documents on which the little plots of land are indicated: 'One of our number who emigrated to Canada still has an old map of the fields. Handkerchief-sized plots, too poor to grow anything.' There is lack, but nothing dissolves. And if their heritage actually was lost – language is gone – the people of Seaford Town know whom to blame.

Hall (1974) and Orizio (2000) both provide detailed accounts of the historical events described in the surviving documents of the period. Both mention brokers who signed rural, low-class Germans into migrating to Jamaica:

> The Germans arrived in Seaford Town in two waves. The first came at the instigation of a certain John Myers, a white Jamaican who was the first to come up with the idea – immediately dismissed as absurd by authoritative newspapers such as the Jamaican Dispatch – of countering the effects of the imminent abolition of slavery by importing European workers. [...] Besides Myers, there was another individual very actively trading in white labour, one Dr William Lemonius [...]. In 1835 the [British] House of Assembly officially gave him the job of finding more German immigrants for the island, and over the next two years Lemonius managed to procure 800, promising a certain amount of land in return for five years' free labour. The Germans [...] were dispersed all over

Jamaica. Like the slaves from Africa and Haiti, they were allocated to the most isolated landowners. (Orizio, 2000: 83–85)

Orizio is very clear about his opinion: this was a case of human trafficking, and these people experienced enslavement. In post-abolitionist Jamaica, free labour and not owning land probably meant just this (Curtin, 2010), and it is very revealing in terms of the same social semiotics still at work that – with the exception of Orizio – no source has explicitly dealt with Seaford Town as a slave settlement.

However, as Hall (1974) and Müller (1981) mention, there were discourses led by the community members that reflected attempts to come to terms with their experiences of intergenerational trauma as a consequence of slavery and human trafficking. These discourses are not simple laments, but considerably impressive in the agency they reveal. Orizio (2000: 85) mentions: 'The inhabitants still refer to Lemonius as the devil and say that had he ever set foot in Seaford he would have been lynched. And there are [...] unexplained feelings of resentment towards the captain of the *Olbers* [the ship with which they came].' An anonymous, well-researched blog on Seaford gives more detailed information on swearing and cursing practices: 'The name Lemonius was used as a swear word among the settlers. "A villain like Lemonius" a thief would be called. Some of the men tied a hanging rope to a tree [...].'[8]

This void is filled with noise: swearing, transgression, mob law. This landscape is not timeless, but it becomes historicised by its inhabitants by making reference to the circumstances of their ancestors' enslavement and trauma handed down to later generations. Hence, this community has turned their shattering experiences into very localised ways of shutting out and of noisy critiquing. Their ruinous history has not been translated into romanticised images of ruins of heritage and cottages, but into discourses on the ruination of the perpetrator, one otherwise evanescent Dr Lemonius.

This blends into the metaphor of ruination used by Stoler (2008, 2013), which stands in stark contrast to the colonial stereotype of the tropics as an ahistorical space. Ruin, Stoler says, is a virulent and very agentive verb, and it expresses the noise of destruction. Ruination is noisy, appalling and unsettling, resulting from disaster, from imperialism which deemed other forms of practice primitive, was noisy as well and set out to make them disappear. The settlers at Seaford Town, it seems, were caught right in these opacities of imperial formations. And the placement of these settlers *in between*, as people who share the experiences of enslavement, of being objectified in complex interwoven racialised discourses as freaks and as weirdly superior to their environment, continues to shape the lives of their descendants. 'To speak of colonial ruination', Stoler says, 'is to trace the fragile and durable substance and signs, the visible and visceral senses in which the effects of empire are reactivated and remain. But ruination is more than a process. It is also a political project that lays waste to certain peoples and places, relations, and things. To think with ruins of empire is to emphasize less the artefacts of empire as dead matter or remnants of a defunct regime than to attend to their re-appropriations and strategic and active positioning within the politics of the present' (2008: 196).

The lives of the people living in these ruins, which surface in the form of names, entanglement and encounters, deserve our attention, not simply as topics of a sociolinguistics of the colonial, but as lives led in ruins that resurrect, as heritage sites and backgrounds to debates on loss and change, and as lives that are continuously moulded and shaped according to the constructs already present in a postcolonial figured world.

An Iridescent Cloud of Words

The motif of the ruinous tropical south has a considerable historical depth. It is a complex metaphor for difference between the colonial self and other, and for the organisation of colonial space, but also between truth and falsity, transparency and secrecy:

> Modern Western history revolves around a deep split in the secret in which truth's dependence on untruth is ethnically and geographically divided between north and south. [...] Purely 'southern', we might say. Villainy, thievery, and of course, *decadence*. (Taussig, 1999: 78 f.)

Michael Taussig here writes about the beach and its southerness. 'This curious contract between truth and falsity, uniting the land mass of Europe along a north–south axis is present in other histories of Europe as well,' he writes (1999: 79), and turns to Thomas Mann's *Death in Venice*. The south has a secret that is revealed at some point in the novella, as a terrible plague creeping into the lives of the tourists and their temporary liminal, inverted existences on the beach. The decadent sexual obsessions of Aschenbach, Taussig argues, are part of the concept of the south as a dissolving space. Not only does the south turn self-control and morale into transgression and lust, but it also requires a price for such experience: 'This sun does *not* give without receiving' (Taussig, 1999: 94). The dissolving tropics here have a sexual, gendered connotation.

The pleasures of the south are forbidden ones, and the price paid for them is high. In Orizio's account of his visit to Seaford Town, there is, almost at the end of this text, a section where the author meets one of the older, disillusioned people who talks about experiences of having been abroad and of meeting the foreigners who now come to Jamaica as tourists: '"We see them, the German girls. They come on holiday to Jamaica hoping to go to bed with a Rasta with dreadlocks." He shakes his head' (2000: 92). Orizio's poetically compounded text ends with where we are today when we travel to places like Jamaica; on the beaches and at tourism resorts, which remain spaces where the passage has not yet ended and the land is already there. As before, people stay in these liminal spaces – the first settlers of Seaford Town with the intention to escape from their miserable situation and move on to America, and the visitors who seek an emotional escape from a monotonous life by hiring a romantic companion.

Being increasingly visited as a heritage site by tourists from beach resorts at Negril and Montego Bay, Seaford Town has become more closely linked to these stages for the enactment of commodified romantic encounters. This link doesn't seem to result in considerable economic change, but it makes particular similarities in racialised heritable class membership and objectification tangible. The sexualised interactions between tourists and Jamaicans working at the beach appear as if they are just another way of making the other strange. This is, however, camouflaged by heritage and consumerism: 'The village, famous for its stuffed roasted pork and yam, becomes a party venue on the weekend for patrons from all over western Jamaica' (Titus, 2011). Whereas a common comment on sex tourism in Jamaica is that this is in principle undisturbing, accepted behaviour and a normal part of touristic encounters, there is also an underlying discourse which frames sex tourism in a more critical way. This discourse prominently surfaces in the naming of the other – the transgressive sex tourist and the male yet feminised sex worker – as figures that blend into pre-existing configurations. Sex tourism here needs to be understood as a contemporary product of imperial formations, and the imperial context of tourism has been identified by Frantz Fanon, who pointed out that the beaches and resorts were developed for a European bourgeoisie, not for the bourgeoisie of the tourism countries, and that the element of sexual exploitation and ruination was built in right from the beginning: 'The casinos in Havana and Mexico City, the beaches of Rio, Copacabana, and Acapulco, the young Brazilian and Mexican girls, the thirteen-year-old mestizas, are the scars of this depravation of the national bourgeoisie. [...] [T]he national bourgeoisie assumes the role of manager for the companies of the West and turns its country virtually into a bordello for Europe' (Fanon, 2004: 101 f.).

In this bordello, there is, again, excess of naming – sex tourists are referred to as *milk-bottles in need of filling, cougars, sugarmamas*, and sex workers as *beach boys, rent-a-rasta, rastitutes, bumsters, sankypankies, sharks* – which fulfils the function of unmaking the protagonists of this liminal play. They appear to be turned into objects and put into place – as just another representation of the postcolonial other who has no control over his or her life. The female sex tourist is portrayed as a physically anti-normative and emotionally unattended person who has no choice but to pay for a partner, and the sex worker as a sexually uncontrolled, yet puerile person who depends on help and guidance.[9] These objects are met with feelings of rejection – they are counter-images of the self, the prototypical inversed existence of the liminal space (Ryan & Hall, 2001; Illouz, 1997).

What strikes me as of chief importance is how these labels for the contemporary poor white translate into popular culture, again citing the freak and notions of exoticism. Globalised hip-hop styles, entertainment formats such as reality TV, as well as blogs and social media provide arenas where poor whites are celebrated as anti-mainstream identity concepts. The labels used for them – *redneck, white trash*, and so on – are 'marked forms of white identity [which] each derive from and respond to the dissonance raised in the American [and, perhaps, globalised] cultural imaginary by linking whiteness and poverty', as John Hartigan Jr. writes (2005: 148). The images associated with these marked forms of white identity conform, he continues, 'to an aesthetic of the grotesque, featuring deranged deer hunters, sex with farm animals, public urination', and so forth (2005: 153). In its marginalised form, whiteness is made strange.

In mobile communication, transgressive images of poor whites now produce their own counterimages. These counterimages might always have been there in the void, but we have no account of those of former times apart from the exiguous mentioning of *white trash* in descriptions of slave discourse, or evidence such as an entry in a lexicon that says there is a *jáaman* besides *jarman*. But finally, we hear names such as *cougar* called by other voices than our own, as a label for the contemporary white other. In blogs operated by writers from the south, the cougar turns into the other's other, and the grotesque again surfaces as a counter-discourse of our times. A Google search on *cougar* reveals how prominent this construction figures, especially in African and Caribbean blogs.

The stories presented there usually combine tabloid news and photographic documentation with elements of sarcasm and irony, resulting in titles, such as *On safari with the Great Northern Cougar*,[10] *Cougars Hunting Nigerians in Thailand*[11] and *Cougars On The Prowl in Kenya*.[12] Such texts are about very young men romantically marrying their 60- to 80-year- old white brides, who will take them to their home countries. The texts usually contain a section about a long period of dating and hoping, culminating in the motif of the redeeming wedding. The reports are often lavishly illustrated with wedding photographs, as if to prove the validity of the post.

The reactions to these texts are almost always riot and noise. Readers post comments that make clear that to them, from their southern perspective, these women are predators who don't simply devour, but buy younger men who have no choice but to sell themselves. One comment explained perceived white superiority as a result of witchcraft (*juju*): 'white women sef Get juju.' Only such practices could explain, this comment suggests, why poor whites might gain such power over other people. A male reader posted a much more transgressive comment in the form of a photograph with a banner reading, 'I will get my green card no matter what.' Such self-deprecating jokes are bitter, sarcastic statements on continued bioracialised class demarcations that produce ruinous relationships. Here, imperial debris falls on both, the *cougar* and her groom, and it is hard for us to see who devours whom.

Figure 6.3 Cougar and groom (nairaland.com)

In most of the other comments, the *cougar* is framed as the Lemonius of our days, and the slaves might be the people who sell themselves at the beach. The *cougar* emanates as a monstrous human trafficker who, after taking her groom to Europe, locks him up. Comments to articles such as *Ugandan Singer, 28, Weds His 68 Year Old American Cougar*[13] come from female readers rather than men, and make it clear that such stories illustrate colonial continuities, such as human trafficking and the slave trade, mental slavery to racist ideologies and marginalisation as an experience of black people:

> African men with their inferiority complex and white skin worshipping! The same African men sold us to slavery 400yrs ago to their white gods!
>
> Una no get shame! Our men are a disgrace since 1600!
>
> Palava dey sha... Desperation in action here 8(
>
> Bye bye to suffering suffering, bye bye to jati jati...
>
> Its now a case of 21st century "slavery" where the "mumu" is captured LIVE thinking he was going to have a life-long pleasure only to discover he is becoming like a "massage machine" to be switched on and off depending on how itchy the "buyer" feels down-below!!LOL

The names attributed to the other continue to evoke, in these comments as well as in the popular coverage of Seaford Town's historical whiteness, roles played by colonial actors. Dorothy Holland and her co-authors have examined the dynamics of the conceptions people develop of themselves as actors in socially and culturally constructed worlds.[14] They refer to these worlds as 'figured worlds': '[...] a socially and culturally constructed realm of interpretation in which particular characters and actors are recognised, significance is assigned to certain acts, and particular outcomes are valued over others' (Holland *et al.*, 1998: 52). The settings under study in colonial linguistics work precisely as figured worlds, historical phenomena to which players continue to be recruited (Holland *et al.*, 1998: 41):

> [...] figured worlds, like activities, are social encounters in which participants' positions matter. They proceed and are socially instanced and located in times and places, not in the 'everywhere' that seems to encompass cultural worlds as they are usually conceived. [...] Figured worlds are socially organized and reproduced; they are like activities in the usual, institutional sense. They divide and relate participants (almost as roles), and they depend upon the interaction and the intersubjectivity for perpetuation. [...] Figured worlds distribute 'us,' not only by relating actors to landscapes of action (as personae) and spreading our senses of self across many different fields of activity, but also by giving the landscape human voice and tone.

It is precisely the distribution of specific roles according to biosemiotic parameters that makes colonial-figured worlds enduring. Imperial debris here covers all – in the form of names, labels and epithets. It seems as if the meaning of these words – of names such as *jaaman* and *cougar* – can only be understood within the colonially figured world. Isn't it here that they unfold their shattering indexicalities? Don't these names capture the power and historical continuity of imperial formations? There seems to be some truth that resonates in them, impossible to hide in the imagined tropical void.

In Conclusion

Even though the diversity of means of addressing another person, or identifying the self, is not at all exclusively restricted to contexts of the postcolony, there seems to be a particular interest in focusing on the semiotics of choice of naming strategies and the ways in which speakers play with categories. Social environments that are characterised by the impact of migration, disruption, social inequality and injustice are environments in which the ability and right to name, to be named and to remain unnamed signify power and social status.

According to Fanon, the subaltern in the postcolonial setting does not have to own a name to be identifiable; the subaltern can be named by others, and the name given can be a generalising common noun or any other possible term. This is part of the epistemic closure that surrounds the players in a figured, postcolonial world, and it is, paradoxically, at the same time a feature of the discursive formations of the postcolony that offers a possibility to historicise such practices and the states of non-being that go along with them.

Visiting heritage tourism sites – the village, for example – means to move, virtually and practically, within a discursively preconfigured arena that allows for various forms of othering and deforming. The semiotics of naming and names alike, the semantic history of terms that designate the self and the other, and the often-ruinous continuities that lie in the use of specific designations and the practices surrounding them are therefore crucial aspects of a linguistics of tourism. These continuing ruinous practices, and the ways in which they are reified and remade continuously by players who clearly reflect these continuities are emblematic linguistic strategies in postcolonial tourism encounters, and gain particular momentum in heritage tourism contexts, where an essentialisation of the other is achieved. I suspect that turning to the emblematic, essentialising terms that are at the centre to unmake persons and places and construct freaks and spaces of otherness instead helps us to arrive at a fresh take on sociolinguistics as a means of considering options where there is 'another human essence than self' (Carson, 1995: 137).

Acknowledgements

I am grateful to Christiane Bongartz and Andrea Hollington for their helpful comments on an earlier version of this chapter and for sharing their ideas and experiences in Jamaica and elsewhere with me. I warmly thank Ana Deumert for an inspiring cooperation, and Angelika Mietzner and Nico Nassenstein for their many stimulating discussions and comments. I am truly indebted to Stefan Engelberg, Thomas Stolz, Erhard Schüttpelz and Paul Kockelman for their many important comments and suggestions on my research on this topic. I remain deeply grateful to Mrs Kameka, Mr Chambers and Mr Groskopf of Seaford Town for their many explanations, and I thank the Global South Studies Center Cologne for the generous research grant that first took me to Jamaica. I am grateful to David Ritter for discussing his experiences as a filmmaker with me and for kindly commenting on this text.

Notes

(1) A very informed source on Lord Seaford is http://ahistoryblog.com/2014/03/16/charles-rose-ellis-1771-1845-come-sing-me-montego-bay/.
(2) Note the singular here, which, as opposed to the plural of "Negroes", articulates difference in ways of being, living, etc. between these bioculturally defined groups.
(3) This was one of several, very similar popular articles on Seaford Town which all appeared around the same time. Others were titled 'Driftwood' (*Strandgut*, *IWZ* 25,

1985) or 'Seaford Town – a German city in Jamaica' (*Seaford Town – eine deutsche Stadt in Jamaica*; Mission 1985).

(4) The original German text reads: "Was Reisende dann zu Beginn unseres Jahrhunderts in Seaford Town vorfanden, war dazu angetan, deutschnationalen Stolz aufs tiefste zu verletzen: Es war ein loser, erbärmlich armer Haufen friedlicher Wilder, der da in Agonie überdauert hatte. Von jenen, die einst der 'Olbers' entstiegen waren, lebten 1911 nur noch zwei. Nicht wenige aber mit blauen Augen und 'flachsenem Haar' mußten zu schwarzen Landbesitzern 'Massa' sagen [...]."

(5) The original German text reads: "Sogar Halbgeschwister gingen vor den Traualtar, und die Kirche, rassentrennungsfreundlich, gab ihren Segen zu den Inzestbeziehungen. Angst vor der feindlichen Umwelt, vielleicht auch der Glaube an weiße Überlegenheit trotz des maladen Lebens, trieb die 'Germans' in die Abkapselung."

(6) German caption translates as: "Alice Kameka with a photograph of her ancestors – a rarity in Seaford Town. For the memory of the forefathers has lapsed, and the language is forgotten." I am grateful to Rainer Drexel for the permission to reproduce this image.

(7) The original German text reads: "Bei den übrigen aber, obwohl von ihrer Umgebung weitgehend isoliert, erloschen alle Traditionen und Erinnerungen nahezu schockartig. [...] Die sozialen Bindungen in der Gemeinde lösten sich restlos auf [...]."

(8) The German original text reads: "Der Name Lemonius wurde unter den Siedlern als Schimpfwort benutzt. 'Ein schufft [sic] wie Lemonius', wurde man als Dieb betitelt. Einige der Männer banden ein Seil an einen Baum [...]" http://www.seafordtown.comoj.com/massengrab_in_seaford_town.html.

(9) Consider Cantet's *Vers le sud* (2005) or Seidl's *Paradies Liebe* (2013) as illustrative examples.

(10) http://stevecockburn.blogspot.co.za/2011/11/on-safari-with-great-northen-cougar.html.

(11) http://ninejathailand.blogspot.de

(12) https://timeinmoments.wordpress.com/2007/11/27/cougars-on-the-prowl-in-kenya-female-sex-tourists/.

(13) At the forum *nairaland.com*.

(14) I am grateful to Ana Deumert for having made me aware of the relevance of this work for my topic.

References

Anchimbe, E. (2011) On not calling people by their names: Pragmatic undertones of sociocultural relationships in a postcolony. *Journal of Pragmatics* 43 (6), 1472–1483.

Austin-Broos, D. (1994) Race/class: Jamaica's discourse of heritable identity. *Nieuwe West-Indische Gids* 68, 213–233.

Benjamin, W. (1968) [1940] Theses on the philosophy of history. In Walter Benjamin, *Illuminations* (pp. 253–264). New York, NY: Schocken.

Bogdan, R. (1988) *Freak Show: Presenting Human Oddities for Amusement and Profit*. Chicago, IL: University of Chicago Press.

Bongartz, C.M. and Storch, A. (2016) Making sense of the noisy. *Critical Multilingualism Studies* 4 (2), 154–173. http://cms.arizona.edu/index.php/multilingual/article/view/104

Brown, F. (2009) History of Seaford Town. *The Gleaner* (30 September).

Cantet, L. (2005) *Vers le sud*. Paris: Haut et Court/France 3.

Carson, A. (1995) *Glass, Irony and God*. New York, NY: New Directions.

Cassidy, F.G. and Le Page, R.B. (2002) *Dictionary of Jamaican English*. Cambridge: Cambridge University Press.

Curtin, M.R. (2010) *The Story of Westmoreland: A Jamaican Parish*. Kingston: Jamaica National Building Society Foundation.

Devonish, H. (1989) *Talking in Tones: A Study of Tone in Afro-European Creole Languages*. London: Karia.
Fabian, J. (2002) [1983] *Time and the Other*. New York, NY: Columbia University Press.
Fanon, F. (1967) [1952] *Black Skin, White Masks*. London: Pluto.
Fanon, F. (2004) [1963] *The Wretched of the Earth*. New York, NY: Grove.
Gordillo, G. (2013) The void: Invisible ruins on the edges of empire. In A.L. Stoler (ed.) *Imperial Debris* (pp. 227–251). Durham, NC: Duke University Press.
Gordon, L.R. (2015) *What Fanon Said*. London: Hurst & Co.
Hall, D. (1974) Bountied European immigration into Jamaica with special reference to the German settlement at Seaford Town up to 1850, Part 2. *Jamaica Journal* 8 (4), 2–9.
Hall, C.M. and Tucker, H. (eds) (2014) *Tourism and Postcolonialism*. London: Routledge.
Hamilton, G. (1973) *To Live and to Let Die*. London: Eon.
Hartigan, J.Jr. (2005) *Odd Tribes: Toward a Cultural Analysis of White People*. Durham, NC: Duke University Press.
Holland, D., Lachicotte, W., Skinner, D. and Cain, C. (1998) *Identity and Agency in Cultural Worlds*. Cambridge, MA: Harvard University Press.
Illouz, E. (1997) *Consuming the Romantic Utopia: Love and the Cultural Contradictions of Capitalism*. Berkeley, CA: University of California Press.
Klieber, A.H. (1913) Verschollene deutsche Katholiken auf Jamaika. *Caritas* 19 (1), 8–12.
Koch, L. (2014) The mystery of 'German Town': A German girl's view of Seaford Town. *The Gleaner* (7 April).
Mbembe, A. (2001) *On the Postcolony*. Berkeley, CA: University of California Press.
Müller, E. (1981) German heritage in Jamaican speech. *Jamaica Journal* 45, 30–33.
Nübling, D., Fahlbusch, F. and Heuser, R. (2012) *Namen. Eine Einführung in die Onomastik*. Tübingen: Narr Francke Attempto.
Orozio, R. (2000) *Lost White Tribes. Journeys among the Forgotten*. London: Secker & Warburg.
Ritter, D. (2015) *German Town: The Lost Story of Seaford Town, Jamaica*. Los Angeles, CA: Photomundo International.
Robinson-Walcott, K. (2009) Deconstructing Jamaican whiteness: A diasporic voice. *Small Axe* 13 (2), 107–117.
Ryan, M.C. and Hall, C. (2001) *Sex Tourism: Marginal People and Liminalities*. London: Routledge.
Sasse, H. and Drexel, R. (1985) Die Gestrandeten. *GEO* 11, 72–90.
Schaffner, F. (1973) *Papillon*. Los Angeles, CA: Allied Artists.
Seidl, U. (2013) *Paradies Liebe*. Vienna: Ulrich Seidl Film Produktion.
Stoler, A.L. (2008) Imperial debris: Reflections on ruins and ruination. *Cultural Anthropology* 23 (2), 191–219.
Stoler, A.L. (2013) Introduction. 'The rot remains': From ruins to ruination. In A.L. Stoler (ed.) *Imperial Debris* (pp. 1–37). Durham, NC: Duke University Press.
Taussig, M. (1999) *Defacement. Public Secrecy and the Labor of the Negative*. Stanford, CA: Stanford University Press.
Titus, M. (2011) The German connection: Westmoreland town strives to maintain European heritage. *The Gleaner* (6 August).
Tusting, K. (2005) Language and power in communities of practice. In D. Barton and K. Tusting (eds) *Beyond Communities of Practice* (pp. 36–54). Cambridge: Cambridge University Press.
Walcott, D. (2014) *The Poetry of Derek Walcott 1948–2013*. New York, NY: Farrar, Straus & Giroux.
Winkler, A.C. (2006) *Going Home to Teach*. Oxford: Macmillan.
Winkler, A.C. (2008) *Trust the Darkness*. Oxford: Macmillan.
Yancy, G. (2012) *Look, A White! Philosophical Essays on Whiteness*. London: Routledge.
Zach, P. (1995) *Insight Guides: Jamaica*. Hong Kong: APA.

Web Addresses

Africa/Answerman Blog at http://africaanswerman.com/onsafari-a-real-village-experience/
Airbnb website at https://www.airbnb.de/rooms/12811644?guests=1&adults=1&children=0&infants=0&s=Cfkm8au6
Germantown Jamaica website at (http://germantownjamaica.com/)
Jamaican National Heritage Trust website at http://www.jnht.com/site_seaford_town.php

7 Postcolonial Performativity in the Philippine Heritage Tourism Industry

Raymund Vitorio

Introduction

Heritage tourism is an indispensable aspect of the tourism industry, especially in postcolonial countries. It relies on many professional practices which capitalise on the consumption of history as an aesthetic and sensory experience, which is situated in various interfaces: the domestic and the foreign, the past and the present and the global and the local. Colonial history simultaneously serves as a backdrop and resource for the active construction of the country as a marketable tourist destination. Images of colonialism and postcolonialism are integrated in banal forms of interaction in the tourism activity, which are integral to how tourists consume heritage tourism attractions. As Thurlow and Jaworski (2010: 9) argue, 'it is at the level of the interpersonal, everyday exchange of meaning where the global and the local interface are negotiated and resolved, be it through processes of cultural absorption, appropriation, recognition, acceptance, or resistance.' These processes of reconciling the global and the local are enacted by the stakeholders involved in the tourism activity.

In this chapter, I investigate how tour guides – a primary stakeholder in the tourism activity – employ various sociolinguistic strategies in order to construct the identity of an effective tour guide. Despite the rapid increase of substitutes for tour guides, such as websites, travel books and crowdsourced forums among tourists, tour guides remain an essential part of the tourism activity. They serve as primary mediators between the global and the local, and function as a bridge between tourists and tourist destinations (Bruner, 2005; Reisinger & Steiner, 2006; Salazar, 2005, 2006). By looking at tour guides in the Philippines, a country which has a long colonial history and a budding tourism industry, I aim to show how tour guides strategically manipulate aspects of colonialism in their guided tours as their way of responding to the 'tourist gaze' (Urry, 1990; Urry & Larsen, 2011) – the visual, sensory and performative '"discursive determinations", of socially constructed seeing or "scopic regimes"'

(Urry & Larsen, 2011: 2) in the activity of tourism that organises how tourists view and interact with the 'other' (Urry & Larsen, 2011: 14). I will investigate the narrative and linguistic aspects of the tour guide performances of tour guides, and how their emblematic use of linguistic resources translate into postcolonial forms of resistance, and how these allow them to construct a strategic position for themselves in the tourism activity. Following the framework of postcolonial performativity (Pennycook, 2001), I argue that while systems of colonialism and oppression may remain strong in the context of heritage tourism, tour guides are not completely devoid of avenues to formulate forms of resistance, even though they may not necessarily be able to completely reconfigure or dismantle the system. These sociolinguistic practices can be construed as a form of semiotic mobility that allows tour guides to develop their own voices with respect to the tourist gaze.

Sociolinguistics, Postcolonialism and the Tour Guide

While earlier research on the role of language and tourism has focused on intercultural communication and on the brokering of cultural exchanges (e.g. Clyne, 1981; Cohen & Cooper, 1986; Ferguson, 1971; Smith, 2001) and on attempts to establish the 'language of tourism' as an object of inquiry (e.g. Dann, 1996; Pritchard & Morgan, 2005), more recent research on the 'sociolinguistics of tourism' (Thurlow & Jaworski, 2010: 1) has paid more attention to the activity of tourism not just in terms of communicative efficiency but also in terms of how it is embedded in different structures of power, inequality, and resistance in light of the changes brought about by globalisation. The richness of semiotic resources in tourism has been approached in various ways, such as in the study of the linguistic features of tourism in marketing (e.g. Dann, 1996; Thurlow & Aiello, 2007); tourism-oriented language learning (e.g. Dörnyei & Csizér, 2005; Phipps, 2007; Thurlow & Jaworski, 2010); authenticity (Coupland & Coupland, 2014; Duchêne & Heller, 2012; Pietikäinen & Kelly-Holmes, 2011); place-making (e.g. Gao, 2012; Kelly-Holmes & Pietikäinen, 2014); linguistic landscapes (e.g. Milani & Levon, 2016; Moriarty, 2015); and the commodification of language (Heller, 2003; Heller *et al.*, 2014).

These studies are based on a few key premises. First, the 'language of tourism' should not be viewed in the traditional sense of 'language,' which is just a collection of linguistic units, but as a collection of multimodal resources which are linked to human activity. Second, language is not a neutral instrument that merely functions as a tool for communication; rather, it is a semiotic resource that is laden with political struggles and embedded in the different scales of interactional activity. Third, the material conditions of the globalised tourism industry spell out new ways of viewing language from the perspectives of the stakeholders of the tourism industry, especially in terms of how it constructs, perpetuates or challenges structures of difference and inequality. Finally, multilingualism has become an important resource in the management of diversity and the construction of various ideologies and identities.

Tourism, Oppression and Resistance

The tourism industry has been criticised for being involved in the propagation of colonial values, such as misrepresenting local cultures for the sake of pleasing the colonising eyes of Western tourists. In a sense, tourism, colonialism, and capitalism are inextricably tied to one another. According to d'Hauteserre (2004: 237):

> Tourism, like postcolonialism, has its roots in colonialism, both as a theoretical construct and as a perceptual mechanism (cf. Temple, 2002). Tourism development, through its approach to Third World destinations (in the form of, for example, resort enclaves and "international standard" hotels), perpetuates colonial forms of interaction that treat the exotic as inferior. Exotic places are controlled by being familiarized and domesticated through a language that locates them in a "universal" (meaning Western system of reference that visitors recognize and can communicate about. Tourist representations draw heavily upon cultural memories produced elsewhere, even though the destination is layered with indigenous cultural inscriptions... Colonial and, today, tourist narratives have strategically functioned to produce geopolitical myths about destinations.

This logic is shared by Nash (1989) when he calls tourism a form of neocolonialism. Palmer's (1994: 792) study of the tourism industry of the Bahamas affirms this idea by claiming that 'by relying on the images of a colonial past, the tourism industry merely perpetuates the ideology of colonialism and prevents the local people from defining a national identity of their own'. She argues that the tourism industry seems to compel local stakeholders in the Bahamas to feel that they have to rely on colonialism in order to effectively stylise themselves as a tourist destination, which comes at the expense of their autonomy to come up with a national identity that works for them.

This is reminiscent of Rosaldo's (1989: 68-90; cf. Bruner, 2001: 71) notion of 'imperialist nostalgia' – which he characterises as the 'process of yearning for what one has destroyed as a form of mystification'. Bruner (2001: 886) follows this point when he claims that 'Tourism performances, throughout the world, regularly reproduce stereotypic images, discredited histories, and romantic fantasies. The past is manipulated to serve the expectations of the tourists and the political interests of those in power [...]'. These criticisms are reasonable given that tourism, especially in postcolonial settings, involves the asymmetrical positioning of the tourist and the host community – with the host community usually being pushed to a disenfranchised position.

These criticisms result in a few questions. First, is there a way for structures of colonialism, capitalism and othering to be contested by the local community? Second, assuming that they can be contested, up to what extent can this happen? Third, given that the local community tends to be in a less ideal position than the tourists in terms of the capitalist setup of the tourism activity, what resources can the local community use in order to contest these structures?

Bruner (2001, also in 2005: 33–100) discusses three different tour performances in three field sites in Kenya, which show the varying extents of agency that the local community have in crafting tour performances. While he claims that the first field site tends to revolve around the satiating of the 'imperialist nostalgia' of the tourists, he argues that the two other field sites accord the performers with more agency. In the second field site, the performers aim to display their nationalism more than just pleasing the nostalgia of the tourists, which allows them to take pride in their work. Finally, in the third field site, performers tweak what are expected of the traditions of the local community by meshing it with tropes from other parts of the world (e.g. *Hakuna Matata*, from the Hollywood film *The Lion King* and a Jamaican reggae version of the song *Kum Ba Yah*, which are now ingrained in the popular culture of the United States despite its African roots), which blurs the line '[...] between us and them, subject and object, tourist and native' (2001: 893).

This study shows the importance of being critical of tour performances while understanding the logic of the local context where they operate in. This is consistent with Heller *et al.*'s (2014) reminder to examine how language paves the way for the assertion of agency and resistance vis-à-vis the seemingly oppressive demands of the tourist gaze. They argue:

> [...] within otherwise normative practices and hegemonic arrangements, there are always opportunities for participants (hosts, locals and tourists alike) to 'speak out' and to 'speak back'. Within the constraints of tourism discourse – its economic structures – there is necessarily room for creativity by which, for example, local communities may promote their own political and personal agendas and may find ways to resist (or just rework) the hierarchies of the symbolic marketplace. (Heller *et al.*, 2014: 448)

This shows that even though tourism is a highly commercial and capitalist activity, it can also be contested by people who may not necessarily have overt economic power through creativity. People are not devoid of agency to find strategic positions for themselves in tourism; they can 'speak out' and 'speak back' (cf. Ashcroft *et al.*, 1989) even though they may not be able to totally reconfigure or dismantle the structures of the tourism industry. As Pennycook (2001: 65) argues, '[...] a critical aspect of critical theorizing needs to incorporate the notion of resistance, ways in which people are not mere respondents to the dictates of social structure and ideology but rather are social actors who also resist sites of oppression.' This gives us leeway to understand how the Other can speak back in tourism (cf. Aitchison, 2001).

Tour Guides as Agents

In this chapter, I investigate how tour guides come up with performances that allow them to resist the seemingly oppressive structures of tourism mentioned previously. Tour guides are a central focus in much research on language and tourism. Earlier works on tour guides problematise their role in the tourism industry (e.g. Cohen, 1985; Holloway, 1981; Pond, 1993), mostly in terms of their status as the professional source of information, socialisation, communication and entertainment and as 'language brokers' (Cohen & Cooper, 1986). Cohen (1985) identifies four major functions of tour guides: Originals, Animators, Tour Leaders and Professionals. Originals are tour guides who primarily cover the basic tasks of guiding, which involve ensuring that tourists find their target destinations and their way back home. Animators are involved in socialising with tourists and making sure that they can effectively connect with them. Tour Leaders assist tourists in intermingling with the people in the local destination. Finally, Professionals take charge in giving nuanced information about the destination and in appreciating the local destinations, practices and experiences of the activity.

More recent research aims to go beyond the communicative and pragmatic utility of tour guides by examining how they actually serve as intermediary between the tourist and the destination. For instance, Reisinger and Steiner's (2006) study enriches earlier works on the communicative aspect of tour guiding by highlighting the role of tour guides in the construction of the feeling of authenticity (e.g. how some tourists feel that they are authentic tourists and not just members of a tour group). This has been picked up by research on the sociolinguistics of tourism (e.g. Hall-Lew *et al.*, 2015; Jack & Phipps, 2005; Jaworski & Pritchard, 2005; Jaworski & Thurlow, 2010; Thurlow & Jaworski, 2010). These studies show the imperative to problematise the supposed roles of tour guides, and why it is important to see tour guides not just as passive participants of the tourism activity but as active frontrunners who strive to assert their own voices. While these works effectively illustrate the forms of communication that take place during the tourism activity and their relevance to tourism discourse, they do not necessarily pay attention to the agentive performances of tour guides.

Salazar's (2005, 2006, among others) works on tourism in Tanzania are good examples of how local stakeholders in the tourism industry exercise agency – albeit momentarily. He argues that tour guides are 'key actors in the process of folkorizing, ethnicizing, and exoticizing a destination' (2006: 834, cf. 2005) and are 'remarkable front-runners of glocalization' (2005: 628). He examines the professional tour guide training that Tanzanian students receive vis-à-vis their actual performances when dealing with foreign tourists, and reports that these students often resort to creative manipulations of the scripts that they learned from their training by shifting their alignments to the 'local' community and the 'global' tourism market, which can be seen as empowering because it shows that their agency as tourism frontrunners manifests itself in the actual interaction. He further argues:

> Although their performance is often staged and routinized, the reproduction of the rehearsed discourses is never complete or devoid of deviation. Tourism tales are not fixed, but are the site of constant contestation of meaning…Guides do not blindly copy the learned canons but use their agency to position themselves strategically on the "us" vs. "them" continuum which is so prevalent in all tourist imaginaries… Even if both tourists and guides are active players in the reproduction of the tourism tautology, there is mediation at every level, and there is always room for alternative or counter-discourses. (Salazar, 2006: 847)

By examining the different semiotic resources that tour guides employ in their performances, I will demonstrate how their sociolinguistic appropriation of postcolonialism serves as a source and product of their agency which allows them to carve a strategic position for themselves in the tourism industry. I argue that that strategic use of sociolinguistic resources can be approached well using the framework of postcolonial performativity (Pennycook, 2001: 68), which will be discussed subsequently.

Postcolonial Performativity and the Global Spread of English

Pennycook (2001: 46–71) proposes the framework of postcolonial performativity as a critical lens in understanding the global spread of English. He envisages postcolonial performativity as a corrective to the insufficiencies of existing frameworks for understanding the global spread of English. He enumerates five existing frameworks (i.e. colonial celebratory, laissez-faire liberalism, linguistic imperialism, language ecology and language rights, and linguistic hybridity) in sociolinguistics that are used to reach this understanding, which can be viewed as parts of a conservatism–liberalism spectrum of how English should be embraced, resisted or interrogated. In this section, I will provide an overview of postcolonial performativity, and how this approach allows us to understand how the tour guide in the study enacts forms of resistance to the seemingly oppressive demands of the tourism industry.

The framework of postcolonial performativity aims to address the gaps of the five frameworks. Inasmuch as the previously mentioned liberal frameworks tend to not appreciate structures of struggle and inequality in their celebration of the global spread of English, the conservative frameworks tend to focus on the rhetoric of activism and oppression at the expense of the possibilities of agency and mobility despite the backdrop of inequality. Postcolonial performativity aims to achieve such level of self-criticality by refusing to romanticise both traditional concepts in sociolinguistics (e.g. communicative competence may need to be revisited in relation to the power structures in the contexts of inquiry) and more recent analytical perspectives (e.g. hybridity needs to be interrogated and not be automatically assumed as inherently emancipatory). It aims to do so by following three key principles: 'the need for an [sic] historical understanding of language use, a view of culture, identity and global politics that avoids essentialism and instead looks at forms of resistance and appropriation, and a need to always work contextually' (Pennycook, 2001: 72). This approach emphasises the need to pay attention to actual linguistic activities of language users, their performative underpinnings and value and the critical understanding of the local context of language use. Starting the analysis from non-essentialist notions with a sensitivity on the reproduction of inequality, this framework opens up possibilities for concrete action and reform by looking at how language use can lead to the creation of third spaces (cf. Kramsch, 1993 cited in Pennycook, 2001) where forms of resistance can take place. This allows us to recognise 'the possibilities of using language against the grain, of taking up and using a language that has been a tool of oppression, colonialism, or rigid identity and turning it against itself' (Pennycook, 2001: 69). This framework also interrogates what language use actually means to people in relation to the material conditions surrounding the linguistic activity.

In this chapter, I explore the potency of postcolonial performativity as a framework for understanding the global spread of English in the context of heritage tourism in the Philippine tourism industry. As a framework, postcolonial performativity highlights the types of imperialist oppression that emerges in the context of tourism, without assuming rigid structural relations or complete freedom of agents. Instead, it foregrounds the performativity of language and discourse as playing a key role in reproducing and transforming colonial relations. The Philippines is a good site of study because of its rich colonial history (i.e. former colony of Spain and the United States and occupied by Japan during the Second World War) and postcolonial struggle (i.e. post-war efforts to create an independent and national identity). I will explore how tour guides take a postcolonial stance in their performances as a semiotic device, such as how they simultaneously discuss and challenge colonialism. I will also tackle how that allows them to strategically position themselves in the tourism industry, which can be viewed as a form of resistance.

The Ethnographic Fieldwork: Charles in Intramuros, Manila

The data that I discuss here are part of the ethnographic fieldwork that I conducted in three fieldwork sites in 2012. This fieldwork was conducted in three of the most important tourism hubs in the Philippines: Manila, Boracay Island and Puerto Princesa City. Recordings of performances of and interviews with ten Filipino tour guides from the said tourism hubs comprise the data. However, in this chapter, I focus on one tour guide, Charles (pseudonym), who conducts tours in Manila, the capital city of the Philippines. His tours are famous in the country; he attracts both local and foreign tourists who are interested in heritage tourism.

Charles has more than ten years of tour guiding experience in Intramuros, a walled city in downtown Manila which was built by Spanish colonisers in the 16th century. He identifies as part of the middle class and has a fairly privileged background – he went to an expensive private school, completed his degree at the country's premier university and has an extensive travel and migration history. His historical knowledge is also backed by his research experience at the Heritage Conservation Society. His involvements in culture and the arts also enabled him to go to different events overseas. He has 'maximum competence' in English and Tagalog and has 'minimal competence' in Spanish (see Blommaert & Backus, 2013 for their discussion of levels of competence), and he has extensive theatre training which made it easy for him to change accents. He is also known in the country as a political activist. The popularity of his tours and civic involvement was recognised by the city government of Manila and made him the city's tourism consultant in 2013. He is probably the most famous tour guide in the Philippines.

In this chapter, I focus on Charles in order to come up with a more ethnographically informed analysis of his performances. Even though Charles' background and style are unusual among the other tour guides in the study, his performances strongly highlight the issues of the imperialist tourist gaze that tour guides need to deal with. Hence, focusing on Charles can be a good way of studying the range of strategies that tour guides may adopt through postcolonial performativity.

Intramuros is in the central area of the City of Manila, which is one of the comprising cities of what is now known as the National Capital Region (NCR) – the economic and political centre of the Philippines. It was constructed to be the seat of the Spanish government in the then Province of Manila. The walls were supposed to defend the city from natural disasters, local insurgents, and other foreign colonisers. Most of Intramuros was destroyed during the Second World War; thus, most of what is left in Intramuros were reconstructed after the war.

Intramuros is regarded as the historical centre of Manila and NCR, and now hosts several universities, government buildings, museums, restaurants and churches – including the famous and grand Manila

Cathedral, and the San Agustin Church, which is one of the baroque churches in the Philippines which are collectively declared as UNESCO World Heritage Sites. Because of its rich history and geographic accessibility, Intramuros is one of the most popular tourist destinations in Manila, and it happens to still have a vibrant tour guiding industry. Given that Intramuros is a site of heritage tourism, tourists tend to benefit from joining guided tours because of the historical explanations that go with them. This shows that tour guides in Intramuros such as Charles mediate structures of colonialism in the tourism activity. Because of this status, Intramuros is a relevant site for an investigation of how postcolonial stances relate to challenging the tourist gaze.

Props, Costumes and the Multimodal Performance of (Post)Colonialism

In this section, I will zoom into the multimodal resources that Charles uses in his tours. He uses a relatively uncommon strategy, at least in the Philippine tourism industry, of using costumes and props in his tours to emphasise his points on Philippine colonial history. He is the only tour guide in my fieldwork who used costumes and props, since all the other tour guides just wore their company or personal clothes. Charles uses them as explicit cultural markers that reflect the different periods of Philippine history. This can be seen in Figures 7.1 to 7.4.

In Figure 7.1, Charles discussed the situation of the Philippines during the Spanish colonial era, while wearing a modern remake of the *Barong Tagalog*, the national costume of the Philippines which is associated with

Figure 7.1 Spanish era (photo RV)   **Figure 7.2** American era (photo RV)

Postcolonial Performativity in the Philippine Heritage Tourism Industry 115

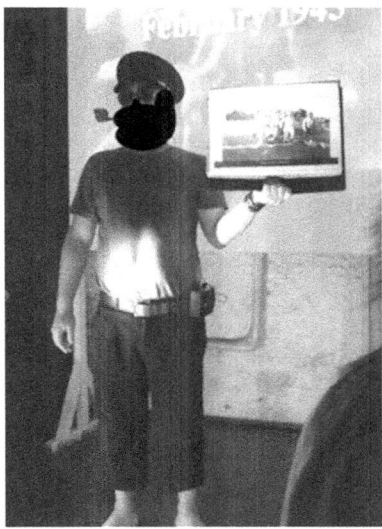

Figure 7.3 Japanese era (photo RV)

Figure 7.4 American flags during the American era discussion (photo RV)

the Spanish era in terms of origin, and a hat which is distinctly European in origin. When he transitioned to the discussion of the American era (as seen in Figure 7.2), he replaced his hat with one that has the American flag on it, which is reminiscent of the iconic hat that the famous character Uncle Sam wears. In the last part of his tour (as seen in Figure 7.3), Charles talked about the Japanese occupation of the Philippines, while noticeably taking off his *Barong Tagalog*, replacing his American hat with a military hat, and putting a tobacco pipe in his mouth. In Figure 7.4, Charles took off his Uncle Sam hat, but he installed two American flags as a backdrop. These costume shifts are noteworthy because it is an uncommon performative strategy in the Philippine tourism industry. His costume changes were done in a highly reflexive way – he unequivocally diverted the audience's attention to the new items that he wears. Charles does not explicitly talk about the costumes; he just uses non-verbal cues to allude to the costumes in order to call attention to them. For instance, he changed his hats very slowly and playfully so that everyone in the tour group would notice it. He also occasionally stopped during the discussion of the Japanese era so that he could pretend that he is smoking his tobacco pipe while repeatedly raising his eyebrows until tourists laugh at what he was doing, which serves as an acknowledgement that the tourists received the message that he was trying to convey. Throughout the tour, Charles uses a compilation of pictures of prominent historical figures (e.g. Philippine war heroes, King of Spain) and landmarks (e.g. Manila Cathedral, Intramuros), as seen in the clear folder that he flashes in Figure 7.4. These props enable Charles to tap on the sensory nature of the tourist gaze by making tourists actually see what he is talking about.

Charles uses multimodal resources to index different colonial periods, which was the governing content and structure of his tour. The costumes and props (i.e. outfit, hats, tobacco pipe, American flag, pictures of prominent places and people) become salient representations of the colonial periods of Philippine history. Given that Charles does not explicitly explain the rationale behind the costumes, he relies on the background knowledge of tourists to understand it. The periodic shifts reflected in the costume changes were well-received by the tourists based on their reactions during the tour, such as their moments of laughter each time Charles would allude to the costumes and props.

Charles does not only use multimodal resources to index the different colonial periods of Philippine History; he also uses them to make markers of local Filipino identity salient. For instance, he began the tour by asking the tour group to sing the Philippine National Anthem with him. This invitation to participate in the multimodal performance of singing the National Anthem is an important interactional activity. It establishes the interactive nature of his tour, which allows him to fulfil the four different functions of tour guides that Cohen (1985) enumerates – especially the function of being a Professional by making tourists appreciate the local context during his performance. This also provides a reversal of the 'imperial nostalgia' (Rosaldo, 1989: 68–90, cf. Bruner, 2001). Instead of presenting tourists with performances of the culture that colonialism has destroyed, he presents them with a strong symbol of the beginning of Philippine independence and postcolonialism: after all, the Philippine National Anthem, written for the proclamation of independence of the Philippines from Spain, condemns colonialism. However, this performance does not explicitly dwell on the postcolonial aspect of the national anthem – especially for the international tourists who do not understand the National Anthem because it was sang in Tagalog. Hence, the singing of the National Anthem enables Charles to allude to colonialism not through the language of the anthem per se, but through its performance and what it entails. It is comparable to Bruner's (2001: 897) point on how performances can construct a 'postmodern image' – by providing interactions that blur the lines between the local and the foreign, and by extension, the colonial and the postcolonial. The focus of the singing was not to explicitly condemn colonialism; rather, the point was to get all the tourists, local and foreign alike, to equally partake in the performance – even though they are from different backgrounds. Hence, the linguistic features of the National Anthem become less important in taking this postcolonial stance; the multimodal nature of actually singing the song fulfils this performative function, which serves as an introductory device for Charles to perform particular stances towards colonialism as he interacts with the tourists.

Metalinguistic Humour and Stylisation

In this section, I will examine the different metalinguistic strategies that Charles uses in his tour in order to take up postcolonial stances: specifically, the use of metalinguistic narratives (i.e. actual discussions about language) and metalinguistic humour (i.e. humour generated through metalinguistic manipulations). These complement his strategy of using multimodal resources in his tours.

Charles does many instances of accent shifts as a form of metalinguistic humour. One of the first few examples of this can be seen in the subsequent extract, when he invited the tour group to sing the Philippine National Anthem, which I discussed previously. During the tour that I recorded, Charles invited the tourists with this spiel:

Extract 1: Charles' invitation to sing the National Anthem

Charles	1	Gentlemen, hats (IPA: [hats]) off [IPA: ɔp]! Stand (IPA: [stand])
	2	straight (IPA: [streɪt]). Hands over (IPA:[oʊbər]) heart. Face
	3	(IPA: [peɪs]) the (IPA: [da]) Filipino (IPA: [pilipinɔ]) flag (IPA: [plag]).
	4	And to the (IPA: [da]) Filipinos (IPA: [pilipinɔs]), you
	5	know the words and ah one two three and...
	6	<tourists laugh>
	7	The Philippine National Anthem. But I guess you
	8	figured out by now, it's not some random song that we Filipinos
	9	decided to sing.

	10	<sarcastic tone> Because a Filipino would never break
	11	out into song for no apparent reason. <laughs>
	12	Ever.
	13	<tourists laugh>
	14	And of course the title of the Philippine National Anthem is...?
Tourist	15	*Lupang Hinirang.*
Charles	16	Very good. Okay.

The joke poked fun at the stereotypical basilectal feature of Philippine English (see Tayao, 2004 for a description of common Philippine English features). This invitation includes some consonantal substitutions, such as [f] to [p] ('off' 'Filipino' 'flag'), [ð] to [d] ('the'), [v] to [b] ('over'). It also has some vowel mergers, such as the [i]/[ɪ] ('Filipinos') and the [æ]/[a] ('stand', 'flag') mergers, which may be a result of the relatively smaller vowel system of Philippine English compared to other native varieties of English.

What is interesting to note here is that Charles' invocation of stereotypical Philippine English features was able to evoke laughter from the audience. This laughter shows the tourists' awareness of the intentional inconsistency of Charles' performed speeches from his usual way of talking, which I would describe as acrolectal (following Tayao, 2004). Charles has maximum competence in English, and in some cases, he can even mimic other English accents, especially the general American and received pronunciation accents. This disjunction between their usual and performed ways of speaking are 'unexpected' (cf. Pennycook, 2012), which definitely appealed to tourists given their laughter. By using the stereotypical features of Philippine English to evoke humour, he performs an instance of stylisation, he does not only use Philippine English for purely referential purposes, but also as a symbolic resource that illustrates localness, and consequently, that his usual speaking style is a marker of globalness. He capitalises on the global understandability of Philippine English, and he simultaneously indexes difference and local authenticity by emphasising the Philippineness of his speech, which becomes even more salient by the context of the singing of the National Anthem, which could be viewed as an activity that makes the local salient. After all, the Philippine National Anthem was written for the proclamation of independence of the Philippines from Spain. The production of the message was informed by his knowledge that Philippine English can be used to both appeal to the global and local scales, and at the same time, create a coherent humorous message that can be received well in that particular tour group. The stylisation can be seen as effective because he was able to evoke humour from the tourists, which complemented the activity of singing the National Anthem. He also employs two famous essentialist jokes in this extract.

The first one is that Filipinos are good at and/or love singing, and he alludes to another point that Filipinos just randomly break out into songs. The second, which would only be understood by Filipino tourists, is that Filipinos usually get the title of the National Anthem wrong. This 'pop quiz' style is quite humorous because it is common knowledge that most Filipinos think that the title of the National Anthem is *Bayang Magiliw*, the first line of the song, instead of *Lupang Hinirang*. This invitation to sing the National Anthem sets the tone for the rest of the tour in a variety of ways: first, tourists can expect that the tour will be about Philippine history and identity; second, it draws the tourists' attention to Charles' accent shifts, so that they can stay focused on his stylistic construction and parody of groups throughout the rest of the tour; third, they also become attuned to Charles' mixing of humour and critical commentary.

In addition to his accent shifts, Charles also directly use metalinguistic discussions in his speeches to create humour. In a way, these jokes function because they lay out some informative value about the periods of Philippine history without explaining their political aspects in depth. This is comparable to how Charles uses costumes and props in the previous discussion. He comes up with narratives that are explicitly about the relationship between colonialism and the linguistic situation in the Philippines, and he does so in lighthearted and playful ways. For instance, he discusses the linguistic influences of Spanish and American English on Philippine English and Tagalog. He names different places in the Philippines which all start with *Santa* or *Santo* (i.e. Spanish words for 'saints') in a Spanish accent, as well as different everyday objects like *papel* 'paper', *lapis* 'pencil', *bombilla* 'light bulb', *tenidor* 'fork' and *cuchara* 'spoon' – all of which were Spanish words which were lexicalised into Tagalog. Similarly, he demonstrates the influence of American English on Philippine English by enumerating names of places, such as Forbes Park, McKinley Road, Taft Avenue, Dewey Avenue – which all allude to key persons of American colonialism in the Philippines – and adds that 'we even have a Beverly Hills in Antipolo (i.e. a city east of Manila).'

In a way, Charles highlights the entanglement of Philippine English, and even Tagalog, in both global and local scales. He later on makes fun of, with his exaggerated Philippine English accent, how Philippine English uses many generic brand names as part of its lexicon, such as the use of Kodak to refer to 'picture' (noun and verb forms), Coke to refer to 'soda,' Frigidaire to refer to 'refrigerator' and Colgate to refer to 'toothpaste'. He later on states in his tour that 'just by the way that we speak, that history (i.e. Philippine colonial history) is made evident once again.'

Charles does not only provide examples of the lexical borrowings of Tagalog from colonial languages. He later on explicitly draws a connection between language and colonialism. He does not only use style shifting for humour; he uses it as an important resource for displaying his political stance towards colonialism. This can be seen in the following extract, where Charles discusses the role of English in Philippine society.

Extract 2: Charles' language ideologies (Bold: American English accent, *Italics: Spanish Accent*, <u>Underline: Philippine English Accent,</u> no format: default way of speaking)

1   And one could look at the presence of English in this country in a good way!
2   And…in a bad. Because in a good way, thanks to them, I'm now speaking
3   to you in English today! And that's why you understand me in English,
4   and why the Philippines is the third largest English-speaking country in
5   the world. And that is also the reason why the Philippines is fast
6   becoming the call centre of planet Earth. That's our number one job
7   growth industry here, just call AT&T or Pizza Hut, you
8   **Don't talk to an American, you talk to one of us! You're talking to some**
9   **man from Malabon in a building in Makati at midnight, pretending to**
10 **have a midwestern accent, sir.** And we could not get an outsourcing
11 job <u>unless we spokening (sic) in English*</u>, but now the Filipino is
12 <u>speaking in English and no longer speakening (sic) in Spanish*</u>.
13 Suddenly any emotional, spiritual or cultural connection we ever could
14 have developed with our Spanish past (unintelligible) 'cause when
15 Filipinos lost the Spanish language, we would lose the words of
16 Cervantes, the poetry of Pablo Neruda, the movies of Almodovar, the
17 original novels of Jose Rizal. They are now inaccessible to you today.
18 Because we lost our connection to Hispanic culture, and now that we

19	were being taught American English, which is apparently completely
20	different from what they speak in England, I hear. It was really only the
21	culture of the Hollywood USA that would become the most readily
22	available cultural canon to the average Filipino, who would literally bid
23	Adios, Cervantes! And hello, Caridad, who's really pretty.

In this extract, Charles explains the role of American colonisation in the embedding of English into Philippine society. He initiates his discussion by hyping the commercial value of English. It should be noted that Charles did not seem to be sarcastic in lines 1-3, as well as in his justification of the benefits of English being imposed on the Filipino people by the American colonisers in lines 4-8. He argues that English paved the way for the transformation of the Philippines as the 'call centre of planet Earth' (line 6), which he associates with American colonialism. He implicitly claims that Filipinos have started to own English by being good at this industry, which is why he said that 'you don't talk to an American, you talk to one of us!' (lines 7-8), which is complemented by his stylised American English accent in lines 9-11. However, as Charles says in lines 1 and 2, the prevalence of English in the Philippines can be seen in a bad way as well. He starts doing this in lines 9-12. The accent shifts that happens in lines 9-12 reflect his evaluative shift of the prevalence of English in the Philippines. In lines 9 and 10, he uses his American accent to suggest that Filipinos can indeed use English to gain economic benefits. In lines 11 and 12, he reverts to the stereotypical, basilectal Philippine English accent – even intentionally using 'spokening' and 'speakening' – common stereotypical features of basilectal Philippine English – in order to show that the prevalence of English comes with a cost, such as Filipinos having to struggle to work with English and Filipinos losing their access to Spanish. In these lines, we can see how Charles' accent shifts are consistent with his value judgement of the English situation in the Philippines.

In lines 15-19, he explains that the move to English meant that Filipinos lost access to Spanish-language literature and media, such as the works of Cervantes, Neruda and Almodovar. He complements this by mimicking the Spanish accent. In lines 19-23, he argues that Filipinos now can just access (American) English literature and media, and even provides a quick critique of American English in lines 19 and 20, when he says that American English is 'different from what they speak in England, I hear.'

While Charles' tour can be seen as very informative and fact-based all throughout the tour, his expression of his political stances was gradually developed in his tour. The metalinguistic jokes built up on each other and allowed him to gradually develop his own political opinions throughout the tour. It is only towards the middle when Charles' own opinions started to manifest themselves in his performance. In a way, it seems that the metalinguistic jokes became the foundation of his eventual critique of colonialism and other ideologies he disagrees with in the Philippines, such as theocracy and a colonial mentality.

In my interview with Charles after the tour, he told me that he does not consider his tours as just a typical tour that allows tourists to get to know a certain place; rather, he considers it as a performance that allows him to use history to try to 'bring the unknown parts of Manila's history, so making what is invisible visible, trying to change the way Manila looks through the way that you look at Manila.' He did this by linking the history of Manila to its current sociopolitical landscape. Doing so gave him enough space to include his own opinions and political stances in his performance, which makes his tour guiding identity a conglomeration of the tour guide functions that Cohen (1985) discusses. This means that Charles is veering away from just being a source of information about the colonial heritage of Intramuros and the Philippines as a whole; rather, he wants to present a critical way of making the tourists learn and understand such information.

One of the most recurrent themes of Charles' tour is the role of the [Philippine] Catholic Church in Philippine history. He approaches this theme from different angles – from the neutral discussion of how Catholicism was one of the driving reasons behind Spanish colonialism, to positive comments about the beauty of Catholic architecture, to highly critical comments about the involvement of the Church in matters of the state. Throughout the tour, he vehemently expressed his critical stance against the [Philippine] Catholic Church – which he consistently called the 'Catholic Taliban.'

This critical view of the Church and of colonialism as a whole is not just delivered in terms of content; they are reflected in his linguistic choices as well. Charles does several accent shifts again in a mocking style, which can be seen in the following extract where he discusses another aspect of Spanish Catholicism.

Extract 3. Charles' discussion of Catholicism and the Spanish era (*Italics* = Spanish accent, **boldface** = exaggerated stereotypical Philippine English accent, <u>underline</u> = local Philippine language accent, <u>broken underline</u> = American accent, no formatting = unmarked Philippine English accent)

1   The Philippines was just literally given away to the Catholic Church. And
2   that's why we don't speak Spanish. Alright, Spanish colony without the
3   Spanish language, how did that happen?
4   <u>And that's because to speak Spanish has always been a King thing,</u>

5	it's never been a Church thing.
6	As a matter of fact, the king ordered the friars to
7	teach Filipinos Spanish since the 18th century.
8	But the priests of Manila said, <shouts> *forget it!*
9	'Cos there really weren't enough priests here to do the job.
10	But more importantly, language is power.
11	And it was the Catholic Church's way of creating a Catholic kingdom…
12	*at the end of the sea.*
13	So instead of teaching Filipinos Spanish, those priests would instead learn
14	***Tagalog, Bicolano, Ilocano, Ilonggo, Tagalog, Bisaya, Kankanaey,***
15	***Waray, Pampangueño, Bisaya, Hiligaynon,*** Ilonggo.
16	Those priests would learn every local dialect and those priests would help
17	save the Philippine languages. Which is one of the reasons
18	why we still speak them. But now it created a very strange situation–
19	wherein the priest could now understand us <laughs> and
20	*we could not understand the priests.* And now more importantly,
21	*we now could not understand (IPA: [ˌandɛrˈstand] the (IPA: [da]) king.*
22	*Because if we understood [ˌandɛrˈstand] the (IPA: [da]) king better,*
23	*we'd see that (IPA: [dat]) the (IPA: [da]) king was on our side*
24	*because the (IPA: [da]) king never wanted the (IPA: [da]) Philippines–*
25	*there's no gold, what's your point?* And even told those friars–
26	*"oh yeah, you friars, who are wasting my money building those seven*
27	*churches from Intramuros. I should see those seven churches*
28	*from Madrid, punyeta (i.e. expletive)."*
29	And the King of Spain would spend an edict to the Philippines to let it go,
30	and the edict will get hijacked by priests. And right in Manila, definitely.
31	So, you can see that the Philippines was really created and controlled more
32	by a parochial friar class than anything else.
33	Controlled by the 18th century *Catholic Taliban.*

In this extract, Charles was able to use five distinctly identifiable accents which, on the surface, fulfil certain functions. He uses his unmarked Philippine English accent as the base accent in this extract and uses the four others in marked ways. He uses Spanish to mimic the Spanish king and friars to perform the coloniser, and he seems to have more disdain for the friars than the king. His extended use of the Spanish accent in lines 25–28 to mimic the king constructs an image of the king which the audience found funny. This simultaneously makes the king appear to be ineffective, which is why he was manipulated by the friars. His use of the exaggerated Philippine English accent evokes self-deprecating humour, as seen in lines 20–24. This accent aids the construction of the image of the Filipino as helpless ('we could not understand the king' in line 21) and dispensable ('the king never wanted the Philippines' in line 24). The American accent is used to make 'matter of fact' assertions, and his unmarked Philippine English accent as the base accent of such hybridity. However, there is more to this style-shifting: these are enactments of different identities which are linked to his own political ideologies about the identities concerned. The complex combination of these style-shifts does not only enable Charles to construct different identities for himself, but to articulate his own postcolonial parody and critique.

He also used these accent shifts in other parts of his tour. As a staunch critic of colonialism and the Catholic Church, Charles codeswitches to Spanish when he wants to create a parody of the Catholic Church. He also switches to an American-accented English when he wants to index the perceived stupidity of Americans (e.g. when he was discussing the failures of the American government during the Second World War). Finally, he switches to a heavily Philippine-accented English when he wants to criticise the attitudes and mindsets of Filipinos that he does not subscribe to (e.g. colonial mentality). It is also worth noting that in line 33, he says 'Catholic Taliban' in a basilectal Philippine English accent, which seems to hype the postcolonial aspect of his parodic critique given that he is using the local variety to do so.

Charles' accent shifts can be construed as a form of parody. Hutcheon (1989: 101) describes parody as follows:

> As a form of ironic representation, parody is doubly coded in political terms: it both legitimizes and subverts that which it parodies. This kind of authorized transgression is what makes it a ready vehicle for the political contradictions of postmodernism at large.

In the previous examples, Charles uses different accents to represent various personas, such as those of the Spanish king, friars, Americans and Filipinos. These representations happen in the supposedly 'factual' context of his historical tour. On the surface, it seems that Charles was just delivering a historical account of what happened in Intramuros and the Philippines in general during the colonial age. However, a closer introspection of his performance would reveal that his representations are rather ironic and critical. Following Hutcheon's previous point, when he represents different types of people by mimicking their accents, he simultaneously legitimises and subverts them. He does not just use accents to create authenticity; he uses the authenticity he creates to go against it and to insert his political opinions and critique of colonialism into his representations.

The framework of postcolonial performativity allows us to understand how this strategy works as a form of resistance. Postcolonial performativity compels us to break away from essentialist assumptions about language and understand what language means to its users and to its local context. The previous examples show that Charles capitalises on his historical understanding of the role of the languages and accents that he uses in his tours in the Philippine setting. He uses them as remarkable markers of colonialism. Moreover, he relies on essentialist notions about the accents that he uses in his tours, but also goes against those essentialist values by critiquing what the accents are supposed to represent. Hence, Charles does not only use the resources mentioned previously to create 'authentic' or 'neutral' markers of the colonial periods of the Philippines; rather, he is using those resources which have '[...] been a tool of oppression, colonialism, or rigid identity and turning it against itself' (Pennycook, 2001: 69). Charles' initial discussions and costume shifts make it seem that he does not have any ulterior motive of criticising colonialism, especially because his costume changes can be construed as ornamental and his accent shifts can be viewed as just playful shifting. However, a historical understanding of how this language use operates, and an investigation of how this simultaneously affirms and challenges essentialist notions, would reveal that his performances use the language of the colonisers in reconciling the global and the local, and in the eventual construction of his political stances.

Amidst all these critical condemnations, Charles also clearly expressed his love for the Philippines, especially the hybrid identity of the Filipino people which resulted from the country's long colonial history. He ended his tour by treating the tourists to a serving of *halo-halo* (transliteration: 'mixed together'), a Filipino dessert which is a mix of various ingredients like red beans, jelly, banana, corn, sweet potato, topped with shaved ice, milk and yam. He told the tourists that the Filipino is a *halo-halo*:

Extract 4: The Philippines as a *halo-halo* (double underline = American accent)

1 ...because of all the intermingling of races, cultures, religions, events,
2 and chromosomes, because of Manila's rich history as a gateway
3 between the East and West, we can truly see that by the 20th century,
4 Manila became Asia's first multicultural society.

5   Manila became the only city in the Far East
6   where you could own an Indian-style bazaar that sold Italian jewellery.
7   You had Malay skin, you had Chinese eyes, you spoke in Spanish,
8   while deep in your heart, [pause] <u>you just wanted to be an American.</u>
9   <laughter>
10   The Filipino had truly and successfully become what we call, a halo-halo.
11   And with that, ladies and gentlemen, we end the journey.
12   And I hope that I've let you all know just a little bit about the enigma
13   that is very misunderstood city of Manila,
14   please use what you've learned, fellow Filipinos,
15   to improve the image of Manila, okay?
16   Because if you really wanna truly change the way that Manila looks, then
17   then what you gotta do
18   is start changing the way that you look at Manila.

Even though Charles' political views against colonialism and theocracy are very resonant in his performances, his love of country remains his most valued, and actually highlighted, advocacy. In the conclusion of his tour, Charles says that people should question the 'legacy' of colonial history in order to better appreciate the Philippines. In Extract 4, he summarises his argument that the core tenet of being Filipino is its diversity brought about by Philippine history.

In Lines 4-8, Charles resorts to using an enumeration of the different cultures that makes Manila 'Asia's first multicultural society.' In Line 8, he once again shifts to an American accent which evoked laughter in Line 9. This is another attempt at parody because the context of the preceding topic was colonial mentality, specifically the running desire of many Filipinos to be American. He uses the *halo-halo* as a concluding metaphor to make tourists understand the Philippines better – to make them understand why the Philippines does not have a singular distinctive and unified cultural image, which he contrasted with Thailand, China and Malaysia; rather, the Philippines has always been about the hybridity of the coloniser and the colonised, and by extension, of the global and the local.

The tourists were later on surprised when Charles' assistants started serving *halo-halo*, which makes the metaphor more effective because the tourists actually got to try the dessert while listening to Charles' discussion. What is more important to note here is that while the actual consumption of the *halo-halo* is not strictly a linguistic activity, it still brings into being certain relations and perspectives on colonialism through the audience's participation. It complements both the multimodal and linguistic strategies enumerated previously. In Bruner's (2005: 33) words, 'tourism gives tribalism and colonialism a new space by bringing them back as representations of themselves and circulating them within an economy of performance.' This is what Charles does – he capitalises on the entanglement of colonial history with the current material conditions surrounding the Philippines and its tourism industry in his performances. This allows him to perform an identity for himself as a tour guide who does not only reaffirm the colonial aspect of his heritage tour, but also as a tour guide who consistently questions that aspect and uses it to 'speak back' (Ashcroft et al., 1989) for his advantage – both in terms of coming up with tours that give him commercial success as a tour guide and by allowing him to integrate his own political stances, such as his condemnation of colonialism and his love of country. This becomes his competitive advantage. He does not directly dismantle the structures of colonialism; he uses them against themselves as a form of postcolonial resistance.

Conclusion

While it is easy to fall into the trap of blindly celebrating this phenomenon as a success of Charles' linguistic performances, we need to remember that postcolonial performativity emphasises the need to critically evaluate this process and to avoid the danger of romanticising such perceived success. Inasmuch as this shows us that the tourist gaze has cracks and gaps that can be exploited by agents like Charles, it does not mean that heritage tourism in the postcolonial world has become an equal space in terms of mobility. Charles comes from a position of privilege unlike most tour guides in the Philippines. Moreover, it would be inaccurate to claim that the colonial aspect of heritage tourism becomes totally dismantled: it is still very much alive, but it can be contested, albeit momentarily or 'fleetingly' (cf. Jaworski & Thurlow, 2010) – which shows that the tourism activity becomes a third space (Kramsch, 1993 cited in Pennnycook, 2001). On the other hand, it would also be unwise to dismiss the idea that this is empowering. This is how the framework of postcolonial performativity provides its value as an interpretive lens: a historical understanding of the linguistic resources that Charles uses in his tours allows us to make sense of how he employs pastiche and parody in his enactment of 'strategic use of essentialism' (Spivak, 1993) and how these linguistic performances work in the local context of the tourism activity. Postcolonial performativity allows us to appreciate the situatedness of agency and mobility in the structures of colonialism and inequality, which is essential to a better understanding of the sociolinguistics of tourism.

References

Aitchison, C. (2001) Theorizing Other discourses of tourism, gender and culture. Can the subaltern speak (in tourism)? *Tourist Studies* 1 (2), 133–147.
Ashcroft, B., Griffiths, G. and Tiffin, H. (1989) *The Empire Writes Back: Theory and Practice in Post-colonial Literatures*. London: Routledge.
Blommaert, J. and Backus, A. (2013) Superdiverse repertoires and the individual. In I. de Saint-Georges and J.J. Weber (eds) *Multilingualism and Multimodality: Current Challenges for Educational Studies* (pp. 11–32). Rotterdam: Sense Publishers.
Bruner, E. (2001) The Maasai and the Lion King: Authenticity, nationalism, and globalization in African tourism. *American Ethnologist* 28 (4), 881–908.
Bruner, E. (2005) *Culture on Tour: Ethnographies of Travel*. Chicago, IL: University of Chicago Press.
Clyne, M.G. (1981) Introduction. *International Journal of Sociology of Language* 28, 5–7.
Cohen, E. (1985) The tourist guide: The origins, structure and dynamics of a role. *Annals of Tourism Research* 12 (1), 5–29.
Cohen, E. and Cooper, R.L. (1986) Language and tourism. *Annals of Tourism Research* 13 (4), 533–563.
Coupland, B. and Coupland, N. (2014) The authenticating discourses of mining heritage tourism in Cornwall and Wales. *Journal of Sociolinguistics* 18 (4), 495–517.
d'Hauteserre, A. (2004) Postcolonialism, colonialism, and tourism. In A. Lew, C.M. Hall and A. Williams (eds) *A Companion to Tourism* (pp. 235–245). Massachusetts: Blackwell.
Dann, G.M.S. (1996) *The Language of Tourism. A Sociolinguistic Perspective*. Oxon: CAB International.
Dörnyei, Z. and Csizér, K. (2005) The effects of intercultural contact and tourism on language attitudes and language learning motivation. *Journal of Language and Social Psychology* 24 (4), 327–357.
Duchêne, A. and Heller, M. (eds) (2012) *Language in Late Capitalism: Pride and Profit*. New York, NY: Routledge.
Ferguson, C.A. (1971) Absence of copula and the notion of simplicity: A study of normal speech, baby talk, foreigner talk, and pidgins. In D. Hymes (ed.) *Pidginization and Creolization of Languages* (pp. 141–150). Cambridge: Cambridge University Press.
Gao, S. (2012) Commodification of place, consumption of identity: The sociolinguistic construction of a 'global village' in rural China. *Journal of Sociolinguistics* 16 (3), 336–357.
Hall-Lew, L., Fairs, A. and Lew, A.A. (2015) Tourist attitudes towards linguistic variation in Scotland. In E. Torgersen, S. Hårstad, B. Mæhlum and U. Røyneland (eds) *Language Variation – European Perspectives V* (pp. 99–110). Amsterdam: Benjamins.
Heller, M. (2003) Globalization, the new economy, and the commodification of language and identity. *Journal of Sociolinguistics* 7 (4), 473–492.
Heller, M., Jaworski, A. and Thurlow, C. (2014) Introduction: Sociolinguistics and tourism – mobilities, markets, multilingualism. *Journal of Sociolinguistics* 18 (4), 425–566.
Heller, M., Pujolar, J. and Duchêne, A. (2014) Linguistic commodification in tourism. *Journal of Sociolinguistics* 18 (4), 539–566.
Holloway, J. (1981) The guided tour: A sociological approach. *Annals of Tourism Research* 8 (3), 377–402.
Hutcheon, L. (1989) *The Politics of Postmodernism*. London: Routledge.
Jack, G. and Phipps, A. (2005) *Tourism and Intercultural Exchange: Why Tourism Matters*. Clevedon: Channel View Publications.
Jaworski, A. and Pritchard, A. (eds) (2005) *Discourse, Communication and Tourism*. Clevedon: Channel View Publications.
Jaworski, A. and Thurlow, C. (2010) Language and the globalizing habitus of tourism: Towards a sociolinguistics of fleeting relationships. In N. Coupland (ed.)

The Handbook of Language and Globalization (pp. 255–286). Massachusetts: Wiley-Blackwell.

Kelly-Holmes, H. and Pietikäinen, S. (2014) Commodifying Sámi culture in an indigenous tourism site. *Journal of Sociolinguistics* 18 (4), 518–538.

Kramsch, C. (1993) *Context and Culture in Language Teaching*. Oxford: Oxford University Press.

Milani, T. and Levon, E. (2016) Sexing diversity: Linguistic landscapes of homonationalism. *Language & Communication* 51, 69–86.

Moriarty, M. (2015) Indexing authenticity: The linguistic landscape of an Irish tourist town. *International Journal of the Sociology of Language* 232, 195–214.

Nash, D. (1989) Tourism as a form of imperialism. In V. Smith (ed.) *Hosts and Guests: The Anthropology of Tourism* (2nd edn) (pp. 179–202). Philadelphia, PA: University of Pennsylvania Press.

Palmer, C. (1994) Tourism and colonialism: The experience of the Bahamas. *Annals of Tourism Research* 21 (4), 792–811.

Pennycook, A. (2001) *Critical Applied Linguistics: A Critical Introduction*. Mahwah, NJ: L. Erlbaum.

Pennycook, A. (2012) *Language and Mobility: Unexpected Places*. Bristol: Multilingual Matters.

Phipps, A. (2007) *Learning the Arts of Linguistic Survival: Languaging, Tourism, Life*. Clevedon: Channel View Publications.

Pietikäinen, S. and Kelly-Holmes, H. (2011) The local political economy of languages in a Sámi tourism destination: Authenticity and mobility in the labelling of souvenirs. *Journal of Sociolinguistics* 15 (3), 323–346.

Pond, K. (1993) *The Professional Guide: Dynamics of Tour Guiding*. New York, NY: Van Nostrand Reinhold.

Pritchard, A. and Morgan, N. (2005) Representations of 'ethnographic knowledge': Early comic postcards of Wales. In A. Jaworski and A. Pritchard (eds) *Discourse, Communication and Tourism* (pp. 53–78). Clevedon: Channel View Publications.

Reisinger, Y. and Steiner, C. (2006) Reconceptualising interpretation: The role of tour guides in authentic tourism. *Current Issues in Tourism* 9 (6), 481–498.

Rosaldo, R. (1989) *Culture and Truth: The Remaking of Social Analysis*. Boston, MA: Beacon Press.

Salazar, N. (2005) Tourism and glocalization. "Local" tour guiding. *Annals of Tourism Research* 32 (3), 628–646.

Salazar, N. (2006) Touristifying Tanzania. Local guides, global discourse. *Annals of Tourism Research* 33 (3), 833–852.

Smith, V.L. (2001) The culture brokers. In V.L. Smith and M. Brent (eds) *Hosts and Guests Revisited: Tourism Issues of the 21st Century* (pp. 275–282). Elmsford: Cognizant.

Spivak, G.C. (1993) *Outside in the Teaching Machine*. New York, NY: Routledge & Kegan Paul.

Tayao, M.L. (2004) The evolving study of Philippine English phonology. *World Englishes* 23 (1), 77–90.

Temple, P. (2002) *The Last True Explorer*. London: Godwit.

Thurlow, C. and Aiello, G. (2007) National pride, global capital: A social semiotic analysis of transnational visual branding in the airline industry. *Visual Communication* 6, 305–344.

Thurlow, C. and Jaworski, A. (2010) *Tourism Discourse: Language and Global Mobility*. Basingstoke: Palgrave Macmillan.

Urry, J. (1990) *The Tourist Gaze: Leisure and Travel in Contemporary Societies*. London Park: Sage.

Urry, J. and Larsen, J. (2011) *The Tourist Gaze 3.0*. Los Angeles, CA: Sage.

8 The Hakuna Matata Swahili: Linguistic Souvenirs from the Kenyan Coast

Nico Nassenstein

Language as Touristic Accessory: Learning Basic Kiswahili

> When traveling to Kenya it is useful to learn some Swahili (or kiswahili) language. Even though your pronunciation may not be perfect, knowledge of some basic words and sentences will pay off in: making contact with locals (they often really appreciate the effort), bargaining and risky or serious situations. So, let's learn some basic Swahili!
>
> Bunch of Backpackers, BoB[1]

The East African beaches, as a sociolinguistic area of interaction, are characterised by a high degree of language contact, a dense occurrence of multilingual resources, rich semiotic landscapes and fluid patterns of translanguaging between hosts and guests. The creative and multilingual encounters between predominantly coastal Mijikenda languages, such as Giryama, Chonyi and Digo-speaking Kenyans with Germans, Italians or French tourists has given rise to new linguistic practices along the coast. While Coasti Slang (Nassenstein, 2016), the language of beach vendors, sex workers and acrobats, constitutes a practice that incorporates German and Italian lexicon, Kiswahili, and Mijikenda words, spoken and performed as a form of genderised business language, Hakuna Matata Swahili (HMS) refers to the basics of Kiswahili, the most widespread language at the East African coast, acquired by tourists in the context of their vacation in Mombasa and Malindi, Kenya.

The recurrent Kiswahili sentences and words, performed in songs such as 'Jambo, jambo bwana...' by Them Mushrooms (1982), with which travellers are often welcomed along the East African coast when arriving at their hotels, mark one of the potential origins of a pidginised Kiswahili that developed in the tourism sector. Another major source, as still to be explained further on, is Walt Disney's movie *The Lion King* from 1994, which has not only increased the popularity of East Africa as a major African tourist destination but has also contributed to a global fame of Kiswahili (however, limited to a few handful of words, expressions and names). *Jambo rafiki* ('hello, friend') and *pole* ('slowly, take it easy, keep calm') or a heartily *maisha marefu* ('cheers/long life') range among the most commonly heard exclamations within a catchy touristic Kiswahili[2] repertoire. Numerous tourists steadily collect words and handy expressions that they encounter as kind of exotic 'linguistic souvenirs'; these bits and pieces convey an indexical meaning in the tourist linguascape (see also Jaworski & Thurlow, 2010: 139–141).

The same partially acquired lexicon is often reproduced online in travel forums, where tourists exchange nostalgic stories, and where male and female sex tourists recommend specific sex workers they have interacted with, whom they often call *amigas*, or *boyfriends*, respectively. Kiswahili words enter photo albums, are noted in diaries and appear on tourists' t-shirts, with a bold print *Mzungu* ('white/European') on the chest. The acquisition of some Kiswahili may serve as travel evidence (see Figure 8.1 from Facebook), and may assumingly also be used to mark the difference between an ignorant tourist and an exploring 'traveller'. Returning with some learnt expressions seems to have an impact on tourists' self-view, representing a travel accessory – as an alternative to safari clothes and binoculars – adorning the narratives of pristine wilderness and adventures that are often included in travelogues from East Africa (see also Wiegand & Knapp, 2014).

HMS, literally 'no problem' Kiswahili,[3] constitutes a simplified form of the language acquired by German, Austrian, French and Italian tourists (among others) during their vacation in Kenya and, to some extent, Tanzania. As the Bantu language with most speakers in Africa, Kiswahili is spoken in Kenya and Tanzania, as well as in several adjacent countries. The basic repertoire of tourists' Kiswahili words, mainly acquired in touristified spaces through interactions with so-called beach boys, namely male sex workers and safari organisers, or hotel employees, and are characterised by their catchiness, their high frequency of use and also, when entire sentences are used, their grammatical simplification. Instead of requiring the speaker to respect the syntactic structure of the

Figure 8.1 Kiswahili on Facebook as travel evidence and souvenir

language or use the noun class system and its concordance correctly, the HMS rather reminds of a juxtaposition of lexemes. From the moment of arrival, tourists are constantly exposed to HMS, both in the hotel resorts as well as at the beaches, local markets, souvenir shops, restaurants and massage parlours, to name just a few.

While the variation of Kiswahili along the Kenyan and Tanzanian coast has been dealt with in numerous dialectological studies (for instance summarised in Möhlig, 1995), processes of linguistic acquisition and performance of Kiswahili in touristic contexts has only been marginally dealt with. In an earlier study on the beach boys' creative language Coasti Slang (Nassenstein, 2016), the acquisition patterns among tourists were mentioned, but had not yet been extensively analyzed. Several other publications that focus on the sociolinguistic interconnectedness of language and tourism in Mombasa are currently in preparation (based on talks given by Mietzner, 2016, 2017; Nassenstein & Rüsch, 2017, each with a different focus). Generally speaking, apart from a range of groundbreaking studies (Phipps, 2007; Thurlow & Jaworski, 2010) or inspiring chapters (Jaworski & Thurlow, 2010), the sociolinguistics of tourism have largely remained understudied until today. This volume, with its broad focus, can therefore be considered an essential contribution to this specific field of study.

Structurally, HMS reveals striking similarities with Kisetla (Vitale, 1980), Kenya Pidgin Swahili (Heine, 1973) or Up-country Swahili (Le Breton, 1936), simplified contact varieties of Kiswahili that emerged out of the interaction of white settlers with Kenyan farm workers in colonial times. However, Kisetla and closely related varieties are mostly colonial products of oppression, due to language contact in settings of extreme inequalities, which is also reflected in the labels given to these varieties (such as *mimi kupiga wewe Swahili* 'I-beat-you-Swahili', see Vitale, 1980: 52), or the lexical inventory they contain, circling around violence, the punishment of servants or extremely hard labour. The touristic scenario in which HMS emerged is clearly in a postcolonial setting as well, and European tourism in Africa often brings out analogies with colonial travellers, 'explorers' and also collectors.

In this chapter, HMS is analyzed in relation to these colonial endeavours of collecting and acquiring word lists and languages, showing that language as a souvenir does have a longstanding historical dimension, and it is by no means a recent traveller practice. The composition of HMS is analysed, and the relation to sex tourism is also discussed. Moreover, commodification processes of language in all-inclusive resorts are dealt with. The preliminary findings are based on qualitative interviews with tourists and beach boys alike, conducted between 2015 and 2017.[4]

A Historical Perspective: On (Post)Colonial Collectors

When focusing on tourists from the Global North, who adopt and scribble down some of the Kiswahili they find spoken around them during their vacation, it is equally necessary to take a look at the practice of collecting word lists and taking notes of foreign languages in colonial times. These notes and observations, which later laid the foundation for prescriptive grammars which were written by missionaries or colonial agents, can be treated as examples of artefactualised language (Blommaert, 2008; Lüpke & Storch, 2013), however minimal they were. Languages were transformed from spoken practice into something that could be listed, stored and taken home. Fabian (1986) states that in the colonisation of the Katanga province (former Shaba) of the DR Congo

> missionaries did not (describe) or even learn African languages simply because 'they were there'; their linguistic scholarly work was embedded [...] in its own internal dynamics [,..] [l]earning from the natives, collecting words and useful phrases, and noting a few grammatical observations, these were the principal activities during an initial phase of settling in and establishing contacts. (Fabian, 1986: 76)

Collecting wordlists was hereby motivated by a striving for knowledge, and by an exoticised desire to find out about a 'missing link', a kind of justification for *l'oeuvre civilisatrice,* which would also linguistically show that many Sub-Saharan African languages were unorganised, messy and lacking structure, with only a minimum of inflectional grammar compared to European languages, and grounded in predominantly oral cultures. In his book *Out of Our Minds*, with its critical view on the madness and obsession of researchers and explorers from the Global North, Fabian (2000: 135) notes that '[t]hey blame difficulties with, and poverty of, communication with Africans on their languages.' The acquisition of language material by colonialists, therefore, often takes a positive notion of good-hearted intellectual support in order to elaborate on the linguistic material in explorers' accounts, and exoticised sounds and grammar shine through the early wordlists which were taken 'home' from Africa. Moreover, acquiring local languages served as an expression of power and Western hegemony, transforming knowledge into an institutionalised system of inequalities, as, for instance, discussed by Bauman and Briggs (2003) concerning various settings in the Global South. Very soon, colonial explorers began to 'lard their prose with native terms', as 'one of the most effective means of displaying authoritative knowledge, aside from lists and tables' (Fabian, 2000: 199), which is reminiscent of German tourists' Facebook pages nowadays, with returning travellers studding their status posts and uploading photographs under which Kiswahili words are tagged, proudly displaying their latest linguistic catch.

In analogy to the colonial and missionary documentation, the partial acquisition of an African language during one's vacation also marks a specific form of ownership over language, and an evidential strategy. The use of HMS here serves as a pinned linguistic map of where one has been, and as the 'exotic' in one's communicative repertoire of German, English and so on. There is no doubt that tourism of European travellers to destinations within Africa reveals strong analogies to the colonial explorations and orientalist myths, and it is based on discursive creations of destinations 'within the context of the historical consumption of places' (Hall & Tucker, 2004: 8). A touristic Kiswahili as an orientalist linguistic souvenir thus contributes to the production of tourist destinations along the Kenyan coast, where exotic(ised) language can be acquired, at least in its basics.

The present insight into HMS also reveals that tourists do not necessarily have to follow the grammatical rules of standard Kiswahili but can speak the basics of Kiswahili as they wish. The collected bits and pieces can be used freely and creatively, regardless of whether forms and structures are 'correct' (oriented at more standardised Kiswahili) or tarzanised, and simply, as long as the basic vocabulary is useful and can possibly reflect a nostalgic travel experience. Vitale (1980), in his study on Kisetla, quotes an article written in 1955, from the *Kenya Weekly News*, summarising the expectations of white settlers towards their African interlocutors, expressing that using the language of the colonised subject is already per se a 'condescending' and thus messy experience for the white traveller.

> If you are not at first understood, shout. If the native addressed still refuses to comprehend, it is mere contumacy and, for the sake of your superior intelligence, should be treated as such. Remember, it is his own language that you are condescending to speak to him. (J.W., *Kenya Weekly News*, 23 December 1955, cited in Vitale, 1980: 52)

Speaking in the tongues of the colonised therefore marks a liminal experience. Power relations are clear, and speaking the Other's language becomes a linguistic adventure, and not only an immersing, but also a degrading experience for the colonial traveller, which has to be rewarded by the colonised local (for instance with assiduity and obedience).

Collecting words is not necessarily always a (post)colonial practice though, but it can also be a way of accumulating or hoarding travel souvenirs, triggered by a burden of proof when it comes to journeys in remote regions of the planet. In Smith's (1989) edited volume, entitled *Hosts and Guests*, Graburn (1989), he defines the souvenirs that tourists bring along as

> tangible evidences of travel that are often shared with family and friends, but what one really brings back are memories of experiences. [...] The chosen style of tourism has its counterpart in types of souvenirs. The Environmental tourist is usually content with pictures and postcards but the Hunter and Gatherer wants rocks and sea shells, or even pieces of an

archaeologic ruin. Bolder members bring back heads of even whole animals to stuff, to testify to their vacation glory. The Ethnic tourist rarely has the opportunity to bring home the 'whole Primitive' but is content with arts or crafts, particularly if they were made by the ethnic for his/her own (preferably sacred) use. (Graburn, 1989: 33)

In regard to Graburn's list of different collectors, another category needs to be added, namely the safari tourist, who collects linguistic souvenirs, either as travel evidence, as proof of their social interaction with Kenyans or Tanzanians, or as a symbolic artefact of exploration and intellectual appropriation or simply in order to conserve a vacation mood (see also Wilkins, 2013 on tourists' souvenirs). This linguistic souvenir of HMS can theoretically be explained with Lipski's (2002) model of 'partial acquisition'. While describing pidginised or simplified forms of Spanish, lacking copulas and with little or no verbal inflection, he points out that

> this model of Spanish 'foreigner talk' has been in existence for at least 500 years and probably much longer. Nor are black Africans the only group to be branded with this type of language; at one time or another, similar reductions of Spanish have been attributed to speakers of Arabic, Berber, Chinese languages, Tagalog, Basque, French, German, English, and a variety of Native American languages. In Renaissance Spain, this was the language of the *moro* or Moor: today, it is the hands-down winner for typecasting the gringo or 'ugly American'. (Lipski, 2002: 118)

A simplified or pidginised form of Spanish, spoken by American tourists, constitutes what he calls gringo lingo ('white tourists' language'), which bears a striking resemblance to the East African HMS. Despite the many social functions of using pidginised speech with second language speakers (according to Lipski) such as being 'based on attitudes, power and influence, and urgency of communication' (Lipski, 2002: 132), he states that deliberately reduced foreigner talk (i.e. natives speaking to non-natives) takes place when natives consider the communication as essential, or have the impression that the non-natives are incapable or unwilling to speak. He points out that this usually occurs regardless of power differences or inequalities, giving examples of Spaniards using pidginised forms with Moors, Latin Americans with *gringo* expatriates, or Turks to German tourists and so on. In the present case, however, partial language acquisition is characterised by striving for (epistemic) power, compressed into tourists' apparent ownership over Kiswahili (as language collectors).

However, traveling to remote countries and immersing in a pool of linguistic diversity also results in challenged worldviews and new opinions. The acquisition of emblematic Kiswahili can therefore be more than just a collection of words, as it is paired with a strong alteration of the traveling self. The linguistic process of alteration, in this case, goes along with a bewildering stay in exotic locations, in a state of ecstasy, marking Kenya as a marginal zone of civilisation, and as the reproduced colonial wild; or in a nutshell, as Africa and all stereotypical associations with it. The alteration process is characterised by pseudo-authentic encounters and experiences, dance shows, performances at the hotel pool, forms of (sexual and narcotic) excess and of encounters with the liminal; lacking hygiene, rural poverty and, whenever possible, thrilling stories of criminality and horror (all this, admittedly, only perceived from a distance). HMS can here serve as a liberating valve: After the challenging tropical journey, which is abundant with danger, intense experiences and adventures, the basics of a newly acquired language may reproduce the vacation mood, sunshine and may also yield exoticised fantasies of Kenya/Tanzania and encounters with Kenyans/Tanzanians.

Minimal Kiswahili, Grassroots Acquisition, and Beach Learners

Tourists' interactions have diversified the Kiswahili found along the East African coast. Distinct from the Kiswahili dialects, which were formerly diffused from southern Somalia down to northern Mozambique, new fluid grassroot practices of Kiswahili have emerged. As described by Schneider (2016) for 'grassroot Englishes' in tourism, with speakers who 'have learnt English in direct interactions rather than through formal education, largely disregarding target variety orientations or concerns about linguistic correctness' (Schneider, 2016: 3), HMS also reveals a salient degree of simplification, which will be dealt with in the following sections, as well as focusing on learning and teaching practices of Kiswahili in touristic interactions. Moreover, the role of simplified Kiswahili in the linguistic landscape of the hotel resorts, its performance by hotel staff and commodification are analysed.

On the Linguistic Inventory and Grammar of Hakuna Matata Swahili

When analysing Kiswahili phrases that tourists acquire at the beach and use in online forums after their return from Kenya or Tanzania, the most common linguistic souvenirs that are found on Facebook, travel blogs and in online forums, constitute examples of phatic communication, such as greetings, terms of address and general positive statements such as *hakuna matata* ('no problem'). It is worth noting that the latter itself is a shortened and simplified form, with different etymological (folk) explanations given when asking individuals from where it has emerged. The commonly used equivalent, in non-touristic interactions, would be *hakuna shida* (a more colloquial expression), or *hakuna matatizo* in more standardised language use. Table 8.1 gives a concise overview of some of the most commonly expressions that make up tourists' HMS inventory.

As becomes evident, the first column contains what most people learn during their vacation, precisely simplified greetings, such as *jambo habari* ('hello, how are you?'), corrupted plural forms such as *rafikis* (instead of *marafiki*, 'friends') as well as the well-known adverb *pole* ('slowly'), with a range of different English translations.

Tourists' frequent question *hi nini?* ('What is that?'), is equally part of the core lexicon of touristified Kiswahili. In standard Kiswahili, by contrast, the demonstrative shows concordance with the referent it points at, varying between *hili, hiki* and so forth (for a concise overview of Kiswahili morphology, see Schadeberg, 1992, among others). When using *hi* as a demonstrative by tourists, usually no distinction in remoteness is made.

Table 8.1 The Basic Lexical Inventory of HMS

Hakuna Matata Swahili	Gloss	Derived from
hakuna matata	'no problem' (general phatic marker in guest–host interactions)	*hakuna matatizo* '(there are) no problems'
hapana	'no', 'I don't want'	*hapana* 'no'
Hi nini?	'What's this?'	*Hii ni nini?* 'What is this?'
iko	'it is'	*-ko* as variable locative copula
jambo [dʒambo/dʒɛmboʊ]	'hello, hi'	*-jambo* as Kiswahili greeting formula, used with negated subject markers
Jambo, habari (gani)?	'How are you?'	*Habari gani?* as most commonly used question about one's state of health/greeting
jambo rafikis	'hello friends'	*rafiki* (NC9), pl. *marafiki* 'friend(s)'
Kuna barafu/balafu?	'Is there/Do you have ice (for my drink)?'	*kuna* 'there is', *barafu* 'ice'
kwa heri 'bye'	'Bye!'	*kwa heri(ni)* 'Goodbye!'
lala salama 'good night'	'Good night!'	Standard Kiswahili, 'sleep well'
maisha marefu	'cheers'	Common toast expressed by people sharing a drink; exaggerated in use due to the high frequency of German *Prost!* among tourists
Mambo?	'How is it going?'	Colloquial Kiswahili
mimi nataka	'I want/give me'	*mimi* '1SG', *nataka* 'I want'
moja, mbili, tatu	'one, two, three'	Kiswahili cardinal numbers (when counting)
ndiyo	'yes'	Standard Kiswahili, 'yes'
Poa?	'How is it going?'	Colloquial Kiswahili 'cool'
pole pole	'slowly, alright, take it easy, slowly slowly'	Standard Kiswahili, 'slowly'
sawa sawa	'alright, easy, cool, no problem'	Standard Kiswahili, 'alright, okay'
Wapi cho?	'Where's the toilet?'	*Choo kiko wapi?* or *Wapi choo?* 'Where are the restrooms?'

In the course of a qualitative interview conducted with a male German tourist in his early thirties, he justified himself for only remembering a few unrelated expressions by uttering, '[I remember] the common things, sorry, nothing remained in my small brain, too much alcohol.'[5] This self-ironic view on his limited acquisition during his vacation at the East African Coast reflects a common view that a few lexical items are sufficient in order to feel like a Kiswahili speaker, or to be able to fully engage in conversations during one's vacation.

In HMS, as becomes obvious in a post in a German online forum,[6] *habari gani* ('How are you/what are the news?') may, at times, be realised as *habari guri,* without being sanctioned or criticised for representing incorrect Kiswahili. Interestingly, also the hosts, namely Kenyan Internet users in online forums, often do not comment on mistakes in Kiswahili posts, maybe due to the fact that rudimentary knowledge is, per se a salient characteristic of HMS, diffused by the hosts themselves, and then acquired by the guests.

A conversation which I witnessed one evening at the hotel bar at the Tiwi Amani Beach included a German woman who had asked the Kenyan barkeeper to hand her two more drinks. The brief interaction shows how tourists have very often mastered brief commands that they use when ordering food or drinks (see Example 1). Asking, or ordering, for the complementary all-inclusive drinks in Kiswahili seems to be a popular strategy of employing freshly acquired lexicon, and also appears to make the encounters with hotel staff, and the overall vacation experience, more authentic.

Example 1

(1) Tourist   *Gin* na *Bitter Lemon* na barafu!   ('Gin with Bitter Lemon and ice!')

Barkeeper   Hakuna *Bitter Lemon.*   ('There is no Bitter Lemon.')

Tourist   *Gin* na *Tonic* na balafu!   ('Gin with Tonic and ice!')

Barkeeper   Hatuna barafu.   ('We do not have ice.')

Tourist   *No ice?* Hakuna matata.   ('No ice? No problem.')

As can be seen in the short interaction, minimal communication held in Kiswahili is mostly limited to the beverage labels or essential terms such as *barafu* (sometimes pronounced as *balafu,* most likely as an alternative to the tap [r], which appears to be hard to pronounce for some speakers of German).

The frequent want statement *mimi nataka* ('I want'; see Table 8.1), at times accidentally realised by tourists with a metathesis **nakata,* marks the personal pronoun of the first person singular *mimi* as obligatory, which cannot be omitted. It therefore has to precede the inflected verb in HMS (see also Example 2), while in standard Kiswahili subject concord such as first person singular *na-* do not require any emphatic personal pronouns.

This feature of HMS can be considered a direct calque from German. The subject markers (*na-, u-, a-*) are often simply omitted or replaced with the emphatic personal pronoun, respectively (see Example 2).

Example 2

    (HMS)

(2) *Wewe sema Swahili?*
    2SG   speak Kisw.
    'Do you speak Kiswahili?'

Similarly, as described by Vitale (1980: 57) Kisetla makes use of a prefix *-na-*, most likely marking present tense, for all persons (see Examples 3a–b), having replaced variable subject prefixes to the verb, as used in standard Kiswahili.

Example 3

    (Kisetla, adapted from Vitale, 1980: 57)

(3a) *mimi nasikia yeye*
    1SG hear OM$_1$
    'I heard him'

(3b) *Wewe nasikia ile?*
    2SG hear DEM
    'Did you hear it?'

When using cardinal numbers, morphologically simplified forms are used. Instead of adapting numbers according to a cross-reference of the head noun to which they refer, usually expressed with prefixed subject markers, the numerals are invariably used (Example 4a), while singular and plural distinctions are not usually made, which is in contrast to standard Kiswahili (Example 4b). In Kisetla, too, numerals are also invariably used or can even replace morphological plural-marking strategies (and thus act as pluratives) (Example 4c).

Example 4

    (HMS)

(4a) *mimi na-taka pombe mbili*
    1SG 1SG-want beer two
    'I would like to have two beers'

(Standard Kiswahili)

(4b) *ni-nge-pend-a   vi-kombe vi-wili vi-a (vya) pombe*
SM$_{1SG}$-COND-love-FV NP$_8$-cup PP$_8$-two PP$_8$-CONN NC$_9$.beer
'I would like to have two beers'

(Kisetla, adapted from Vitale, 1980: 55)

(4c) *kitu moja   kitu mbili*
'one thing'   'two things'

The same is the case with qualitative adjectives (Example 5a), they are often invariable in HMS, despite their dependency upon the head noun of the noun phrase in standard Kiswahili. In the Kiswahili spoken by tourists, adjectives, such as *muzuri* ('good) and *mubaya* ('bad') are used, in addition to numerous English adjectives. Similar examples are also typical of Kisetla (Example 5b), where invariable adjectives often take the concordance patterns of noun class prefix seven (*ki*).

Example 5

(HMS)

(5a) *Gin Tonic   i-ko   muzuri*
G. T.   SM-COP   good
'(this) Gin Tonic tastes good'

(Kisetla, adapted from Vitale, 1980: 56)

(5b) *ni-li-nunua   mkate   kidogo*
SM$_{1SG}$-PAST-buy   bread   small
'I bought a small (loaf of) bread'

In Disney's animated movie *The Lion King,* a pidginised – and to some extent invented – Kiswahili is also used. The monkey Rafiki (whose name in-itself already constitutes an example of HMS with the term for 'friend' as a symbolic association with its embodied character) uses simplified and ungrammatical or unintelligible language, which is no longer standard Kiswahili (Example 6).

Example 6

(HMS)

(6) *asante   sana   squash banana   wewe   nugu   mimi   hapana*
    Thank you very   2SG   baboon   1SG   NEG
    'thanks a lot (squash banana), you-baboon, me-not'

This corrupted and banal rhyme, to be translated with 'you are a baboon, I am not' is reminiscent of infantile language. The word *nugu* is not of Kiswahili origin, but potentially stems from the Kenyan Bantu language Kikuyu or another closely-related language of the area. It is not clear whether this was actually a translation mistake that occurred with Walt Disney's language consultants, or if this was intended. The negation *mimi hapana* (supposed to mean 'me-not') reveals a pidginised structure. While a negative copula would be expected here in standard Kiswahili, the lexeme *hapana* ('no') serves as negator, which is a recurrent feature in specific varieties of Kiswahili which have been in contact with non-Bantu languages, such as Bunia Swahili from the Democratic Republic of the Congo (see Dimmendaal & Nassenstein, forthcoming) or West Nile Swahili from Uganda. Also, Vitale (1980: 57) analyses a similar simplified negation pattern for Kisetla (see Example 7), where 'verb forms are negativized by the negative element hapana'.

Example 7

(Kisetla, adapted from Vitale, 1980: 57)

(7) *mimi   hapana   anguka*
    1SG   NEG   fall
    'I will not fall'

The catchy slogan in Example (6) has, in a short time, spread all over the world, being printed on t-shirts and cups, and can be referred to as, what Halliday (2014) calls, 'The (mis)use of Kiswahili in Western popular culture'. The hosts, namely Kiswahili speakers from Kenya, have had their share in the popularisation of this simplified language practice and, in coastal areas, have themselves begun to converse with tourists using HMS.

Beach Learners, Pool Learners and Metalinguistic Exchange on Kiswahili

Language learning on the beach and in interaction with hotel staff follows its own rules, and it takes place at pools, at the breakfast buffet or in the evenings at the counters of hotel bars. As already indicated, the

Figure 8.2 Tourists and their wordlists at the pool bar (Tiwi Amani, 2017)

acquisition of basic Kiswahili can serve practical reasons of communication or can be a pastime activity in the all-inclusive resort besides solving riddles, reading tourist guides and so on, where everything is otherwise taken care of. Learning Kiswahili can be understood by learners themselves as striving for authenticity, for a specific linguistic reality beyond the artificiality of the hotel (without realising that HMS actually *is* a constructed and simplified way of speaking, and it *is* part of the all-inclusive experience). Speaking basic Kiswahili may then become part of the 'tourist gaze' (Urry, 2002), which allows immersion on the one hand and Orientalism on the other (seen from the perspective of an alleged savant with more profound insights). Apart from authentic vacation experience, language learning may symbolise one's striving for epistemic power, for ownership over language and longing for exotic accessories.

During my stay at Tiwi Beach, a German woman in her late fifties sat together with the pool bar employee James every day and scribbled down all new words in a small notebook, from which she would usually revise while relaxing in the sunshine. Her conversational partner explained me how he taught her Kiswahili day after day:

> That woman, she has a big book, she writes all the words down. I tell her 'how are you', 'good morning', 'good evening', the next day she knows it all. Some people like learning some words. (J. A., 2017)

One day, during their lesson at the pool bar, I approached them to find out more about the grassroots learning that took place at the bar and all around the resort (see Example 8).[7]

Example 8

(8) Tourist   *Sixty?*

   Barkeeper Sitini.   ('Sixty.')

NN	*Oh, you're learning Swahili… together?*	
Tourist	*Yeah* (laughs). *Seventy?*	
Barkeeper	Sabini.	('Seventy.')
Tourist	Nanini?	('Eighty?')
Barkeeper	(corrects her) Themanini.	('Eighty!')
NN	*Da sind Sie aber schon weit gekommen mit den Zahlen.*	('You have already reached far with the numerals.')
Tourist	*Wir üben ja auch schon eine Weile.*	('We have been practicing for a while now.')
NN	*Klasse, es sind ja wenige Leute, die hier Kiswahili lernen.*	('Great. There are few people here who learn Kiswahili.')
Tourist	*Ja, aber ich finde, in so einem Land kann man ja immer ein bisschen…*	('Yes, but I think in a country like this, you can always a bit…')
NN	*Stimmt.*	('Right.')
Tourist	(to barkeeper) *When I met the young lady at the soup, I asked* Habari? *She says* Nzuri sana! *and then? She asked me …*	
Barkeeper	Na wewe?	('And you?')
Tourist	*I don't think it was* Na wewe? *– Can you write it?* (barkeeper writes it down) *In that moment, I don't have a pencil. And when I don't have a pencil and can't write it down, I have forgotten.* (to me) *Ja, es fing an, im Prinzip, when I made – damit er das auch versteht – Water Gymnastik, they count. So I heard the first numbers, and I asked him, and so we learnt together.*	(' … yes, it all actually started when – so that he can also understand – I did water aerobics …')
NN	*It's rare to see someone really trying, because usually the things people know are only this* hakuna matata*…*	

Tourist	...*maybe* habari ...
NN	Yes, *maybe* habari. *But maybe it's always good to take something home?*
Tourist	*Yes! Ten years ago, when I were the first time in Kenya, eh, we had every day a Swahili lesson in the hotel. After ten years, I forgot. Everything.*
NN	*Yes, of course. But that's nice. And I think you have a good teacher!*
Tourist	(laughs) *Yes, I have, I have. I can tell everyone my room number, and they are all impressed.*
NN	*So ten years ago the Swahili classes were organised by the hotel?*
Tourist	*Yes, in Dominican Republic and Mexico, it's also, some hotels, they have water aerobic, dart, and they also have a lesson of their language. Same way, I have learnt a lot of Spanish.*
Barkeeper	*They used to have Swahili class here, too.*

The brief interview with the German lady and the barkeeper at the pool bar, who acts as her informal Kiswahili teacher, shows how important writing is in these contexts. Kiswahili can, building on a European tradition of language acquisition in formalised contexts of language classes, only be acquired when newly learnt words enter notebooks, are scribbled down and revised later. In a materialised form, they turn into useful and tangible souvenirs, mastered by the eagerly learning tourist, and into linguistic artefacts (see Blommaert, 2008). When uttered over a soup, without being written down, they remain meaningless, strange, unintelligible. Moreover, the brief conversation clarifies how basic language learning has become (a commodified) part of the vacation experience in contexts of package tourism, as if Spanish learnt by the pool in Mexico or Kiswahili acquired in Mombasa, individualised the travel experience. Hotels thus offer language classes in order to satisfy the seemingly intellectual hunger of tourists, who aim to immerse themselves in the local culture and language.

Figure 8.3 *Moja, mbili, tatu* – Beach learners (Tiwi beach, 2017)

Other tourists strive for more complexity and are not content with a handful of emblematic expressions but attempt to memorise entire sentences or grammatical forms. Figure 8.3 shows a Ukrainian woman at Tiwi Beach, revising notes from her Kiswahili class. The heading 'Swahili Classes' reveals that the endeavour is taken seriously, and some of the example sentences demonstrate that some of them were translated from other pocket guides into Kiswahili (such as 'we are staying for two weeks' and 'thank you for your help,' among others).[8]

Metalinguistic exchange about Kiswahili is important in order to show how deeply a tourist has already become immersed within the surrounding cultural sphere. This is achieved through guessing games, what specific Kiswahili words could potentially mean or where one had already potentially come across Kiswahili terms in popular (German) culture. Example 9 shows the conversation of several German tourists in the hotel pool, where HMS is discussed and alleged knowledge is shared. Very often these words or expressions stem from the few early TV productions which were diffused on German television or from romantic popular novels.

Example 9

(9) Tourist 1 *Kennen Sie ein paar Swahiliworte?* ('Do you know some words of Kiswahili?')

Tourist 2 *Jambo.*

Tourist 3 *Hakuna matata.*

Tourist 1 *… ein ganz berühmtes, aus einem Film?* ('… a very famous one, out of a movie?')

Tourist 2 *Nee.* ('Nah.')

Tourist 1	Hatari, hatari *heißt 'Gefahr'. Und, was noch?... Daktari!*	('Hatari, hatari means 'danger'. And, what else? ... Daktari!')
Tourist 2	*Ah,* daktari.	('Ah, daktari.')
Tourist 1	Daktari, *das ist der Tierarzt. Da kennen wir schon zwei Wörter aus unserer Literaturvergangenheit.*	('Daktari, that's the 'vet'. There we already know two words from our literary past.')

In the short exchange on Kiswahili knowledge and grassroots acquisition, it becomes obvious that one's own vacation experience is directly related to images of East Africa that were produced for television with a strong colonial taste, such as CBS's family drama *Daktari* from 1966, focusing on wildlife and white protagonists' adventures in a natural African setting. A tourist's travel becomes therefore directly linked to a pervasive idealised copy of Africa made in Hollywood.[9]

Teaching HMS in the All-Inclusive Resort: Commodified and Performed Language

Language in the tourism sector, however, is not uniquely about beach language learning but also about beach teachers and their practices. Speaking and teaching Kiswahili is known to be part of the touristic experience, and some of the staff such as bartenders, pool attendants (often called 'pool boys') and restaurant waiters do not only serve beverages, food or help with towels, but also provide snippets of Kiswahili. In Example 10, an elderly woman slowly approached the pool bar at Tiwi Amani and was greeted by the Kenyan bartender in Kiswahili.

Example 10

(10)	Barkeeper	Jambo. Unataka nini?	('Hello. What do you desire?')
	Tourist	*I want a beer, please. A cold one.*	
	Barkeeper	(serves beer silently)	
	Tourist	*Danke.*	('Thank you.')

James, the barkeeper at the Mbuyuni Pool Bar, when asked in an interview what he thought about HMS, stated that he did not mind it and would at times also use it, when it appeared to be suitable, and when pleasing tourists who were interested in learning some Kiswahili words. Using it would help to create a positive atmosphere and build good relationships with the guests (and might also result in some much-needed tips, given the low salaries of most of the hotel staff). Using HMS may also make the encounter easier, due to the fact that only basic and necessary communication is exchanged, and that performance comes into play. Hotel workers can turn into actors who play along as part of the paper-maché scenery in which the postcolonial safari play is performed for tourists.

All in all, the hotel offers touristified Kiswahili as part of the overall all-inclusive experience, which can be seen in the restaurant areas of specific hotels along the beaches of the Kenyan South Coast. Around the vast buffet area of the Tiwi Amani Beach Resort small signposts were attached to the plants and samples of staple foods such as beans (*maharagwe*), see Figure 8.4. This allowed the foreign guest to engage not only in the apparently exotic shows and evening events, such as Maasai dances or acrobatics, but to also discover the East African coast in a culinary manner, served by white-liveried staff.

Figure 8.4 Swahili translations of plants offered in the hotel restaurant

This accoutrement of the touristified space also affects the menus of bars and restaurants, for instance, 'Hakuna Matata' is also the name of a non-alcoholic drink which is served in numerous hotels along the coast. Containing only passion fruit juice, grenadine syrup and ice, it is actually as 'unproblematic' as its name, regardless of the amount of one's consumption. As explained by a Kenyan bartender, the drink is very popular, to some extent specifically because of its name, since this would insinuate 'no problem, no hangover' (B.A. 2017, interview excerpt). Kiswahili is consumed excessively, just like the free drinks, buffet food and other 'all inclusive' offerings, and is, moreover, often sold in the form of exoticised souvenirs; it can also be interpreted as a specific type of lifestyle, beyond all sorrows and problems. According to one German tourist, whom I interviewed at Tiwi Beach, *hakuna matata* means more than simply 'no problem', but stands for a specific Kenyan mentality:

I like the Hakuna Matata, *leben und leben lassen* ('to live and let live'), but Kenyan work is not like German work, *es ist halt nicht das gleiche* ('it is just not the same'). (T. 2017, interview excerpt)

The slogan here turns into the characterisation of the absolute Other with apparent laziness, inefficiency and a form of southern lethargy. While *hakuna matata* often seems to serve as a performance, masque and tourist play (performed by hotel staff, beach boys as a comforting strategy of the foreign visitors), it may also be conceptualised and mistaken by tourists as a lifestyle, as a way of living a laid-back way and laisser-faire, marking a highly controversial concept (see also Mietzner, 2017).

HMS is very prominent in linguistic landscapes around the resort, too. Strategically placed trees planted for return-guest are meant to encourage visitors to come back the following year. Some hotels, with a high number of these signposts on their lawn between pools and restaurants, look like gigantic graveyards, with travellers' names, travel memories and simplified bits of acquired Kiswahili buried in the garden areas (see Figure 8.5).

The shops in hotel resorts, the airport and touristic core areas of Mombasa, such as Fort Jesus, all offer items for sale which are decorated with commodified HMS. Apart from these Kiswahili souvenirs printed on t-shirts, photographs, *kitenge* fabrics sold in hotels or along the beach, the global '*Lion King*' industry has turned Kiswahili into a fashionable item that is found in abundance all around the globe. Moreover, HMS is increasingly tattooed onto travellers' bodies (cf. Nassenstein & Rüsch, 2017), who may have *sawa sawa* ('alright') inked on their legs or, for instance, an image of the lion cub from Disney's movie paired with a playfully drawn *hakuna matata*. This sort of inerasable body modification represents a special form of embodied linguistic souvenir.

Figure 8.5 Tourist trees, planted as a reward for return-guests at the resort (Tiwi Amani Beach Resort, 2017)

It is increasingly common to hear HMS used in and around the hotel pools, not just by the hotel workers, but also by the growing number of home-grown Kenyan tourists; used within a group of friends as a way of mocking other tourists or as a sort of linguistic fashion. While tourists to the East African coast used to originate from Europe, with a large number of them coming from Germany, Austria, Switzerland and Italy, the increasing attacks of the Somalian Al-Shabaab militia in coastal areas has had an impact and reduced the numbers of European tourists. Kenyan tourists, especially from Nairobi, have thereafter replaced them in some of the beach resorts. In my field diary I summarised my observation of a group of young Kenyan tourists in the pool as follows:

> Kenyan tourists in hotel pool in front of Mbuyuni Bar, pulling each other in the water. Guys pulling girls on inflatable toy, they all use simple Kiswahili: *"Pole pole."* *"Eh, pole pole."* Another one replies *"Twende safarini!"* [Let's go on a safari!] Laughter in the group. A girl imitates a European accent: *"Unataka ona lion?"* [Do you want to see a lion?] Whole group bursts out laughing. (Tiwi Amani Beach Resort, 10 March 2017)

While at first sight HMS appears to be owned by the visitors only, enabling tourists from the Global North to acquire apparent authenticity in the touristic encounter, and serving as a pleasurable linguistic souvenir, a second interpretation of roles and motivation is possible. The diffusion and mantra-like repetition of simplified sentences by sex workers, hotel employees, beach vendors or Kenyan tourists (see the previously mentioned) can be understood as a postcolonial critique. The use of HMS criticises tourists, marks them as the Others, and it gives us a glimpse of how the colonial explorers viewed African languages, as tarzanised speech, as 'baby talk', or as linguistic practices too unorganised to be prescriptively rectified. This 'foreigner talk' (Lipski, 2005) is not only based on urgency in communication, but it changes the perspective and redirects the lens of Othering, through which the Northern tourist often sees the allegedly exotic southerner, who provides the northern guest with a linguistic repertoire of 'baby talk'. Instead of requiring exoticised vocabulary and linguistic souvenirs, (s)he acquires a deconstructed version of his/her own language ideology, tarzanised and twisted. A Kiswahili speaker from Tanzania argued that the form of Kiswahili produced by locals towards tourists could possibly serve as a critique and emblematic simplified form, stating

> I would never say *pole pole, hakuna matata*. It's *hakuna shida*. That's just for tourists. [...] Yes, it might be possible that they are aware that the constant repetition of *pole pole, hakuna matata* gets on people's nerves... anyhow, I think they do it in the first place to teach them some basics, and maybe it sounds cute to them. (A. B. 2016)

It can therefore hypothetically be assumed that the hosts mimetically employ HMS in order to mark the tourist as the Other, who then learns the word or catchy phrase and marks himself/herself, unknowingly, as a rudimentary learner, who will never come close to being an authentic speaker of Kiswahili. The underlying language ideologies of keeping standard Kiswahili and HMS apart can be a meaningful strategy of differentiation. Keeping the linguistic resources of one's repertoire apart, using more standardised Kiswahili among friends or at home, while speaking HMS with tourists (and teaching HMS in the resort), can be seen as a form of colonial mimesis. Standard Kiswahili, elaborated in the colonial system, now constitutes the epistemic power of the ostracised East African over the safari tourist, who speaks and performs the pidginised and infantile language. This play with mock forms of simplified language also has an indexical value. Referring to colonialists' modalities of acquisition, Errington (2008: 96) states that

> [b]ut to acquire the languages they needed for that work, they had to engage with the lives of those languages' speakers in their entirety, what one American missionary more recently referred to in the jargon of social science as 'the totality of a social system'. To refuse full engagement with a community would produce linguistic knowledge as a broken, pidgin idiom [...]

Tourists in the coastal resorts do not fully engage with the local population. Shared social practices are restricted to business transactions, at times to even barter with/trade worn socks or underwear for drinks or carved handicrafts, transactions which contain a strong neo-colonial image. In the worst cases, the sharing of social practices and local engagement is limited to sexual intercourse. According to Errington's (2008) idea, a very limited engagement in social activities, with a lack of empathy and will to integrate, will necessarily limit the colonialist's – or here, the tourist's – repertoire to a simplified emblematic reflection of his own avoidance of social interaction and integration. The use of HMS by Kenyans in the hotel resorts thus reflects a critical assessment of the tourists' interactions with their surroundings, as seen from a postcolonial angle, and confronting them with their own discursive ruins.

Learning and speaking German versus learning and speaking basic Kiswahili evokes critical questions about valuing languages according to common hegemonic views. Knowing 'good German' in the tourism sector seems to be much more essential and more valued in contrast to knowing 'good Kiswahili', which rather constitutes as a linguistic luxury or an exotic souvenir. At one coastal resort pool, I was able to observe two elderly German ladies who exchanged ideas about their safari guide, who had organised a trip for them, and about his language skills, summarising '[d]a ist Rashid, der hat uns alles organisiert. Er spricht gut

Deutsch. Was heißt gut? Nicht richtig gut. Aber er versteht und er kann mit dir sprechen.' ('there is Rashid, he organised everything for us. He speaks good German. Well, what is 'good'? Not really good. But he understands and can speak to you.'). The assumption that the Kenyan conversational partner speaks only basic German seems to legitimise the speaker's use of *du*, an informal term of address in German, instead of the more formal *Sie*. Using this informal term of address is common practice in the guest/host interaction within the resorts.

Looki Looki for Jiggi Jiggi: On Language and Sex Tourism

The twofold distinction of banal touristic expressions and sexualised language seems to be surprising at first sight, but makes sense when considering that, especially along the East African coast, fluid language practice is often bound to genderising language, to language acquired through sexual encounters (Nassenstein, 2016) and bound to business transactions. This is by no means a recent phenomenon, based only on the increasing sex tourism on Kenya's coast (see Kibicho, 2009; Kiungu-Neu, 2012), but can also be seen as being grounded in colonial foundations, as becomes evident when reading Fabian's (2000: 81–82) account of Jêrome Becker's (1997) interrelatedness of sexual exploitation and language acquisition, showing a clear connection between sex and language.

> Our joyful and frequent exchanges with the dames d'honneur of the chief of Konko, our increasingly intimate relations with the natives, our conversations with the men of our escort and our studies, assisted by the immediate help we had from our personal servants, appointed language teachers, made me amazingly competent in the Swahili dialect. Already [around September 1881] I no longer need an interpreter (2: 51). The transition from erotic banter to serious language study that Becker describes puts 'sex' into a perspective of close social relations that were vital to the enterprise of exploration. The intimate and relatively lasting relations some of the explorers seem to have had with African women were not necessarily limited to the satisfaction of sexual needs. They were part of daily life, of days filled with travel and domestic chores that had to be planned and discussed with companions, male and female. (Fabian, 2000: 81–82, quoting Becker, 1887)

Similar relations between language exchange and sex work become obvious when analyzing the most common sex talk in online forums, where European sex tourists to the Kenyan coast share stories and pictures, and where lexical items from Kiswahili and Kenyan English are equally shared, as a form of sexualised souvenirs (see Table 8.2).

Among the most frequent items are *mzungu* or the variation *langzeitmzungu*, as well as terms that should serve as a compliment such as *pendeza sana, nakupenda* or *muzuri sana* and the term *amiga* for female sex workers, with *boyfriend* as the male equivalent. Also *butterfly* and *malaya* ('female sex worker') are included among the recurrent terms that can be heard in the beach areas, and the pidginised *looki for jiggi jiggi* ('looking out for sex') stands out as an emblematic term for 'sexual intercourse'.

Some of the listed sexualised terms are furthermore found in the following brief narrative, taken from an online travel blog (my emphasis):

> Da ich von Natur aus sehr neugierig bin und auch ein wenig swahili spreche habe ich die Storys aus erster Hand erfahren. Da war Cindy von Nairobi, ihr afrikanischer *Boyfriend* fand einen Studienplatz in Deutschland. Also ging sie nach Mombasa fand einen *Mzungu*, der sie auch prompt nach Germany einlud. Sie sagte mir, eine Woche nett sein zu ihm reichte ihr finanziell, dann kaufte sie sich ne Fahrkarte und fand ihren *Boyfriend*, zwar mit einer anderen im Bett, aber sie konnte bei ihm untertauchen. Stellah, eine andere *Malaya* aus Mtwapa, kam nach Berlin. Ja aber was sollte sie den ganzen Tag machen wenn ihr *Mzungu* auf Arbeit war?

Table 8.2 Sexualised linguistic souvenirs in HMS

Hakuna Matata Swahili	Gloss	Derived from
mzungu	'white person, rich person, foreign person'	*mzungu* 'white person'
langzeitmzungu	'retired white people who have no contact with Africans apart from their bed companions; returning sex tourist'[10]	*mzungu* ('European, white') and German *lange Zeit* 'long time', also used in Coasti slang by beach boys (Nassenstein 2016)
pendeza sana	'beautiful, good-looking' (adjectival use)	*kupendeza sana* 'to appeal to somebody very much'
jambo nakupenda	'hello beautiful/hello lovely' (term of address)	*jambo* as common greeting (see Table 8.1) and *nakupenda* 'I love you'
amiga	'female sex worker'	Italian *amica* 'female friend', most probably used in Malindi, North Coast
boyfriend	'male sex worker'	English
muzuri sana	'very nice, very beautiful (woman)'	*nzuri sana* 'very good' with inserted epenthetic vowel, making the word allegedly easier to pronounce for speakers with limited practice
butterfly	'occasional sex worker'	euphemism, English (flying from flower to flower)
malaya	'occasional sex worker'	*malaya* 'prostitute'
looki looki for jiggi jiggi	'looking out for sex, sex-seeking'	*looky* 'to look' in vendor-customer encounters worldwide; *jiggi* 'onomatopoetic word denoting the sexual act'

Fernsehen? Sie konnte ja kaum ein Wort deutsch. Also *looki for jiggi jiggi* und siehe da, da kann man ja richtig Kohle machen hier in Deutschland.

[Since I am very curious by nature and also speak a bit of swahili I got to know the stories at first hand. There was Cindy from Nairobi, her African boyfriend found an occasion to study in Germany. So she went to Mombasa, found a *Mzungu*, who invited her then to Germany. She told me to be nice to him for one week would be sufficient financially, then she bought a ticket and found her boyfriend, well, with another girl in bed, but she could stay with him. Stellah, another whore from Mtwapa, came to Berlin. But what was she supposed to do all day long when *Mzungu* was at work? Watching TV? She could barely speak a word of German. So just *looki for jiggi jiggi* and behold, you can really make some cash with that in Germany.][11]

In the quoted example, *mzungu* is used as a self-ironic label, through which mutual Othering processes between hosts and guests (or sex workers and sex tourists) are made visible. Language, and especially derogatory HMS terms, no longer serve as travel evidence or pleasant souvenirs, as shown in the preceding paragraphs, but as a strategy of verbal marginalisation. The potential for disappointment around false promises, intercultural problems beyond the vacation romance or quick sexual encounters, and the general inequalities concerning the encounters of sex tourists with sex workers, are reflected in some of the terms. While specific lexemes, such as *butterfly*, constitute euphemistic ways of referring to sex workers, the pidginised *looki for jiggi jiggi* does not mark the limited proficiency of the tourist, but ostracises the Kenyan Kiswahili speaker, whose simplified language use appears infantile.

The terminology used in online forums and in exchanges among sex tourists shows the inherent potential of Orientalism in touristic interactions in a postcolonial world (see Hall & Tucker, 2004), and takes the collected linguistic souvenirs discussed in the preceding sections a step further, providing a basis for exclusion and ostracism.

Concluding Thoughts

This chapter has intended to provide a first insight into simplified Kiswahili as learnt, taught and used in the tourism sector in East Africa. Discussed both in terms of its value as a touristic souvenir for European travellers, in analogy with the colonial practices of Northern 'explorers' and as a sexualised linguistic practice resulting from an increasing sex tourism on the Kenyan coast (cf. Kibicho, 2009), HMS has been analyzed as a recent linguistic phenomenon bound to package tourism and to the apparent ideologies of minimal language acquisition in host-guest interactions.

Starting off from this preliminary view on simplified language practice as a linguistic souvenir, and as part of an all-inclusive performance in hotel resorts, more profound studies will need to focus on language in relation to processes of touristic commodification, especially in regard to Kiswahili. The sociolinguistics of tourism, a rather recent field of study (as it seems when considering the paucity of extensive ethnographic studies), still requires a stronger focus on the beach and hotel areas as salient sociolinguistic contact zones.

In this regard, it may be specifically helpful to assess the impact of sex tourism as a driving force for sociolinguistic change along the East African coast. Moreover, it will be essential to include postcolonial approaches to language in upcoming studies on language variation and touristic interactions in beach areas, taking into consideration the colonial mimesis, language ideologies and linguistic performance of the various actors in the tourism sector.

Notes

(1) See https://www.bunchofbackpackers.com/basic-swahili/ (accessed 12 December 2017).
(2) Kiswahili and Swahili both stand for the same language. While Kiswahili [sw] is the full language name with a nominal prefix *ki-* denoting 'language', Swahili is a shortened form that has been increasingly used over the last century and is known as a widespread abbreviation. In this paper, Kiswahili is used when no specific dialect of the language is referred to, while Hakuna Matata Swahili or Kenyan Swahili usually carry the shortened label.
(3) Whilst I assume authorship of the designation *Hakuna Matata Swahili*, this label was rather the result of numerous inspiring conversations with my interlocutors, Wilson and Tela at Bamburi Beach, Amadou from Tiwi Beach, as well as with colleagues from the University of Cologne, first and foremost the editors of the present volume. However, the label does not attempt to imply that Hakuna Matata Swahili is a language on its own, nor a distinctive variety of Kiswahili, but rather it represents a fluid touristified practice that is recurrent along the East African coast.
(4) As already stated, I am particularly grateful to Anne Storch and Angelika Mietzner for all inspiration and shared valuable ideas. Moreover, I warmly thank all interlocutors during two research stays at the Kenyan coast at Bamburi Beach (North Coast) and along Tiwi Beach (South Coast). I am grateful to Agnes Brühwiler, Maren Rüsch and Drulvin Carl. First and foremost, I am indebted to Vivianne for accompanying me to Kenya, assisting and constantly inspiring me. Zoë Braven-Giles is warmly thanked for correcting my English. However, the common disclaimers apply.
(5) In German, he uttered „*das Übliche (...), sorry, in meinem kleinen Hirn ist nix hängen geblieben, zuviel Alkohol*' (S. S., 2016).
(6) See http://www.reisebineforum.de (accessed April 2016).
(7) While all German sentences are translated into English, the tourists' English, as used by German travelers, has not been modified in terms of grammar or choice of words in order to keep it as authentic as possible. This explains certain apparent mistakes.
(8) Moreover, this seems to be the handwriting of somebody from Kenya. This means that sheets with the most essential sentences and phrases are already prepared for language classes, or they may be sold to interested tourists. While I first thought that these were handwritten notes by the tourist, it can actually be assumed that some classes are very well organised with distributed papers and listed sentences based

on the intended use. I am particularly grateful to Angelika Mietzner for sharing this observation with me.
(9) See http://www.imdb.com/title/tt0059977/ (accessed 10 December 2017).
(10) Both of the latter are taken from the website http://ninahmouse.de, and were then translated into English (by myself).
(11) See http://ninahmouse.de/index.html (accessed 28 April 2016).

References

Bauman, R. and Briggs, C.L. (2003) *Voices of Modernity. Language Ideologies and the Politics of Inequality.* Cambridge: Cambridge University Press.
Becker, J. (1887) *La vie en Afrique; ou trois ans dans l'Afrique centrale.* Brussels: J. Lebègue.
Blommaert, J. (2008) Artefactual ideologies and the textual production of African languages. *Language & Communication* 28, 291–307.
Dimmendaal, G.J. and Nassenstein, N. (forthcoming) Bunia Swahili and emblematic language use. *Journal of Language Contact.*
Errington, J. (2008) *Linguistics in a Colonial World. A Story of Language, Meaning and Power.* Malden: Blackwell.
Fabian, J. (1986) *Language and Colonial Power: The Appropriation of Swahili in the Former Belgian Congo 1880–1938.* Berkeley, CA: University of California Press.
Fabian, J. (2000) *Out of our Minds: Reason and Madness in the Exploration of Central Africa.* Berkeley, CA: University of California Press.
Graburn, N.H.H. (1989) Tourism: The sacred journey. In V.L. Smith (ed.) *Hosts and Guests. The Anthropology of Tourism* (pp. 21–36). Philadelphia, PA: The University of Pennsylvania Press.
Hall, C.M. and Tucker, H. (2004) Tourism and postcolonialism: An introduction. In C.M. Hall and H. Tucker (eds) *Tourism and Postcolonialism: Contested Discourses, Identities and Representations* (pp. 1–24). London: Routledge.
Heine, B. (1973) *Pidgin-Sprachen im Bantubereich.* Berlin: Dietrich Reimer.
Jaworski, A. and Thurlow, C. (2010) Language and the globalising habitus of tourism: Toward a sociolinguistics of fleeting relationships. In N. Coupland (ed.) *The Handbook of Language and Globalization* (pp. 255–286). Oxford: Blackwell.
Kibicho, W. (2009) *Sex Tourism in Africa. Kenya's Booming Industry.* Burlington, VT: Ashgate Publishing.
Kiungu-Neu, S.W. (2012) Colonial ideologies in tourism: Examples from Kenya. B.A thesis, University of Cologne.
LeBreton, F.H. (1936) *Up-Country Swahili: For the Soldier, Settler, Miner, Merchant and their Wives, and for All who Deal with Up-Country Natives without Interpreters.* Richmond: Simpson.
Lipski, J.M. (2002) 'Partial' Spanish. Strategies of pidginization and simplification (from Lingua Franca to 'Gringo Lingo'). In C.R. Wiltshire and J. Camps (eds) *Romance Phonology and Variation: Selected Papers from the 30th Linguistic Symposium on Romance Languages,* Gainesville, Florida February 2000 (pp. 117–143). Amsterdam: Benjamins.
Lüpke, F. and Storch, A. (2013) *Repertoires and Choices in African Languages.* Berlin: Mouton de Gruyter.
Mietzner, A. (2016) North meets South: Moral threat, shame, disgust and Kenya's sex tourism. Paper presented at the Workshop on Disgust, University of Cologne, 15–16 February 2016.
Mietzner, A. (2017) The Hakuna matata tourist. Paper presented at the conference *The Other's Other: Performance and Representation in Language,* Cologne, Germany, September 25–26.
Möhlig, W.J.G. (1995) Swahili Dialekte. In W.J.G. Möhlig and G. Miehe (eds) *Swahili Handbuch* (pp. 41–62). Cologne: Köppe.

Nassenstein, N. (2016) Mombasa's Swahili-based 'Coasti Slang' in a super-diverse space: Languages in contact on the beach. *African Study Monographs* 37 (3), 117–143.

Nassenstein, N. and Rüsch, M. (2017) Skinscape souvenirs and globalized bodies: Tattoo tourism and body art as travel narratives. Paper presented at the *Tattoo Workshop*, Morphomata/University of Cologne, 1–2 December 2017.

Phipps, A. (2007) *Learning the Arts of Linguistic Survival: Languaging, Tourism, Life.* Clevedon: Channel View Publications.

Schadeberg, T. (1992) *A Sketch of Swahili Morphology.* Cologne: Köppe.

Schneider, E.W. (2016) Grassroots Englishes in tourism interactions. *English Today* 32(3), 2–10.

Thurlow, C. and Jaworski, A. (2010) *Tourism Discourse. Language and Global Mobility.* London: Palgrave Macmillan.

Urry, J. (2002) *The Tourist Gaze.* London: Sage.

Vitale, A. (1980) KiSetla: Linguistic and sociolinguistic aspects of a Pidgin Swahili in Kenya. *Anthropological Linguistics* 22, 47–65.

Wiegand, F.K. and Knapp, M. (2014) Wild inside: Uncanny encounters in European traveller fantasies of Africa. In D. Picard and M.A. Di Giovine (eds) *Tourism and the Power of Otherness: Seductions of Difference* (pp. 158–175). Bristol: Channel View Publications.

Wilkins, H. (2013) Souvenirs and self-identity. In J. Cave, L. Jolliffe and T. Baum (eds) *Tourism and Souvenirs: Glocal Perspectives from the Margins* (pp. 40–48). Bristol: Channel View Publications.

Web Addresses

Bunch of Backpackers website at https://www.bunchofbackpackers.com/Halliday, C. (2014) The (mis)use of Kiswahili in Western popular culture. Accessed 30 May 2016. http://thisisafrica.me/misuse-kiswahili-western-popular-culture/

Lipski, J. (2005) "Me want cookie": Foreigner talk as monster talk. Unpublished manuscript. Accessed 21 October 2017. http://www.personal.psu.edu/jml34/monster.pdf

Ninahmouse. Accessed 28 April 2016. http://ninahmouse.de/index.html

Abbreviations

COND	conditional
CONN	connective
COP	copula
DEM	demonstrative
FV	final vowel
HMS	Hakuna Matata Swahili
NEG	negation
NP$_1$	nominal prefix 1
OM	object marker
PAST	past tense
PP	pronominal prefix
SG	singular
SM	subject marker

Afterword: Between Silence and Noise: Towards an Entangled Sociolinguistics of Tourism

Adam Jaworski

Setting the Scene

The starting point of my reflections on the preceding chapters comes from Angelika Mietzner and Anne Storch's Introduction, where they comment on tourism, especially in postcolonial contexts, as a bundle of historically rooted entanglements – linguistic, ideological and economic – which require the sociolinguistics of tourism to turn its attention 'to the settings in which the discovery of ourselves as well as the production of the Other takes place – contexts of power inequalities, resistance and subversion, social injustice and struggle' (Mietzner and Storch[1]). This is a demanding but increasingly urgent task; we need to engage more widely and systematically with questions of our own self-positionality *vis-à-vis* the people, practices and places of the tourist sites we choose to study and write about.

Many chapter authors provide self-reflexive food for thought by thematising their own positions, perceptions and practices while conducting fieldwork, interacting with informants (both tourists and hosts), and writing up their research. Christiane M. Bongartz problematises her own motivations for directing her analytic gaze towards specific types of linguistic displays, and not others. Her focus on the linguistic landscape of Jamaica is firmly set on the manifestations of what she perceives as localness, non-standardness, difference and exoticism, which, by her own admission, risks leading her to interpret Jamaica as 'local', 'non-standard', 'different' and 'exotic'. Luís Cronopio experiments with academic writing as genre by eschewing a typical scholarly format for his critique of backpacking in favour of a more personal, dramaturgic piece of writing that unfolds the stages of being a 'backpacker' who belongs to the privileged class of a globally mobile elite (cf. Doorne & Ateljevic, 2005). Tawona Sitholé and Alison Phipps subvert the academic essay genre further by resorting to poetry, which, unlike academic writing, is typically valued for its ambiguity. In this sense, poetry may well be a viable response to the relative impenetrability of the 'noise of history' residing in, and the 'silence of awe' arising from, tourist visits at former slave trading posts in West Africa. Sara Zavaree describes her own preparations to witness the performance of a Zār ceremony of spiritual healing on Hormoz Island, one brought to Iran by Africans in the 19th century. She deliberates whether her integrity as a researcher is compromised as her search for anthropological verisimilitude gets mixed up with the anticipation of a therapeutic fix alongside other middle-class internationals flocking to the show.

Remaining contributions to the volume continue asking difficult questions about the linguistic, ideological and economic entanglements of tourism by juxtaposing linguistic forms and their use in relation to social structure as mediated by linguistic and cultural ideologies – or what Silverstein (1985) has termed the 'total linguistic fact'. Angelika Mietzner turns her anthropological (and photographic) lens onto philanthropic German tourists in rural Kenya who are seeking encounters with the beneficiaries of their charitable giving only to find themselves mediating these encounters through set performances, exchanges of limited formulaic expressions, and distancing themselves from their potential interlocutors by another mediational tool – the photographic camera. In the end, it's the photographic record of the trip that becomes the trip's own rationale and key evidence justifying future philanthropic-touristic activity. Such charitable trips cannot alleviate the sharp divisions between the touring and the toured. 'One cruel result of the twentieth century's mobility is the transformation of poor regions into stage sets on which their citizens act like the forebears for the benefit of those who feel superior because they have lost touch with their own backgrounds' (Lippard, 1999: 34). And it's clear that the self-perception of philanthropic tourists – with their good intentions and righteous motivation to travel – does not always match their perception by hosts. Bruner (1996) comments on the ironies of the mostly wealthy, middle-class African Americans visiting the former slave trade post at Elmina Castle in Ghana. The tourists who come to Ghana in a quest for their roots are typically perceived by Ghanaians as economically better off – and, in a sense, better off for having had their ancestors taken as slaves.

> The situation is full of ironies. When diaspora blacks return to Africa, the Ghanaians call them *obruni*, which means 'whiteman,' but the term is extended to Europeans, Americans, and Asians regardless of skin color, so it also has a meaning of foreigner. This second meaning is also ironic, since the diaspora blacks see themselves as returning 'home.' So the term *obruni* labels the African Americans as both white and foreign, whereas they see themselves as black and at home. (Bruner, 1996: 295)

Thus, Richards (2005) argues, despite African-American tourists seeing themselves as family members returning to a welcoming home, the former slave trade centres must be seen as postcolonial contact zones (Pratt, 1992) with many disparate histories, competing representations and interpretations.

Anne Storch examines Seaford Town, Jamaica, a heritage (or heritagised) site populated by the descendants of German migrants who were brought there in the 1830s after the Slavery Abolition Act of 1833 had created a shortage of labour on plantations. This group of effectively enslaved migrants and their disadvantaged descendants are positioned by typical tourism texts – such as guidebooks, travelogues, blogs, tourist comments and so on – as 'freaks', the ultimate 'Other'. The role of these texts in framing objects of display (whether people or artefacts) is not a new phenomenon: 'The priority of objects over texts in museum settings was reversed during the second half of the 19th century. [Dr George Brown Goode, director of the US National Museum] operated according to the dictum "the most important thing about an exhibition was the label [Goode, 1989: 433]"' (Kirshenblatt-Gimblett, 1998: 30). In other words, museum exhibitions, folkloric festivals, displays of religious or secular rituals, cultural or ethnic 'living villages' and so on, whether exhibiting people or objects, are 'guided by a poetics of detachment, in the sense not only of material fragments but also of a distanced attitude. The question is not whether an object is of visual interest, but rather how interest of any kind is created. All interest is vested' (Kirshenblatt-Gimblett, 1998: 30). This is why we cannot just collect our data and display it back to our audiences, academic or otherwise, without any commentary. What we write as academic papers and book chapters are the labels we then use for exhibits in our printed 'museums' of data. By taking on the role of ethnographer–linguist–tourist, we also take on responsibility for our actions; detachment from our informants, sites, objects and data is not an option (Bongartz). We need to take a stand and go on the record with our own privilege, complicity and benefit from the work (Thurlow & Jaworski, 2010, 2017). 'There is no "view from nowhere," no gaze that is not positioned' (Irvine & Gal, 2000: 36). Or, as argued by Mitchell (1986: 38), '…there is no vision without purpose…the innocent eye is blind' for the 'world is already clothed in our system of representation'.

Power Inequalities

The semiotic, intangible nature of the consumables produced by and for the tourism industry has long been acknowledged. A myriad of signs and texts or metacultural displays that mediate and mediatise culture, heritage, landscape and the local 'Other' are caught up in complex, dynamic processes of self- and other-positioning by hosts and tourists – whether it's tokens of language (Bongartz; Nassenstein), interactions (Cronopio; Mietzner), narratives, memories, and voices (Sitholé; Phipps; Storch; Vitorio), or rituals (Zavaree). And there is no way of getting away from the fact that, other things being equal, the tourist experience is always part of an economic contract. For tourists, access to locals is overwhelmingly not a 'free good' (Goffman, 1967). Even the apparent ethos of egalitarianism of backpacker tourism has not displaced its Orientalist, postcolonial, capitalist frame as a mode of travel and consumption of place. Cronopio starts his essay with a vignette of 'booking a flight', an inevitable first step in most genres of tourism. The credit card underpins the backpacker experience in Cronopio's account, whereby the exotic is only a scenic backdrop against which the backpacker seeks 'an-Other' from among equally motivated fellow travellers only to be disappointed by their uniform and normative orientation to their 'alternative' hippie identity (cf. Davidson, 2005). Storch refers to sex tourism in Jamaica as 'commodified romantic encounters' (p. 98). Bongartz states clearly that doing linguistic fieldwork is a form of academic tourism which requires economic power to secure a tourist welcome from hosts (Jaworski, 2014) and to enjoy the frisson of a pleasurable adventure ahead. And just as with all elective forms of travel, the academic-tourist is free to leave again and return home when the time is right, or when the funds run out (Jaworski & Thurlow, 2010).

Nico Nassenstein examines the contexts and consequences of tourist language learning, which turns Kiswahili into a 'linguistic souvenir'. He draws parallels between the political economies of tourist and 'local' languages, and the colonising and colonised languages in Africa. Nassenstein argues that the simplified, limited register of Kiswahili typically learnt by European tourists in East Africa – *Hakuna Matata Swahili* (HMS) – and its intertextual links to American popular culture (the movie *The Lion King*) are emblematic of tourists' limited engagement with and lack of empathy for the local population, like the colonisers that came before them.

In other contexts, economic power dominates tourist–host interactions quite explicitly. Mietzner documents and critiques modes of interaction between German tourists and Kenyan villagers afforded to the former by their philanthropic activity of sponsoring the schooling of children in the local community. Most encounters are devoid of face-to-face interaction, except one at the end of the visit that allows the tourists (sponsors) and hosts (sponsored children and their families) to spend time in a reasonably intimate, small group, attempting to talk, typically via an interpreter. All such encounters involve relentless photo-taking of local people, their homes and their possessions, predominantly foregrounding their poverty to aid future fundraising activities in Germany. As Mietzner concludes, 'all those who serve as the exotic other profit financially from the situation' (p. 78). Bongartz mentions a group of German tourists who, after a disappointing visit to the Dominican Republic where they 'had found the staff standoffish and not very welcoming' (p. 21), derived much enjoyment from the relationships they struck with their Jamaican servers. Returning there on subsequent visits, they 'bonded with their Jamaican butler, and sponsored him when he had a financial emergency' (p. 23). Tourism may be a unique area of social life where there is an expectation and an acceptance of friendship built on monetary exchange, the potential for sponsorship or even the promise of an invitation to the tourist's home country (cf. Lawson & Jaworski, 2007). Perhaps it's the liminality of tourism that allows us to confuse the purchase of assistance and favours that are normally provided by family and friends (care, intimacy, trust, etc.) with *real* friendship (Sandell, 2012).

In fairness, Bal Krishna Sharma (2018) suggests that it may be too simplistic to reduce the sociability of tourist–host relations to the mechanics of economic transactions. Citing Ortner (1999) on the anthropology of sponsorship in the Himalayas, Sharma explains

> that for ethnic Tamangs, Sherpas and Tibetans, finding a sponsor is a part of 'cultural schema' of coming-of-age for young men. Known as *zhindak*, looking for a financial supporter for monasteries, communities and individuals is a traditionally accepted practice in those communities. *Zhindak*, in this sense, is a patron or a protector who helps a weaker person to succeed. Traditionally, the relationship is less hierarchical and more reciprocal: the lesser person also serves and takes care of the protector. (Sharma, 2018a: 96)

The suggestion that patterns of present-day global tourism may be syncretically mapped onto traditional, local forms of patronage and sponsorship is certainly plausible. There are other likely candidates for this sort of comparison (cf. Irvine, 1989). However, as Sharma states, the traditional relationships of sponsorship in the Himalayas are 'less hierarchical and more reciprocal'. My initial sense is that, in most tourist contexts, especially in the Global North/Global South contact zones, tourist–host encounters are predominantly hierarchical and non-reciprocal, which does not preclude the participants from enjoying a degree of *conviviality* (e.g. Blommaert & Varis, 2015; Williams & Stroud, 2013), or some instances of tourist–host encounters developing into longer term relationships. This topic merits further investigation.

Vitorio, Zavaree and Nassenstein provide other examples of host–tourist contact, or performance of contact (Jaworski & Thurlow, 2010), in which the economic element of the interaction is its indispensable precondition. Vitorio examines the discourse of a Manila-based tour guide, a typical 'language worker' (Heller, 2003) of the tourist industry. Commenting on the re-emergence of Zār ceremonies in Iran after a relative decline following the Shah's policy of westernisation in the 1960s and 1970s and the Islamic Revolution of 1979, Zavaree observes that their resurgence is largely motivated by the demand for spiritual tourism driven by international, middle class tourists. This has not only led to the economic competition between rival Zār communities; in broader terms, the economic demand for and supply of this vanishing cultural practice enables its preservation and transmission. As Barbara Kirshenblatt-Gimblett observes, 'heritage and tourism show what cannot be seen – except through them...' (Kirshenblatt-Gimblett, 1998: 166).

Nassenstein's analysis situates HMS learning by German tourists in East African oceanside resorts within the tradition of colonial transformations of local languages into systems of knowledge which institutionalised inequalities (Bauman & Briggs, 2003; Irvine, 2001). Nassenstein argues that vacation 'language learning may symbolise [the tourist's] striving for epistemic power, for ownership over language, and longing for exotic accessories' (p. 142). There is a vignette in the chapter of a pool bar employee providing a tourist with (free?) instruction in Kiswahili. This is reminiscent of the exploitation of the multilingualism of low-skilled workers when a need for free translation arises in emergency situations – at airports, for example (Duchêne, 2011) – or the voluntary language work typical of the globalised, flexible, precarious workforce (Dlaske, 2016). One can only hope that the linguistic services of the pool bar worker were rewarded by a hefty tip before the tourist's departure.

Maria João Cordeiro (2011) situates mainstream tourist ideology (and practice, to some degree) of learning the languages of travel destinations from guidebooks, travelogues, glossaries and other tourist texts as part of the promise of, or desire for, a true, authentic experience – meeting the local 'Other' (see also Thurlow & Jaworski, 2010, 2011). However, Cordeiro considers the representation of tourist languages (in her case, Portuguese) in tourist texts as a 'mystification' hovering between the exotic and the familiar. Nassenstein's notion of 'linguistic souvenirs' is reminiscent of Cordeiro's comments on the souvenirisation of local languages, which, like places, can be miniaturised, simplified and reduced to a few identifiable symbols, most typically greeting formulae (Jaworski, 2009). All of these examples invoke the idea of tourists, like ethnographers, selecting, picking up, watching and collecting fragments from which some putative cultural wholes are supposed to emerge. People and objects become signs of themselves. Such representations are essentialising, standing in for the quintessence of a 'culture', and totalising, a part standing in metonymically for a whole (Kirshenblatt-Gimblett, 1998: 55).

Resistance and Subversion

However, power is not a static attribute for any specific type of structure or relationship. Foucault (1980: 98) argues against the idea of individuals as inert or consenting targets of power; rather, they are always also agents of its articulation. Because power is located within an acting subject, it is closely followed by resistance, and anyone confronted by power can resort to an array of responses, available reactions and resisting possibilities (Foucault, 1982). Thus, power is 'a set of potentials which, while always present, can be variably exercised, resisted, shifted around and struggled over by social agents' (Hutchby, 1999: 586). Foucault's model of power is 'productive' (Mills, 1997). For him, power is dispersed throughout all social relations; and, as a force which prevents some actions but enables others (e.g. the power to show resistance by a minority member), it has the ability to bring about social change.

The performative nature of contact between hosts and tourists creates particularly fertile ground for hosts to resist tourists' power and to subvert the dominant ideologies of tourism (Jaworski & Thurlow, 2010; Salazar, 2006). As has been suggested previously, ethnographers and tourists create their own versions of entire cultures from ethnographic and touristic fragments. When these heterogeneous stylistic resources, their context-sensitive meanings and conflicting ideologies are selected and put on display by hosts in artful performances for tourists, they enter a 'reflexive arena where they can be examined critically' (Bauman & Briggs, 1990: 60). Or, as suggested by Coupland (2010: 110), stylisation, just like any other form of verbal performance, may bring 'conflicting identities and realities into contact with each other, making them available for reassessment' (Coupland, 2010: 110). These semiotic opportunities for performance are documented in various forms by the chapter authors. Zavaree suggests that the performances of Zār ceremonies can be treated as African Iranians' instantiations of struggle and resistance against Islamic dogma and discrimination.

Raymund Vitorio demonstrates how Charles, a Manila tour guide, manages to subvert traditional, dominant, colonial and national narratives of history, identity and power relations. The guide overlays the genre of the guided tour with an artful, multimodal and humorous performance in which differently enregistered accents, dialects and languages, like his other props and costumes, are subversively deployed for parodic styling of different historical personas and figures of authority. Charles' artful guided tours of Intramuros in Manila (the 16th century walled city built by the Spanish) become multi-voiced, vari-directional (Bakhtin, 1981) performances in which he is able to contest the dominant narratives of (post)colonial history and the hegemonic ideologies of the Philippine state and church. Likewise, Nassenstein argues that the adoption of Hakuna Matata Swahili (HMS) – the mock Kiswahili spoken by tourists – by Kenyan hotel and sex workers, beach vendors or Kenyan tourists in fleeting, parodic performances becomes a way of speaking back to the tourists, ridiculing their half-hearted and feeble attempts at speaking Kiswahili.

Social Injustice and Struggle

Social inequality is cited as one of the key motivations for the emergence of sociolinguistics in the 1960s and 1970s (Heller & McElhinny,

2017: 195). The relentless valorisation of languages and linguistic diversity in tourist destinations (Bongartz; Cronopio; Zavaree; Storch; Vitorio; Nassenstein) is one of the key sources or ways of legitimizing social injustice (Piller, 2016). Mainstream mediatisation of the linguistic market of tourism perpetuates the image of Othered, silenced hosts with their languages typically 'part of an authentic background noise for the audience' (Sharma, 2018b: 16; see also Chen, 2016; Jaworski et al., 2003).

Storch unravels sociolinguistic mechanisms of marginalisation and othering of the inhabitants of Seaford Town, a heritage site. She demonstrates how tourism discourse, through naming or categorising practices, renders the enslaved *jaamans* (Germans) who were brought to Jamaica in the first half of the 19th century and their present-day descendants as racialised, hence marked, and deformed, hence incomprehensible, voiceless and inhuman. Although self-categorisation within communities can be highly contested (Zavaree), the naming of colonised peoples has long been recognised as a power-wielding practice in colonial expansion:

> Colonial expeditions were not just a form of invasion; nor was their purpose just inspection. They were determined efforts at *in-scription*. By putting regions on a map and native words on a list, explorers laid the first, and deepest, foundations for colonial power. By giving proof of the 'scientific' nature of their enterprise they exercised power in a pure subtle form – as the power to name, to describe, to classify. (Fabian, 1986: 24)

Metaphorically, *jaamans* are positioned between the silence of Othering and marginalisation, and the noise of ruination of their lives' destruction. Silence and noise appear to be productive metaphors in the sociolinguistics of tourism (Bongartz & Storch, 2016). Tourism, as Hall (2010; cited in Poon, 2018) argues, simultaneously empowers and silences minority voices. Noise may indeed signify ruination, but it is also a vehicle of disruption in societies of control (Deumert, 2015).

In view of the pervasiveness of racism, Bongartz sees the possibility of redressing the balance between the oppressed and the privileged in the latter's recourse to silence or deep, reflexive listening. Cronopio invokes silence as part of backpackers' anxiety in their search for experiences beyond the quotidian. Sitholé positions the inconceivable events of slave trade at the Cape Coast Castle between the multilayered noise of history and the 'long unbroken silences' of those reflecting on it. Mietzner comments on the worldlessness of German tourists' philanthropy in approaching their rural Kenyan hosts 'already named as "the Other"' (p. 69). Nassenstein comments on the predominantly transactional nature of tourist–host interactions, where '[i]n the worst cases, the sharing of social practices and local engagement is limited to sexual intercourse' (p. 150).

The legacy of colonialism and the economic disparities that underpin tourism from Global North to Global South do not remain unchallenged.

As has been mentioned, Vitorio demonstrates how a tour guide's performances for tourists become sites of struggle whereby the inequalities and injustices brought about by colonial exploitation, stereotyping and erasure are exposed, critiqued and challenged. There's probably more that sociolinguists can learn from the performances, actions and provocations of visual artists who have turned their objectifying gaze back onto the tourists and critiqued the hegemonic ideologies of tourism and its postcolonial and Orientalising legacy (Dahlgren *et al.*, 2005; Demeester *et al.*, 2005; Lippard, 1999; Storch *et al.*, 2017). Performance art will certainly not bring an end to the long history of postcolonial inequality and exploitation evident in many forms of contemporary tourism. But it may bring hope and closure for some. With the magic of poetry, Sitholé and Phipps conjure up a cast of characters, human and non-human – the enslaved, the slave traders, the clergy, the whitewashed walls, the rooms, the tourists – all mingling together in an unlikely, ghostly procession on a judgment day that will never come, seeking justice and redemption.

Acknowledgements

Thank you, Anne Storch and Angelika Mietzner, for inviting me to the stimulating seminar 'Entanglements, Emblematic Codes and Languaging in Tourism' at the University of Cologne, 30 May 2016. Thank you, Jenn Gresham, for your invaluable help in making my prose just a bit more fluent.

Note

All references without the year of publication refer to the chapters in this book: Angelika Mietzner and Anne Storch (eds) 2019 *Language and Tourism in Postcolonial Settings*. Bristol: Channel View Publications.

References

Bakhtin, M.M. (1981) *The Dialogic Imagination*. Austin, TX: University of Texas Press.
Bauman, R. and Briggs, C.L. (1990) Poetics and performance as critical perspectives on language and social life. *Annual Review of Anthropology* 19, 59–88.
Blommaert, J. and Varis, P. (eds) (2015) *Multilingual Dislocations*. Special issue of *Multilingual Margins: A Journal of Multilingualism from the Periphery* 2 (1).
Bongartz, C.M. and Storch, A. (2016) Making sense of the noisy. *Critical Multilingualism Studies* 4 (2), 154–173.
Bruner, E.M. (1996) Tourism in Ghana. The representation of slavery and the return of the black diaspora. *American Anthropologist* 98 (2), 290–304.
Chen, X. (2016) Linguascaping the Other: Travelogues' representations of Chinese languages. *Multilingua* 35 (5), 513–534.
Coupland, N. (2010) The authentic speaker and the speech community. In C. Llamas and D. Watts (eds) *Language and Identities* (pp. 99–112). Edinburgh: Edinburgh University Press.
Cordeiro, M.J. (2011) Portuguese 'to go': Language representations in tourist guides. *Language and Intercultural Communication* 11 (4), 377–388.

Dahlgren, K., Foreman, K. and Van Eck, T. (2005) *Universal Experience: Art, Life, and the Tourist's Eye*. Chicago, IL: Museum of Modern Art.

Davidson, K. (2005) Backpacker India: Transgressive spaces. In A. Jaworski and A. Pritchard (eds) *Language, Communication, Tourism* (pp. 28–52). Clevedon: Channel View Publications.

Demeester, A., Laurence P. and Cantor, M. (2005) *Global Tour: Art, Travel & Beyond*. Amsterdam: W139.

Deumert, A. (2015) Wild and noisy publics OR The continuation of politics by other means. Plenary lecture delivered at the 6th Language and the Media Conference, University of Hamburg, 7–9 September 2015.

Dlaske, K. (2016) Shaping subjects of globalisation: At the intersection of voluntourism and the new economy. *Multilingua* 35 (4), 415–440.

Doorne, S. and Ateljevic, I. (2005) Tourism performance as metaphor: Enacting backpacker travel in the Fiji Islands. In A. Jaworski and A. Pritchard (eds) *Discourse, Communication and Tourism* (pp. 173–198). Clevedon: Channel View Publications.

Duchêne, A. (2011) Néolibéralisme, inégalités sociales et plurilinguismes: l'exploitation des ressources langagières et des locuteurs. *Langage & Société* 136, 81–106.

Fabian, J. (1986) *Language and Colonial Power: The Appropriation of Swahili in the Former Belgian Congo 1880–1938*. Cambridge: Cambridge University Press.

Foucault. M. (1980) *Power/Knowledge: Selected Interviews and Other Writings, 1972–1977*. Edited by C. Cordon. Brighton: Harvester Press.

Foucault, M. (1982) The subject and power. *Critical Inquiry* 8 (4), 777–795.

Goffman, E. (1967) *Interaction Ritual: Essays on Face-to-Face Behavior*. New York, NY: Doubleday Anchor.

Goode, G.B. (1989) The museums of the future. *Annual Report of the Board of Regents of the Smithsonian Institution...for the Year Ending June 30, 1889: Report of the National Museum*. Washington, D.C.: Government Printing Office.

Hannerz, U. (1992) *Cultural Complexity: Studies in the Social Organisation of Meaning*. New York, NY: Columbia University Press.

Hall, C.M. (2010) Power in tourism: Tourism in power. In D.V.L. Macleod and J.G. Carrier (eds) *Tourism, Power and Culture: Anthropological Insights* (pp. 199–213). Bristol: Channel View Publications.

Heller, M. (2003) Globalization, the new economy, and the commodification of language and identity. *Journal of Sociolinguistics* 7 (4), 473–492.

Heller, M. and McElhinny, B. (2017) *Language, Capitalism, Colonialism: Toward A Critical History*. Toronto: University of Toronto Press.

Hutchby, I. (1999) Power in discourse: The case of arguments on a British talk radio show. In A. Jaworski and N. Coupland (eds) *The Discourse Reader* (pp. 576–588). London: Routledge. [originally published in *Discourse & Society* 7 (4), 481–497].

Irvine, J.T. (1989) When talk isn't cheap: Language and political economy. *American Ethnologist* 16, 248–267.

Irvine, J.T. and Gal, S. (2000) Language ideology and linguistic differentiation. In P.V. Kroskrity (ed.) *Regimes of Language: Ideologies, Politics, and Identities* (pp. 35–83). Santa Fe, NM: SAR Press.

Jaworski, A. (2009) Greetings in tourist–host encounters. In N. Coupland and A. Jaworski (eds) *The New Sociolinguistics Reader* (pp. 662–679). Basingstoke: Palgrave Macmillan.

Jaworski, A. (2014) *Welcome*: Synthetic personalization and commodification of sociability in the linguistic landscape of global tourism. In B. Spolsky, O. Inbar and M. Tannenbaum (eds) *Challenges for Language Education and Policy: Making Space for People* (pp. 214–231). London: Routledge.

Jaworski, A. and Thurlow, C. (2010) Language and the globalizing habitus of tourism: Towards a sociolinguistics of fleeting relationships. In N. Coupland (ed.) *Handbook of Language and Globalisation* (pp. 255–286). Oxford: Wiley-Blackwell.

Jaworski, A., Thurlow, C. and Heller, M. (eds) (2014) *Sociolinguistics and Tourism*. Special issue of the *Journal of Sociolinguistics* 18 (4).
Jaworski, A., Thurlow, C., Lawson, S. and Ylänne-McEwen, V. (2003) The uses and representations of local languages in tourist destinations: A view from British TV holiday programmes. *Language Awareness* 12 (1), 5–29.
Kirschenblatt-Gimblett, B. (1998) *Destination Culture. Tourism, Museums, and Heritage*. Berkeley, CA: University of California Press.
Lawson, S. and Jaworski, A. (2007) Shopping and chatting: Reports of tourist–host interactions in The Gambia. *Multilingua* 26, 67–93.
Lippard, L. (1999) *On the Beaten Track: Tourism, Art, and Place*. New York, NY: The New Press.
Mills, S. (1997) *Discourse*. London: Routledge.
Mitchell, W.J.T. (1986) *Iconology: Image, Text, Ideology*. Chicago, IL: University of Chicago Press.
Piller, I. (2016) *Linguistic Diversity and Social Justice: An Introduction to Applied Sociolinguistics*. New York, NY: Oxford University Press.
Poon, B. (2018) Tourism discourse in Hong Kong. Unpublished MPhill thsis. University of Hong Kong.
Pratt, M.L. (1992) *Imperial Eyes: Travel Writing and Transculturation*. London: Routledge.
Pratt, M.L. (1987) Linguistic utopias. In N. Fabb, D. Attridge, A. Durant and C. MacCabe (eds) *The Linguistics of Writing* (pp. 48–66). Manchester: Manchester University Press.
Rampton, B. (2009) Speech community and beyond. In N. Coupland and A. Jaworski (eds) *The New Sociolinguistics Reader* (pp. 694–713). Basingstoke: Palgrave Macmillan.
Richards, S.L. (2005) What is to be remembered?: Tourism to Ghana's slave castle-dungeons. *Theatre Journal* 57 (4), 617–636.
Salazar, N.B. (2006) Touristifying Tanzania: Local guides, global discourse. *Annals of Tourism Research* 33 (3), 833–852.
Sandell, M.J. (2012) *What Money Can't Buy: The Moral Limits of Markets*. London: Penguin.
Sharma, B.K. (2018a) English and discourses of commodification among tourism workers in the Himalayas. *Journal of Sociolinguistics* 22 (1), 77–99.
Sharma, B.K. (2018b) Discursive representations of difference and multilingualism in Himalaya with Michael Palin. *International Journal of Multilingualism*. Published online 29 January, 1–16.
Silverstein, M. (1985) On the pragmatic 'poetry' of prose. In D. Schiffrin (ed.) *Meaning, Form and Use in Context*. Washington D.C.: Georgetown University Press.
Storch, A., Nassenstein, N., Traber, J., Mietzner, A. and Schneider, N. (eds) (2017) Normalities: Artefacts from various Souths and Norths. *The Mouth* 1.
Thurlow, C. and Jaworski, A. (2010) *Tourism Discourse: Language and Global Mobility*. Basingstoke: Palgrave Macmillan.
Thurlow, C. and Jaworski, A. (2011) Tourism discourse: Languages and banal globalization. *Review of Applied Linguistics* 2, 285–312.
Thurlow, C. and Jaworski, A. (2017) Word-things and thing-words: The transmodal production of privilege and status. In J.R. Cavanaugh and S. Shankar (eds) *Language and Materiality: Ethnographical and Theoretical Explorations* (pp. 135–203). Cambridge: Cambridge University Press.
Williams, Q. and Stroud, C. (2013) Multilingualism in transformative spaces: Contact and conviviality. *Language Policy* 12, 289–311.

Bookend

cape ghost

For Obed

Alison Phipps

Which one haunts you?
Is it an ancestor
or the captive screaming of today?

Is there whiteness in your skin,
Is there blame?

Which voices do you hear
from the death mask's whisper?
Was the blood you share
a trader?
Was the blood you share
a slave?

Which shadows do you see
in the gate of no return
behind the door of no return?

Are you the one he saw,
chose,
bathed and
screaming through
a trap door
screaming
from the trapped door
bore his now creaming child?

Are you the one whose eye
was choosing, following
skin and limb and
glowering

holding hand to hip
to mouth
in the tearingtaking
that is war?

Are you the trader who
measured angles
clasped shackles
taking the way of wrangles?

Are you the girl child,
the boy child
your mother plucked
for the fields of the south,
and you for lands to the north
her memory a brand
like the one
on your skin?

Are you the preacher
of Zion
blessing abomination
before you proudly trade
in the name of a god?

Are you the guide, traveller
in time, telling the flattened
endlessly repeating
tales of terror,

closing the door
of no return
on those
who pay to know?

Cape Coast

the sea is coming to
greet you,

which ghost
are you?

Index

Advertise, advertisement 6, 9, 81, 83
Africa 1ff, 8, 14, 26, 41, 49ff, 57ff, 68f, 71, 82, 84, 88, 96
Australia 9ff
Authenticity 9, 11, 12, 29, 38, 57, 82, 91, 107, 118, 125, 142, 149

Backpacker/Backpacking 14, 38ff, 46f, 130, 157, 160, 164
Beach 1ff, 25, 45, 49, 56, 67, 81, 97f, 130, 132, 136, 141, 145ff, 152, 154, 163
Beach Boy 2f, 98, 131f, 148, 152
Beach vendor 2, 130, 149, 163

Cannibal 1ff
Cape Coast x, xi, xvi, 13f, 164, 165
Caribbean 26, 81, 88, 99
China 27, 57, 126
Chinese 27, 30, 126, 135
Chow, Rae 29, 54, 57f
Colonialism 5, 7, 15, 25, 29, 32, 57, 106ff, 112, 114, 116f, 119ff, 164
Commodification 3, 6, 11, 107, 132, 136, 154
Cougar 98ff

Diani Beach 1f, 5
Digo 67, 130
Dixon, Bob 10f
Drugs in tourism 41ff

English 3, 7, 11, 19ff, 23, 25, 27ff, 73, 87, 91, 93, 111ff, 118ff, 124, 134ff, 140, 151
Egypt 8, 26, 61

Festival 50ff, 56, 58, 159
Food, culinary discourse 10, 73f, 138, 146ff, 157,
Freak 15, 83, 85, 90, 91, 93f, 9, 99, 102, 159

German 1ff, 15, 29, 43, 56, 58, 66ff, 70, 73, 77, 84, 87ff, 91f, 94f, 97, 130f, 133f, 135, 137ff, 142, 144f, 147f, 149ff, 158ff, 162, 164,
Ghana 2, 14, 158,
Giryama 130

Hakuna Matata 15, 109, 130, 136f, 138, 143, 145, 147ff, 154, 160, 163
Heritage 10, 14f, 58ff, 69, 81ff, 85, 87, 89, 91, 94ff, 97, 102, 106, 112f, 122, 127, 155, 162, 164
Hormoz 14, 49f, 53, 55f, 61f, 158

Indian Ocean 50, 67
Iran 14, 49ff, 158, 161, 163

Jamaica 15, 19f, 23, 25, 32, 34f, 81, 83ff, 91f, 94f, 96ff, 102, 109, 157, 159ff, 164

Kenya 1, 6, 9f, 15, 66ff, 71ff, 76, 99, 109, 130ff, 134f, 138, 141, 146ff, 153, 158, 160, 163f
Kikuyu 141

Linguistic landscape 13, 24f, 27f, 31, 34, 107, 136, 148, 157
Literacy 21, 27

Maasai 2, 9f, 147
Manila 15, 113f, 116, 122f, 125f, 161, 163
Maroon 21
Migrant 5, 15, 51, 92, 159,
Migration 5, 14, 91, 101, 113
Mombasa 67, 69, 130, 132, 144, 148, 152f
Morocco 45, 60

Noise 10f, 13f, 54, 96, 99, 157, 164

Patwa 19, 25, 27, 29, 88, 93, 95
Performance 5ff, 9, 11, 13f, 38, 40, 42, 45, 50, 52ff, 58f, 61, 72, 82, 107ff, 116f, 122, 125f, 127, 132, 136, 147f, 154, 158, 161, 163, 165
Performativity 5, 13, 15, 60, 106f, 111f, 125, 127
Pharaonic 8
Philippines 15, 106, 112ff, 118f, 120ff
Photography 13f, 67, 77ff
Poor Whites 89, 99
Poverty 25, 68f, 77ff, 87ff, 93, 97, 99, 133, 136, 160
Pro-poor 1, 15, 66, 68

Racism 29, 31, 51, 83, 164
Rastafari 88

Ritual 50, 52f, 53f, 56f, 59ff, 120, 159
  -spiritual 14, 54
  -access 4f
  -trance 55

Sex tourism 98, 132, 151, 153f, 160
Silence xv, 30, 41, 43f, 157ff, 164
Souvenir 1f, 9, 45, 56, 59, 132, 134f, 144, 147, 151, 153
  -linguistic 130f, 134ff, 148ff, 152ff, 160, 162
Spirit 14, 49ff, 120, 158
  -possession 50, 54
  -tourism 161
Swahili 2ff, 6f, 15, 50, 60, 139ff, 160, 162f

Tagalog 113ff, 119, 123, 135
Tjapukai 9ff
Tourist gaze 9, 18, 78, 106f, 109, 113f, 116, 127, 142
Tourist guide 14f, 142
Tourist guidebook 83, 91f
Trump, Donald 31, 43

Walcott, Derek 26f, 30, 33ff, 89
White guilt 5f, 29, 32

Zar 14, 49ff, 158, 161, 163

For Product Safety Concerns and Information please contact our EU Authorised Representative:

Easy Access System Europe

Mustamäe tee 50

10621 Tallinn

Estonia

gpsr.requests@easproject.com